Software Development and Professional Practice

John Dooley

Apress®

President and Publisher: Paul Manning
Lead Editor: Dominic Shakeshaft
Technical Reviewer: John Zukowski
Editorial Board: Steve Anglin, Mark Beckner, Ewan Buckingham, Gary Cornell, Jonathan Gennick, Jonathan Hassell, Michelle Lowman, James Markham, Matthew Moodie, Jeff Olson, Jeffrey Pepper, Frank Pohlmann, Douglas Pundick, Ben Renow-Clarke, Dominic Shakeshaft, Matt Wade, Tom Welsh
Coordinating Editor: Adam Heath
Copy Editor: Tracy Brown
Compositor: Bytheway Publishing Services
Indexer: Toma Mulligan
Artist: April Milne
Cover Designer: Anna Ishchenko

Distributed to the book trade worldwide by Springer Science+Business Media, LLC., 233 Spring Street, 6th Floor, New York, NY 10013. Phone 1-800-SPRINGER, fax (201) 348-4505, e-mail orders-ny@springer-sbm.com, or visit www.springeronline.com.

For information on translations, please e-mail rights@apress.com, or visit www.apress.com.

Apress and friends of ED books may be purchased in bulk for academic, corporate, or promotional use. eBook versions and licenses are also available for most titles. For more information, reference our Special Bulk Sales–eBook Licensing web page at www.apress.com/info/bulksales.

The source code for this book is available to readers at www.apress.com. You will need to answer questions pertaining to this book in order to successfully download the code.

For Diane, who is always there;
for Patrick, the best son a guy could have; and
for Margaret Teresa Hume Dooley (1926–1976),
the first one is for you, Mom.

Contents at a Glance

Contents

About the Author

 **John Dooley** wrote his first program 40 years ago – on punch cards in Fortran IV. Since then, he's spent more than 18 years in industry, working for companies such as Bell Labs, IBM, McDonnell Douglas, and Motorola, along with the obligatory stint at a start-up. He's also spent 17 years teaching computer science to undergraduates, including at Knox College in Galesburg, Illinois, where he is chair of the Computer Science Department and has taught for the last 10 years. As a software professional, he has written everything from device drivers to compilers to embedded phone software to financial applications. He has also managed teams of from 5 to 30 developers in companies large and small. He holds degrees in mathematics, computer science, and electrical engineering.

About the Technical Reviewer

 **John Zukowski** has been developing software professionally for over 20 years now. He first started programming in BASIC on a Commodore Vic-20, before moving on to a Commodore 64. He's developed with FORTRAN on a VAX/VMS system, in C and C++ on early Sun3/4 Solaris boxes, and, for the past 15 years, with the Java platform on micro-devices, desktops, and servers. John is also the author of ten books related to Java technologies, from his first, *Java AWT Reference* (O'Reilly, 1997) to his most recent, *Java 6 Platform Revealed* (Apress, 2006). In his spare time, you may find John enjoying Mob Wars on Facebook or entering contests on Twitter (@JavaJohnZ).

Acknowledgments

I'd like to thank Dominic Shakeshaft of Apress for encouraging me and making this book possible. The staff at Apress, especially Adam Heath, Matthew Moodie, and Tracy Brown have been very helpful and gracious. The book is much better for their reviews, comments, and edits.

I owe huge debt of gratitude to Professor Dominic Soda, who taught me most of the mathematics I know and shared his deep love of learning with me while I was his student and, later, his colleague.

Thanks also to all my students in CS 292 over the last four years who have put up with successive versions of the course notes that became this book. And to Knox College for giving me the time and resources to finish this book.

Finally, I owe everything to Diane who hates that I work nights, but loves that I can work at home.

Preface

What's this book all about? Well, it's about how to develop software, from a personal perspective. We'll look at what it means for you to take a problem and produce a program to solve it from beginning to end. That said, this book focuses a lot on design. How do you design software? What things do you take into account? What makes a good design? What methods and processes are there to designing software? Is designing small programs different from designing large ones? How can you tell a good design from a bad one?

Next, it's about code construction. How do you write programs and make them work? "What," you say? "I've already written eight gazillion programs! Of course I know how to write code!" Well, in this book, we'll explore what you already do, and we'll investigate ways to improve on that. We'll spend some time on coding standards, debugging, unit testing, modularity, and characteristics of good programs. We'll also talk about reading code and what makes a program readable. Can good, readable code replace documentation? How much documentation do you really need?

Third, it's a bit about software engineering, which is usually defined as "the application of engineering principles to the development of software." What are "engineering principles?" Well, first, all engineering efforts follow a defined *process*. So we'll be spending a bit of time talking about how you run a software development project and what phases there are to a project. All engineering work has a basis in the application of science and mathematics to real-world problems. So does software development. As I said already, we'll be spending *a lot* of time examining how to design and implement programs that solve specific problems.

By the way, there's at least one person (besides me) who thinks software development is not an engineering discipline. I'm referring to Alistair Cockburn, and you can read his paper, "The End of Software Engineering and the Start of Economic-Cooperative Gaming" at http://alistair.cockburn.us/The+end+of+software+engineering+and+the+start+of+economic-cooperative+gaming.

Finally, this book is about professional practice, the ethics and the responsibilities of being a software developer, social issues, privacy, how to write secure and robust code, and the like. In short, those fuzzy other things one needs in order to be a *professional* software developer.

This book covers many of the topics described for the ACM Computing Curricula 2001 course C292c Software Development and Professional Practice (www.acm.org/education/education/curricula-recommendations). It is designed to be both a textbook and a manual for the working professional. Although the chapter order generally follows the standard software development sequence, one can read the chapters independently and out of order. I'm assuming that you already know how to program and that you are conversant with at least one of Java, C, or C++. I'm also assuming you are familiar with basic data structures, including lists, queues, stacks, maps, and trees, along with the algorithms to manipulate them.

I use this book in a junior-level course in software development. It has grown out of the notes I've developed for that class over the past five years. I developed my own notes because I couldn't find a book that covered all the topics I thought were necessary for a course in software development as opposed to one in software engineering. Software engineering books tend to focus more on process and project management than on design and actual development. I wanted to focus on the design and writing of real code rather than on how to run a large project. Before beginning to teach, I spent over 18 years in the computer industry, working for large and small companies, writing software, and managing other people who wrote software. This book is my perspective on what it takes to be a software developer on a small- to medium-sized team and help develop great software.

I hope that by the end of the book you will have a much better idea of what the design of good programs is like, what makes an effective and productive developer, and how to develop larger pieces of software. You'll know a lot more about design issues. You'll have thought about working in a team to deliver a product to a written schedule. You'll begin to understand project management, know some metrics, know how to review work products, and understand configuration management. I'll not cover everything in software development by a long stretch, and we'll only be giving a cursory look at the management side of software engineering, but you'll be in a much better position to visualize, design, implement, and test software of many sizes, either by yourself, or in a team.

Introduction to Software Development

"Not only are there no silver bullets now in view, the very nature of software makes it unlikely that there will be any — no inventions that will do for software productivity, reliability, and simplicity what electronics, transistors, and large-scale integration did for computer hardware. We cannot expect ever to see twofold gains every two years."

— Frederick J. Brooks, Jr.[1]

So, you're asking yourself, why is this book called *Software Development and Professional Practice*? Why isn't it called *All About Programming* or *Software Engineering*? After all, isn't that what software development is? Well, no. Programming is a part of software development, but it's certainly not all of it. Likewise, software development is a part of software engineering, but it's not all of it.

Here's the definition of software development that we'll use in this book: software development is the process of taking a set of requirements from a user (a problem statement), analyzing them, designing a solution to the problem, and then implementing that solution on a computer.

Well, isn't that programming, you ask? Well, no. Programming is really the implementation part, or possibly the design and implementation part, of software development. Programming is central to software development, but it's not the whole thing.

Well, then, isn't it software engineering? Again, no. Software engineering also involves a process and includes software development, but it also includes the entire management side of creating a computer program that people will use. Software engineering includes project management, configuration management, scheduling and estimation, baseline building and scheduling, managing people, and several other things. Software development is the fun part of software engineering.

So software development is a narrowing of the focus of software engineering to just that part concerned with the creation of the actual software. And it's a broadening of the focus of programming to include analysis, design and release issues.

---

[1] Brooks, Frederick. "No Silver Bullet." *IEEE Computer* (1987). 20(4): 10-19.

What We're Doing

It turns out that, after 60 or so years of using computers, we've discovered that developing software is hard. Learning how to develop software correctly, efficiently, and beautifully is also hard. You're not born knowing how to do it, and most people, even those who take programming courses and work in the industry for years, don't do it particularly well. It's a skill you need to pick up and practice – a lot. You don't learn programming and development by reading books – not even this one. You learn it by doing it. That, of course, is the attraction; working on interesting and difficult problems. The challenge is to work on something you've never done before, something you might not even know if you can solve. That's what has you coming back to create new programs again and again.

There are probably several ways to learn software development. But I think that all of them involve reading excellent designs, reading a lot of code, writing a lot of code, and thinking deeply about how you approach a problem and design a solution for it. Reading a lot of code, especially really beautiful and efficient code, gives you lots of good examples about how to think about problems and approach their solution in a particular style. Writing a lot of code lets you experiment with the styles and examples you've seen in your reading. Thinking deeply about problem solving lets you examine how you work and how you do design, and lets you extract from your labors those patterns that work for you; it makes your programming more intentional.

So, How to Develop Software?

Well, the first thing you should do is read this book. It certainly won't tell you everything, but it will give you a good introduction into what software development is all about and what you need to do to write great code. It has its own perspective, but that's a perspective based on 20 years writing code professionally and another 16 years trying to figure out how to teach others to do it.

Despite the fact that software development is only part of software engineering, software development is the heart of every software project. After all, at the end of the day what you deliver to the user is working code. That code is usually created by a team of developers working in concert. So to start, maybe we should look at a software project from the outside and ask what does that team need to do to make that project a success?

In order to do software development well you need the following

> *A small, well integrated team.* Small teams have fewer lines of communication than larger ones. It's easier to get to know your teammates on a small team. You can get to know your teammates' strengths and weaknesses, who knows what, and who is the "go to guy" for particular problems or particular tools. Well-integrated teams have usually worked on several projects together. Keeping a team together across several projects is a major job of the team's manager. Well-integrated teams are more productive, they are better at holding to a schedule, and they produce code with fewer defects at release. The key to keeping a team together is to give them interesting work to do and then leave them alone.

> *Good communication among team members.* Constant communication among team members is critical to day-to-day progress and successful project completion. Teams that are co-located are better at communicating and communicate more than teams that are distributed geographically (even if they're just on different floors or wings of a building). This is a major issue with larger companies that have software development sites scattered across the globe.

Good communication between the team and the customer. Communication with the customer is essential to controlling requirements and requirements churn during a project. On-site or close-by customers allow for constant interaction with the development team. Customers can give immediate feedback on new releases and be involved in creating system and acceptance tests for the product. The Extreme Programming agile development methodology requires that a customer be part of the development team and be on site daily. See Chapter 2 for a quick introduction to Extreme Programming.

A _process_ that everyone buys into. Every project, no matter how big or small, follows a process. Larger projects and larger teams tend to be more plan-driven and follow processes with more rules and documentation required. Larger projects do require more coordination and tighter controls on communication and configuration management. Smaller projects and smaller teams will, these days, tend to follow more agile development processes, with more flexibility and less documentation required. This certainly doesn't mean there is *no* process in an agile project, it just means you do what makes sense for the project you're writing so that you can satisfy all the requirements, meet the schedule, and produce a quality product. See Chapter 2 for more details on process and software life cycles.

The ability to be flexible about that process. No project ever proceeds as you think it will on the first day. Requirements change, people come and go, tools don't work out, and so on. This point is all about handling risk in your project. If you identify risks, plan to mitigate them, and then have a contingency plan to address the event where the risk actually occurs, you'll be in much better shape. Chapter 4 talks about requirements and risk.

A _plan_ that every one buys into. You wouldn't write a sorting program without an algorithm, so you shouldn't launch a software development project without a plan. The project plan encapsulates what you're going to do to implement your project. It talks about process, risks, resources, tools, requirements management, estimates, schedules, configuration management, and delivery. It doesn't have to be long and it doesn't need to contain all the minute details of the everyday life of the project, but everyone on the team needs to have input into it, they need to understand it, and they need to agree with it. Unless everyone buys into the plan, you're doomed. See Chapter 3 for more details on project plans.

To know where you are at all times. It's that communication thing again. Most projects have regular status meetings so that the developers can "sync up" on their current status and get a feel for the status of the entire project. This works very well for smaller teams (say, up to about 20 developers). Many small teams will have daily meetings to sync up at the beginning of each day. Different process models handle this "spot" meeting differently. Many plan-driven models don't require these meetings, depending on the team managers to communicate with each other. Agile processes often require daily meetings to improve communications among team members and to create a sense of camaraderie within the team.

To be brave enough to say, "hey, we're behind!" Nearly all software projects have schedules that are too optimistic at the start. It's just the way we are. Software developers are an optimistic bunch, generally, and it shows in their estimates of work. "Sure, I can get that done in a week!" "I'll have it to you by the end of the day." "Tomorrow? Not a problem." No, no, no, no, no. Just face it. At some point you'll be behind. And the best thing to do about it is to tell your manager right away. Sure, she might be angry. But she'll be angrier when you end up a month behind and she didn't know it. Fred Brooks' famous answer to the question of how software projects get so far behind is "one day at a time." The good news, though, is that the earlier you figure out you're behind, the more options you have. These include lengthening the schedule (unlikely, but it does happen), moving some requirements to a future release, getting additional help, etc. The important part is to keep your manager informed.

The right tools and the right practices for this project. One of the best things about software development is that every project is different. Even if you're doing version 8.0 of an existing product, things change. One implication of this is that for every project one needs to examine and pick the right set of development tools for *this* particular project. Picking tools that are inappropriate is like trying to hammer nails with a screwdriver; you might be able to do it eventually, but is sure isn't easy or pretty, and you can drive a lot more nails in a shorter period of time with a hammer than with a screwdriver. The three most important factors in choosing tools are the application type you are writing, the target platform, and the development platform. You usually can't do anything about any of these three things, so once you know what they are, you can pick tools that improve your productivity. A fourth and nearly as important factor in tool choice is the composition and experience of the development team. If your team are all experienced developers with facility on multiple platforms tool choice is much easier. If, on the other hand, you have a bunch of fresh-outs and your target platform is new to all of you, you'll need to be careful about tool choice and fold in time for training and practice with the new tools.

To realize that you don't know everything you need to know at the beginning of the project. Software development projects just don't work this way. You'll always uncover new requirements; other requirements will be discovered to be not nearly as important as the customer thought; still others that were targeted for the next release are all of a sudden requirement number 1. Managing requirements churn during a project is one of the single most important skills a software developer can have. If you are using new development tools (say that new web development framework) you'll uncover limitations you weren't aware of and side-effects that cause you to have to learn, for example, three other tools to understand them. (That web development tool is Python based, requires a specific relational database system to run, and needs a particular configuration of Apache to work correctly.)

Conclusion

Software development is the heart of every software project, and it is the heart of software engineering. Its objective is to deliver excellent, defect-free code to users on time and within budget –all in the face of constantly changing requirements. That makes development a particularly hard job to do. But finding a solution to a difficult problem and getting your code to work correctly is just about the coolest feeling in the world.

> *"[Programming is] the only job I can think of where I get to be both an engineer and an artist. There's an incredible, rigorous, technical element to it, which I like because you have to do very precise thinking. On the other hand, it has a wildly creative side where the boundaries of imagination are the only real limitation. The marriage of those two elements is what makes programming unique. You get to be both an artist and a scientist. I like that. I love creating the magic trick at the center that is the real foundation for writing the program. Seeing that magic trick, that essence of your program, working correctly for the first time, is the most thrilling part of writing a program."*

— Andy Hertzfeld (designer of the first Mac OS)[2]

References

Brooks, Frederick. "No Silver Bullet." *IEEE Computer* (1987). 20(4): 10-19.

Lammers, Susan. *Programmers at Work.* (Redmond, WA: Microsoft Press, 1986).

---

[2] Lammers, Susan. *Programmers at Work.* (Redmond, WA: Microsoft Press, 1986).

CHAPTER 2

Process Life Cycle Models

If you don't know where you're going, any road will do.
If you don't know where you are, a map won't help.

- Watts Humphrey

Every program has a life cycle. It doesn't matter how large or small the program is, or how many people are working on the project – all programs go through the same steps:

1. Conception

2. Requirements gathering/exploration/modeling

3. Design

4. Coding and debugging

5. Testing

6. Release

7. Maintenance/software evolution

8. Retirement

One's program may compress some of these steps, or combine two or more steps into a single piece of work, but all programs go through all steps.

Although every program has a life cycle, there are many different process variations that encompass these steps. Every life cycle model, however, is a variation on two fundamental types. In the first type, the project team will generally do a complete life cycle – at least steps 2 through 7 – before they go back and start on the next version of the product. In the second type, which is more prevalent these days, the project team will generally do a partial life cycle – usually steps 3 through 5 – and iterate through those steps several times before proceeding to the release step.

These days the management of software development projects generally fall into two different types, traditional *plan-driven models*,[1] and the newer *agile development* models.[2] In the plan-driven models, the process tends to be stricter in terms of process steps and when releases happen. Plan-driven models have more clearly defined phases, and more requirements for sign-off on completion of a phase before moving on to the next phase. Plan-driven models require more documentation of each phase and verification of completion of each work product. These tend to work well for government contracts for new software with well-defined deliverables. The agile models are inherently incremental, and make the assumption that small, frequent releases produce a more robust product than larger, less frequent ones. Phases in agile models tend to blur together more than in plan-driven models, and there tends to be less documentation of work products required, the basic idea being that code is what is being produced and so documentation efforts should focus there. See the Agile Manifesto web page at http://agilemanifesto.org to get a good feel for the agile development model and goals.

We'll take a look at several life cycle models, both plan-driven and agile, and compare them. There is no one best process for developing software. Each project must decide on the model that works best for its particular application and base that decision on the project domain, the size of the project, the experience of the team, and the timeline of the project.

A Model That's not a Model At All: Code and Fix

The first model of software development we'll talk about isn't really a model at all. But it is what most of us do when we're working on small projects by ourselves, or maybe with a single partner. It's the *code and fix Model*.

The code and fix model, shown in Figure 2-1, is often used in lieu of actual project management. In this model there are no formal requirements, no required documentation, no quality assurance or formal testing, and release is haphazard at best. Don't even think about effort estimates or schedules when using this model.

Code and fix says take a minimal amount of time to understand the problem and then start coding. Compile your code and try it out. If it doesn't work, fix the first problem you see and try it again. Continue this cycle of type-compile-run-fix until the program does what you want with no fatal errors and then ship it.

Every programmer knows this model. We've all used it way more than once, and it actually works in certain circumstances: for quick, disposable tasks. For example, it works well for proof-of-concept programs. There's no maintenance involved and the model works well for small, single-person programs. It is, however, a *very dangerous* model for any other kind of program.

With no real mention of configuration management, little in the way of testing, no architectural planning, and probably little more than a desk check of the program for a code review this model is good for quick and dirty prototypes and really nothing more. Software created using this model will be small, short on user interface niceties, and idiosyncratic.

---

[1] Paulk, M. C. *The Capability Maturity Model: Guidelines for Improving the Software Process.* (Reading, MA: Addison-Wesley, 1995.)

[2] Martin, R. C. *Agile Software Development, Principles, Patterns, and Practices.* (Upper Saddle River, NJ: Prentice Hall, 2003.)

That said, this is a terrific way to do quick and dirty prototypes and short, one-off programs. It's useful to validate architectural decisions and to show a quick version of a user interface design. Use it to understand the larger problem you're working on.

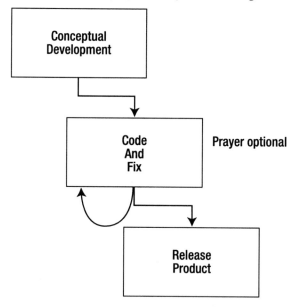

Figure 2-1. *The code and fix process (non) model*

Cruising over the Waterfall

The first and most traditional of the plan-driven process models is the *waterfall* model. Shown in Figure 2-2, it was created in 1970 by Winston Royce,[3] and addresses all of the standard life cycle phases. It progresses nicely through requirements gathering and analysis, to architectural design, detailed design, coding, debugging, system testing, release, and maintenance. It requires detailed documentation at each stage, along with reviews, archiving of the documents, sign-offs at each process phase, configuration management, and close management of the entire project. It's a model of the plan-driven process.

---

[3] Royce, W. W. *Managing the Development of Large Software Systems.* Proceedings of IEEE WESCON, IEEE Press. (1970)

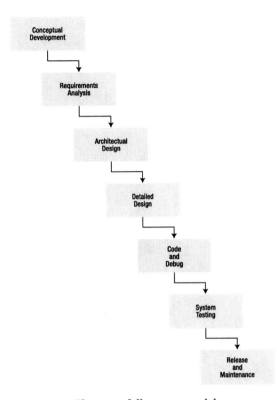

Figure 2-2. The waterfall process model

It also doesn't work.

There are two fundamental and related problems with the waterfall model that hamper its acceptance and make it very difficult to implement. First, it generally requires that you finish phase N before you continue on to phase N+1. In the simplest example, this means that you must nail down *all* your requirements before you start your architectural design, and finish your coding and debugging before you start anything but unit testing, etc. In theory, this is great. You'll have a complete set of requirements, you'll understand exactly what the customer wants, and everything the customer wants, so you can then confidently move on to designing the system.

In practice, this never happens though. I've never worked on a project where all the requirements were nailed down at the beginning of the work. I've never seen a project where big things didn't change somewhere during development. So finishing one phase before the other begins is problematic.

The second problem with the waterfall is that, as stated, it has no provision for backing up. It is fundamentally based on an assembly-line mentality for developing software. The nice little diagram shows no way to go back and rework your design if you find a problem during implementation. This is similar to the first problem above. The implications are that you really have to nail down one phase and review everything in detail before you move on. In practice this is just not – practical. The world doesn't work this way. You never know everything you need to know at exactly the time you need to know it. This is why software is a wicked problem.

All this being said, the waterfall is a terrific theoretical model. It isolates the different phases of the life cycle and forces you to think about what you really do need to know before you move on. It's also a good way to start thinking about very large projects; it gives managers a warm fuzzy because it lets them think they know what's going on (they don't, but that's another story). It's also a good model for inexperienced teams working on a well-defined, new project because it leads them through the life cycle.

So because the waterfall is not a good practical model, it immediately morphs into a slightly different one.

Backing Up the Waterfall

The first thing that happens to the waterfall model is that it changes into the waterfall with feedback, shown in Figure 2-3. This is an admission that a straight-line waterfall doesn't work and that you need the ability to back up to a previous phase when you discover a problem in the current phase.

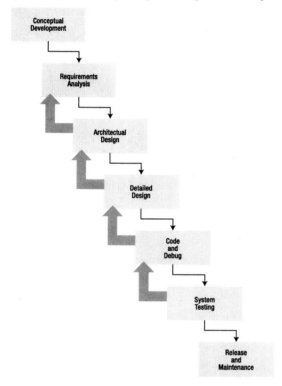

Figure 2-3. Waterfall with feedback process model

The waterfall with feedback model recognizes that you have to start work with incomplete requirements, design, test plan, and so on. It also explicitly builds in the idea that you will have to go back to previous process steps as new information about your project is uncovered. The new information can be new requirements, updated requirements, design flaws, defects in testing plans, and the like. Any of these will require that you revisit a previous process step to rectify the problem.

This process model is still quite rigid, and it still has the same advantages of a waterfall model when it comes to very large, new projects and inexperienced teams. The two main disadvantages with the waterfall with feedback model are that it really messes with your scheduling big time, and it makes it harder to know when you're finished. It messes with your schedule because in any phase there can be unexpected moves back to a previous phase of development. This also means it's harder to know when you are done.

Because of these disadvantages, the waterfall with feedback model also morphs into a new model, one that attempts to address the scheduling and uncertainty issues.

Loops Are Your Friend

The best practice is to iterate and deliver incrementally, treating each iteration as a closed-end "mini-project," including complete requirements, design, coding integration, testing, and internal delivery. On the iteration deadline, deliver the (fully-tested, fully-integrated) system thus far to internal stakeholders. Solicit their feedback on that work, and fold that feedback into the plan for the next iteration.

(from "How Agile Projects Succeed"[4])

While the waterfall with feedback model recognizes that all the requirements aren't typically known in advance, and that mistakes will be made in architectural design and detailed design, it doesn't go far enough in taking those realizations into the process. Iterative process models make this required change in process steps more explicit and create process models that build products a piece at a time.

In most iterative process models, you'll take the known requirements – you'll take a snapshot of the requirements at some time early in the process – and prioritize them, typically based on the customer's ranking of what features are most important to deliver first.

You then pick the highest priority requirements and plan a series of iterations, where each iteration is a complete project. For each iteration, you'll add a set of the next highest priority requirements (including some you may have discovered during the previous iteration) and repeat the project. By doing a complete project with a subset of the requirements every time at the end of each iteration you end up with a complete, working, and robust product, albeit with fewer features than the final product will have.

According to Tom DeMarco, these iterative processes follow one basic rule:

Your project, the whole project, has a binary deliverable. On the scheduled completion day, the project has either delivered a system that is accepted by the user, or it hasn't. Everyone knows the result on that day.

The object of building a project model is to divide the project into component pieces, each of which has this same characteristic: each activity must be defined by a deliverable with <u>objective completion criteria</u>. The deliverables are demonstrably done or not done."[5]

So what happens if you estimate wrong? What if you decide to include too many new features in an iteration? What if there are unexpected delays?

---

[4] www.adaptionsoft.com/on_time.html

[5] DeMarco, T. *Controlling Software Projects: Management, Measurement and Estimation.* (Upper Saddle River, NJ: Yourdon Press, 1983.)

Well, if it looks as if you won't make your iteration deadline there are only two realistic alternatives: move the deadline, or remove features. We'll come back to this problem when we talk about estimation and scheduling.

The key to iterative development is "live a balanced life – learn some and think some and draw and paint and sing and dance and play and work every day some,"[6] or in the software development world, *analyze* some and *design* some and *code* some and *test* some every day. We'll revisit this idea when we talk about the agile development models.

Evolving the Incremental Model

The traditional way of implementing the incremental model is known as *evolutionary prototyping*.[7] In evolutionary prototyping, one prioritizes requirements as they are received and produces a succession of increasingly feature-rich versions of the product. Each version is refined using customer feedback and the results of integration and system testing. This is an excellent model for an environment of changing or ambiguous requirements, or a poorly understood application domain. This is the model that evolved into the modern agile development processes. See Figure 2-4.

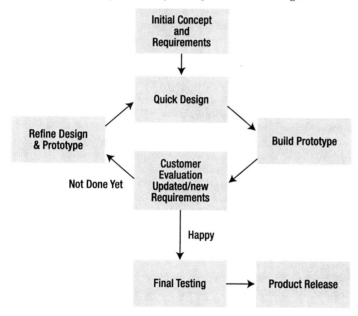

Figure 2-4. Evolutionary prototyping process model

---

[6]Fulghum, R. *All I Really Need to Know I Learned in Kindergarten.* Revised Edition. (New York, NY: Ballantine Books, 2004.)

[7]McConnell, S. *Rapid Development: Taming Wild Software Schedules.* (Redmond, WA: Microsoft Press, 1996.)

Evolutionary prototyping recognizes that it's very hard to plan the full project from the start and that feedback is a critical element of good analysis and design. It's somewhat risky from a scheduling point of view, but when compared to any variation of the waterfall model it has a very good track record. Evolutionary prototyping provides improved progress visibility for both the customer and project management. It also provides good customer and end user input to product requirements and does a good job of prioritizing those requirements.

On the downside, evolutionary prototyping leads to the danger of unrealistic schedules, budget overruns, and overly optimistic progress expectations. These can happen because the limited number of requirements implemented in a prototype can give the impression of real progress for a small amount of work. On the flip side, putting too many requirements in a prototype can result is schedule slippages, because of overly optimistic estimation. This is a tricky balance to maintain. Because the design evolves over time as the requirements change, there is the possibility of a bad design, unless there's the provision of re-designing – something that becomes harder and harder to do as the project progresses and your customer is more heavily invested in a particular version of the product. There is also the possibility of low maintainability, again because the design and code evolve as requirements change. This may lead to lots of re-work, a busted schedule, and increased difficulty in fixing bugs post-release.

Evolutionary prototyping works best with tight, experienced teams who have worked on several projects together. This type of cohesive team is productive and dexterous, able to focus on each iteration and usually producing the coherent, extensible designs that a series of prototypes requires. This model is not generally recommended for inexperienced teams.

Agile Is as Agile Does

Starting in the mid 1990s, a group of process mavens began advocating a new model for software development. As opposed to the heavyweight plan-driven models mentioned above and espoused by groups like the Software Engineering Institute (SEI) at Carnegie Mellon,[8] this new process model was lightweight. It required less documentation and fewer process controls. It was targeted at small to medium-sized software projects and smaller teams of developers. It was intended to allow these teams of developers to quickly adjust to changing requirements and customer demands, and it proposed to release completed software much more quickly than the plan-driven models. It was, in a word, agile.[9]

Agile development works from the proposition that the goal of any software development project is working code. And because the focus is on working software, then the development team should spend most of their time writing code, not writing documents. This gives these processes the name lightweight.

Lightweight methodologies have several characteristics. They tend to emphasize writing tests before code, frequent product releases, significant customer involvement in development, common code ownership, and refactoring – rewriting code to make it simpler and easier to maintain. Lightweight methodologies also suffer from several myths. The two most pernicious are probably that lightweight processes are only good for very small projects, and that you don't have to have any process discipline in a lightweight project.

The truth is that lightweight methodologies have been successfully used in many small and medium-sized projects – say up to about 500K lines of code. Lightweight methodologies also require process discipline, especially in the beginning of a project when initial requirements and an iteration cycle are created and in the test-driven-development used as the heart of the coding process.

---

[8]Paulk, M. C. (1995)

[9]Cockburn, A. *Agile Software Development*. (Boston, MA: Addison-Wesley, 2002.)

We'll look at two lightweight/agile methodologies, eXtreme Programming, and Scrum.

eXtreme Programming (XP)

eXtreme Programming was created around 1995 by Kent Beck and Ward Cunningham. XP is a "lightweight, efficient, low-risk, flexible, predictable, scientific, and fun way to develop software."[10]

XP Overview

XP relies on the following four fundamental ideas:

- *Heavy customer involvement:* XP requires that a customer representative be part of the development team and be on site at all times. The customer representative works with the team to create the contents of each iteration of the product, and she creates all the acceptance tests for each interim release.

- *Continuous unit testing* (also known as test-driven development [TDD]): XP calls for developers to write the unit tests for any new features before any of the code is written. In this way the tests will, of course, initially all fail, but it gives a developer a clear metric for success. When all the unit tests pass, you've finished implementing the feature.

- *Pair programming:* XP requires that all code be written by pairs of developers. In a nutshell, pair programming requires two programmers – a driver and a navigator – who share a single computer. The driver is actually writing the code while the navigator watches, catching typos, making suggestions, thinking about design and testing, and so on. The pair switches places periodically (every 30 minutes or so, or when one of them thinks he has a better way of implementing a piece of code). Pair programming works on the "two heads are better than one" theory. While a pair of programmers is not quite as productive as two individual programmers when it comes to number of lines of code written per unit of time, their code usually contains fewer defects, and they have a set of unit tests to show that it works. This makes them more productive overall. Pair programming also provides the team an opportunity to re-factor existing code – to re-design it to make it as simple as possible while still meeting the customer's requirements. Pair programming is not exclusive to XP, but XP was the first discipline to use it exclusively.

---

[10]This is a very short description of how XP works; for a much more eloquent and detailed explanation, really the bible of XP, see:

Beck, K. *Extreme Programming Explained: Embrace Change.* (Boston, MA: Addison-Wesley, 2000.)

- *Short iteration cycles and frequent releases:* XP typically uses release cycles in the range of just a few months and each release is composed of several iterations, each on the order of 4–6 weeks. The combination of frequent releases and an on-site customer representative allows the XP team to get immediate feedback on new features and to uncover design and requirements issues early. XP also requires constant integration and building of the product. Whenever a programming pair finishes a feature and it passes all their unit tests, they immediately integrate and build the entire product. They then use all the unit tests as a regression test suite to make sure the new feature hasn't broken anything already checked in. If it does break something, they fix it immediately. So in an XP project, integrations and builds can happen several times a day. This process gives the team a good feel for where they are in the release cycle every day and gives the customer a completed build on which to run the acceptance tests.

XP Motivation

Risk is the most basic problem in software. Risk manifests itself in many ways: schedule slips, project cancelation, increased defect rates, misunderstanding of the business problem, false feature rich (you've added features the customer really doesn't want or need), and staff turnover. Managing risk is a very difficult and time-consuming management problem. Minimizing and handling risk are the key areas of risk management. XP seeks to minimize risk by controlling the four variables of software development.

The Four Variables

The four variables of software development projects are as follows:

- Cost
- Time
- Features
- Quality

Cost is probably the most constrained; you can't spend your way to quality or schedule, and as a developer you have very limited control over cost. Cost also is where Brooks' law gets invoked (adding programmers to a late project just makes it later).

Time is your delivery schedule and is unfortunately usually imposed on you from the outside. For example, most consumer products (be they hardware or software) will have a delivery date in late summer or early fall in order to hit the holiday buying season. You can't move Christmas. If you are late, the only way to fix your problem is to drop features or lessen quality; neither of which is pretty.

Quality is the number and severity of defects you are willing to release with. You can make short-term gains in delivery schedules by sacrificing quality, but the cost is enormous. It will take more time to fix the next release and your credibility is pretty well shot.

Features (also called *scope*) is what the product actually does. This is what developers should always focus on. It's the most important of the variables from the customer's perspective and it is also the one you as a developer have the most control over. Controlling scope allows you to provide managers and customers control over quality, time, and cost.

XP recognizes that to minimize risk, developers need to control as many of the variables as possible, but especially they need to control the scope of the project. XP uses the metaphor of "learning to drive." Learning to drive is not pointing the car in the right direction. It's pointing the car, constantly paying attention and making the constant minor corrections necessary to keep the car on the road. In programming, the only constant is change. If you pay attention and cope with change as it occurs, you can keep the cost of change manageable.

The Four Values

In order for XP to be a viable discipline of development everyone who is involved in an XP project needs to buy into a common set of values that will permeate all the rules that make up the discipline. In XP there are the following four core values that enable it to work:

- Communication

- Simplicity

- Feedback

- Courage

Communication really means spreading the collective knowledge of the group around to all the members. Keeping the XP team small facilitates communication by keeping the number of lines of communication small. Pair programming and collective ownership of the code also facilitate communication by spreading the knowledge of the entire code base around the entire team. XP developers are encouraged to fix bugs they find and to redesign features to make them simpler (see below); this spreads knowledge of the code widely among the team.

Simplicity is key. XP focuses on developing the simplest piece of software that solves today's task. XP developers bet that "...it is better to do a simple thing today and pay a little more tomorrow to change it if it needs it, than to do a more complicated thing today that may never be used anyway." All developers on an XP team are allowed and encouraged to redesign code to make it simpler at any time. This practice is called "refactoring." "Concrete *feedback* about the current state of the system is absolutely priceless. Optimism is an occupational hazard of programming. Feedback is the treatment."[11] XP programmers are required to write tests before they write the code, so that they always have immediate feedback about their code and its impact on the system. Also, the customer is writing functional (acceptance) tests so those are available to measure how well the system is adhering to the "stories" used to develop it.

XP developers must have *courage*. They must be willing to make changes at any time when the design no longer fits. They need to be prepared to throw code away if it doesn't work. Simplicity supports courage because you're less likely to break a simple system. XP team members track the schedule daily and involve the customer in re-prioritizing features as soon as needed.

The 15 Principles

From the four values described above XP derives some basic principles. The list looks like the following:

> *Rapid feedback*: Get feedback, interpret it, and put it back into the system as quickly as possible. Automated tests are crucial here because you can run unit tests all the time and you can run the entire regression suite whenever you want to integrate your changes.

---

[11]Beck, K. (2000)

Assume simplicity. Focus on today's task and solve it in the simplest way possible. This also means that you should be looking for ways to simplify the code whenever you're making changes. Refactoring keeps the code as simple as possible and reduces defects.

Incremental change. Integrate your new code into the system every day. In fact, integrate whenever you finish a task. This allows you to find interface and interaction errors quickly and gives the customer a new baseline to examine at least once a day.

Embracing change. It's gonna happen, so be prepared for it. The whole basis of agile methodologies like XP is that change is a constant in software development and the more your discipline accommodates change, the better your development process will be.

Quality work. Quality isn't free; strive for defect-free code. Pair programming gives you the two heads are better than one gift and test-driven development focuses your code on satisfying requirements. Both of these help lead to fewer defects in your code.

Teach learning. Teach how to learn to do testing, refactoring, and coding better rather than set down a set of rules that say, "you must test this way."

Small initial investment. The emphasis here is on small teams, particularly at the beginning of a project to manage the resources carefully and conservatively. If you start with fewer resources and a tight budget, it will focus your thinking on lean design and code. This reinforces simplicity.

Play to win. As opposed to playing not to lose. If you don't worry about schedules, or requirements churn, your days will be more relaxed, you'll be able to focus on the problems at hand (and not on the next deadline) and your code will be cleaner, you'll be more relaxed and more productive. Just relax and win.

Concrete experiments. Every abstract decision (requirements or design) should be tested. In XP and in other agile methodologies, you're encouraged to produce something called a *spike.* A spike is a quick and dirty proof-of-concept piece of code that implements at least the outline of your decision so you can see if you're actually right. Or, if you're wrong, you've not wasted lots of time figuring that out.

Open, honest communication. You have to be able to criticize constructively and be able to deliver bad news as well as good. This is the foundation of a good design or code review. The culture of the team must be that you can offer constructive criticism at any time. The idea is two-fold; first, you're all trying to improve the code, so criticism is a good thing, and second, common code ownership means that everyone is entitled to make changes without fear of hurting someone else's feelings.

Work with people's instincts, not against them. People generally like to win, like working with others, like being part of a team, and especially like seeing their code work. Don't do things that go against this.

Accepted responsibility. The team as a whole is responsible for the product. Responsibility is accepted by the entire team and tasks are not assigned, they're requested. Common code ownership leads to common project ownership. XP teams typically do not have managers that assign work; they have a coach to help with the process and a project manager to take care of the administrative tasks. The development team members themselves select tasks and make sure they get done.

Local adaptation: Change XP to fit your local circumstances and project. This is an application of accepted responsibility. The team owns the project, so the team also owns the process and they reach consensus on adaptations.

Travel light: The team and process artifacts you maintain should be few, simple, and valuable. This implies that you should be willing to change directions quickly and jettison things (code, design) that aren't working for ones that do.

Honest measurement: Measure at the right level of detail and only measure what makes sense for your project. Remember the difference between accuracy and precision.

The Four Basic Activities

In order for XP to take the values and principles just described and create a discipline out of them, we need to describe the activities we'll use as the foundation. XP describes four activities that are the bedrock of the discipline.

- *Coding:* The code is where the knowledge of the system resides so it's your main activity. The fundamental difference between plan-driven models and agile models is this emphasis on the code. In a plan-driven model, the emphasis is on producing a set of work products that together represent the entire work of the project with code being just one of the work products. In agile methodologies, the code is the sole deliverable and so the emphasis is placed squarely there; in addition, by structuring the code properly and keeping comments up to date, the code becomes documentation for the project.

- *Testing:* The tests tell you when you are done coding. Test-driven development is crucial to the idea of managing change. XP depends heavily on writing unit tests before writing the code that they test and on using an automated testing framework to run all the unit tests whenever changes are integrated.

- *Listening:* To your partner and to the customer. In any given software development project there are two types of knowledge. The customer has knowledge of the business application being written and what it is supposed to do. This is the domain knowledge of the project. The developers have knowledge about the target platform, the programming language(s), and the implementation issues. This is the technical knowledge of the project. The customer doesn't know the technical side and the developers don't have the domain knowledge, so listening – on both sides – is a key activity in developing the product.

- *Designing*: Design while you code. "Designing is creating a structure that organizes the logic in the system. Good design organizes the logic so that a change in one part of the system doesn't always require a change in another part of the system. Good design ensures that every piece of logic in the system has one and only one home. Good design puts the logic near the data it operates on. Good design allows the extension of the system with changes in only one place."[12]

Implementing XP: The 12 Practices

We (finally) get to the implementation of XP. Here are the rules that every XP team follows during their project. The rules may vary depending on the team and the project, but in order to call yourselves an XP team, you need to do some form of these things. The practices described here draw on everything previously described: the four values, the 15 principles, and the four activities. This is really XP.

- *The planning game*: Develop the scope of the next release by combining business priorities and technical estimates. The customer and the development team need to decide on the stories (read features) that will be included in the next release, the priority of each story, and when the release needs to be done. The developers are responsible for breaking the stories up into a set of tasks and for estimating the duration of each task. The sum of the durations tells the team what they really think they can get done before the release delivery date. If necessary, stories are moved out of a release if the numbers don't add up. Notice that estimation is the responsibility of the developers and not the customer or the manager. In XP *only* the developers do estimation.

- *Small releases*: Put a simple system into production quickly, and then release new versions on a very short cycle. Each release has to make sense from a business perspective, so release size will vary. It is far better to plan releases in durations of a month or two rather than six or twelve. The longer a release is, the harder it is to estimate.

- *Metaphor*: "A simple shared story of how the whole system works." The metaphor replaces your architecture. It needs to be a coherent explanation of the system that is decomposable into smaller bits – stories. Stories should always be expressed in the vocabulary of the metaphor and the language of the metaphor should be common to both the customer and the developers.

- *Simple design*: Keep the design as simple as you can each day. Re-design often to keep it simple. According to Beck, a simple design (1) runs all the unit tests, (2) has no duplicated code, (3) expresses what each story means in the code, and (4) has the fewest number of classes and methods that make sense to implement the stories so far.[13]

---

[12]Beck, K. (2000)
[13]Beck, K. (2000)

- *Testing:* Programmers constantly write unit tests. Tests must all pass before integration. Beck takes the hard line that "Any program feature without an automated test simply doesn't exist."[14] Although this works for most acceptance tests and should certainly work for all unit tests, this analogy breaks down in some instances, notably in testing the user interface in a GUI. Even this can be made to work automatically if your test framework can handle the events generated by a GUI interaction. Beyond this, having a good set of written instructions will normally fill the bill.

- *Refactoring:* Restructure the system "without changing its behavior" to make it simpler – remove redundancy, eliminate unnecessary layers of code, or to add flexibility. The key to refactoring is to identify areas of code that can be made simpler and to do it while you're there. Refactoring is closely related to collective ownership and simple design. Collective ownership gives you permission to change the code and simple design imposes on you the responsibility to make the change when you see it needs to be made.

- *Pair programming:* All production code written in an XP project must be written by two programmers at one machine. Any code written alone is thrown away. Pair programming is a dynamic process. You may change partners as often as you change tasks to implement. This has the effect of reinforcing collective ownership by spreading the knowledge of the entire system around the entire team. It avoids the "beer truck problem," where the person who knows everything gets hit by a beer truck and thus sets the project schedule back months.

- *Collective ownership:* The team owns everything, implying that anyone can change anything at any time. In some places this is known as "ego-less programming." Programmers need to buy into the idea that anyone can change their code and that collective ownership extends from code to the entire project; it's a team project, not an individual one.

- *Continuous integration:* Integrate and build every time a task is finished, possibly several times a day (as long as the tests all pass). This helps to isolate problems in the code base; if you're integrating a single task change, then the most likely place to look for a problem is right there.

- *40-hour week:* Work a regular 40-hour week. Never work a second week in a row with overtime. The XP philosophy has a lot in common with many of Tom DeMarco's *Peopleware* arguments. People are less productive if they're working 60 or 70 hours a week than if they are working 40 hours. When you're working excessive amounts of overtime, several things happen. Because you don't have time to do chores and things related to your "life," you do them during the workday. Constantly being under deadline pressure and never getting a sustained break also means you get tired and then make more mistakes, which somebody then needs to fix. But being in control of the project and working 40-hours a week (give or take a few) leaves you with time for a life, time to relax and recharge, and time to focus on your work during the work-day, making you more productive, not less.

---

[14]Beck, K. (2000)

- *On-site customer.* A customer is part of the team, is on-site, writes and executes functional tests, and helps clarify requirements. The customer's ability to give immediate feedback to changes in the system also increases team confidence that they are building the right system every day.

- *Coding standards.* The team has 'em, follows 'em, and uses 'em to improve communication. Because of collective code ownership the team must have coding standards and everyone must adhere to them. Without a sensible set of coding guidelines, it would take much, much longer to do refactoring and it would decrease the desire of developers to change code. Notice that I said sensible. Your coding standards should make your code easier to read and maintain: they shouldn't constrict creativity.

The XP Life Cycle

The XP life cycle contains all the phases of the generic life cycle described at the start of the chapter, but it compresses the middle three phases – design, code, and test – into a single implementation phase. A productizing phase is added after implementation to allow the code to be stabilized before release. The XP life cycle shows how producing code is the centerpiece of the methodology.

9. *Exploration:* Exploration is done when "the customer is confident that there is more than enough material on the story cards to make a good first release and the programmers are confident that they can't estimate any better without actually implementing the system."[15] During exploration, the team's main goal is to get as many requirements (story cards) written as they can. This is also the time when they can explore the architecture possibilities by doing a quick spike of the system. Estimate all tasks done during exploration to practice your estimation skills. In most projects Exploration is the "fuzzy front-end" of the project. You're not quite sure how long it will take and you're gathering requirements and trying to figure out what the product will actually *do*.

10. *Planning game.* The Planning game is the tail end of your release exploration phase. In the planning game you need to identify your top priority, high-value stories and agree with the customer which ones will be in the next release. Releases should be from two to six months duration each. Any shorter and you're not likely to get any significant work done and any longer is just plain too hard to plan. Then you need to plan the first few iterations for the release; iterations are 1 to 4 weeks each. Each iteration produces functional test cases for each story scheduled for the iteration. The first iteration helps you nail down your metaphor for the project and puts the architecture in place. Subsequent iterations add new features based on the prioritized list of stories. Reschedule as necessary.

11. *Implement:* Design, code, test, or actually, design, test, code. One task at a time until all the tasks for a story are complete, and one story at a time until all the stories for this iteration are complete. Need we say more?

---

[15]Beck, K. (2000)

12. *Productizing*: Occurs in the last iteration before your release is done. At this point you should freeze new functionality and focus on stabilizing the product, tuning performance, if necessary, and running acceptance tests.

13. *Maintenance/evolution*: Well, according to the agile philosophy, you're always in maintenance mode. Here though, you've released something the customer will use and you now must "simultaneously produce new functionality, keep the existing system running, incorporate new people into the team, and bid farewell to members who move on."[16]

14. *Death*: If the customer can't come up with new stories, mothball the code. If the system can't deliver anymore, mothball the code and start over.

Scrum, mate

The second agile methodology we'll look at is *Scrum*. Scrum derives its name from rugby, where a scrum is a means of restarting play after a rules infraction. The scrum uses the eight forwards on a rugby team (out of 15 players in the rugby union form of the game) to attempt to (re)gain control of the ball and move it forward towards the opposing goal line. The idea in the agile Scrum methodology is that a small team is unified around a single goal and gets together for sprints of development that move them towards that goal.

Scrum is, in fact, older than XP, with the original process management idea coming from Takeuchi and Nonaka's 1986 paper, "The New New Product Development Game."[17] The first use of the term scrum is attributed to DeGrace and Stahl's 1990 book *Wicked Problems, Righteous Solutions*.[18] Scrum is a variation on the iterative development approach and incorporates many of the features of XP. Scrum is more of a management approach than XP and doesn't define many of the detailed development practices (like pair programming or test-driven development) that XP does, although most scrum projects will use these practices.

Scrum uses teams of no more than 10 developers. Just like other agile methodologies, scrum emphasizes the efficacy of small teams and collective ownership.

Scrum is characterized by the *sprint*, an iteration of between one and four weeks. Sprints are time-boxed in that they are of a fixed duration and the output of a sprint is what work the team can accomplish during the sprint. The delivery date for the sprint does not move out. This means that sometimes a sprint can finish early, and sometimes a sprint will finish with less functionality than was proposed. A sprint always delivers a usable product.

Scrum requirements are encapsulated in two backlogs. The product backlog is the prioritized list of all the requirements for the project; it is created by the scrum team and the product owner. The sprint backlog is the prioritized list of requirements (say user stories) for the current sprint. Once the sprint starts, only the development team may add items to the sprint backlog – these are usually bugs found during testing. No outside entity may add items to the sprint backlog, only to the product backlog.

---

[16]Beck, K. (2000)

[17]Takeuchi, H. and I. Nonaka. "The New New Product Development Game." *Harvard Business Review* **64**(1): 137-146. (1986)

[18]DeGrace, P. and L. H. Stahl. Wicked Problems, Righteous Solutions: A Catalogue of Modern Software Engineering Paradigms. (Englewood Cliffs, NJ: Yourdon Press, 1990.)

Scrum projects are facilitated by a ScrumMaster whose job it is to manage the backlogs, run the daily Scrum meetings, and to protect the team from outside influences during the sprint. The scrum master is usually not a developer.

Scrum projects have a daily scrum meeting, which is a stand-up meeting of 15–30 minutes duration where the entire team discusses sprint progress. The daily Scrum meeting allows the team to share information and track sprint progress. By having daily Scrum meetings, any slip in the schedule or any problems in implementation are immediately obvious and can then be addressed by the team at once. "The Scrum master ensures that everyone makes progress, records the decisions made at the meeting and tracks action items, and keeps the Scrum meetings short and focused."[19]

At the Scrum meeting, each team member answers the following three questions in turn:

1. What tasks have you finished since the last Scrum meeting?

2. Is anything getting in the way of your finishing your tasks?

3. What tasks are you planning to do between now and the next Scrum meeting?

Discussions other than responses to these three questions are deferred to other meetings. This meeting type has several effects. It allows the entire team to visualize progress towards the sprint and project completion every day. It reinforces team spirit by sharing progress – everyone can feel good about tasks completed. And finally, it verbalizes problems – which can then be solved by the entire team.

The development team itself is self-organizing; the members of the Scrum team decide among themselves who will work on what user stories and tasks, assume collective ownership of the project, and decide on the development process they'll use during the sprint. This organization is reinforced every day at the Scrum meeting.

Before the first sprint starts, Scrum has an initial planning phase that creates the list of the initial requirements, decides on an architecture for implementing the requirements, divides the user stories into prioritized groups for the sprints, and breaks the first set of user stories into tasks to be estimated and assigned. They stop when their estimates occupy all the time allowed for the sprint. Tasks in a sprint should not be longer than one day of effort.

After each sprint, another planning meeting is held where the Scrum master and the team re-prioritize the product backlog and create a backlog for the next sprint. With most Scrum teams, estimates of tasks become better as the project progresses primarily because the team now has data on how they have done estimating on previous sprints. This effect in Scrum is called "acceleration;" the productivity of the team can actually increase during the project as they gel as a team and get better at estimating tasks. This planning meeting is also where the organization can decide whether the project is finished, or whether to finish the project at all.

After the last scheduled sprint, a final sprint is done to bring closure to the project. This sprint implements no new functionality, but prepares the final deliverable for product release. It fixes any existing bugs, finishes documentation, and generally productizes the code. Any requirements left in the product backlog are transferred to the next release A Scrum retrospective is held before the next sprint begins to ponder the previous sprint and see if there are any process improvements that can be made.Scrum is a project management methodology and is typically silent on development processes. Despite this, Scrum teams typically use many of the practices described above in the XP practices

---

[19]Rising, L. and N. S. Janoff. "The Scrum Software Development Process for Small Teams." *IEEE Software* **17**(4): 26-32. (2000)

section. Common code ownership, pair programming, small releases, simple design, test-driven development, continuous integration and coding standards are all common practices in Scrum projects.

Conclusion

As can be seen from the methodologies described in this chapter, iteration is the key, whether you are using an evolutionary plan-driven process or an agile development one. Recognize that the best way to build a complex piece of software is incrementally. Learn that designing, writing, testing, and delivering incrementally better code is your first step to writing great software.

References

Beck, K. *Extreme Programming Explained: Embrace Change.* (Boston, MA: Addison-Wesley, 2000.)

Cockburn, A. *Agile Software Development.* (Boston, MA: Addison-Wesley, 2002.)

DeGrace, P. and L. H. Stahl. *Wicked Problems, Righteous Solutions: A Catalogue of Modern Software Engineering Paradigms.* (Englewood Cliffs, NJ: Yourdon Press, 1990.)

DeMarco, T. *Controlling Software Projects: Management, Measurement and Estimation.* (Upper Saddle River, NJ: Yourdon Press, 1983.)

Martin, R. C. *Agile Software Development, Principles, Patterns, and Practices.* (Upper Saddle River, NJ: Prentice Hall, 2003.)

McConnell, S. *Rapid Development: Taming Wild Software Schedules.* (Redmond, WA: Microsoft Press, 1996.)

Paulk, M. C. *The Capability Maturity Model: Guidelines for Improving the Software Process.* (Reading, MA: Addison-Wesley, 1995.)

Rising, L. and N. S. Janoff. "The Scrum Software Development Process for Small Teams." *IEEE Software* **17**(4): 26-32. (2000)

Royce, W. W. *Managing the Development of Large Software Systems.* Proceedings of IEEE WESCON, IEEE Press. (1970)

Takeuchi, H. and I. Nonaka. "The New New Product Development Game." *Harvard Business Review* **64**(1): 137-146. (1986)

Project Management Essentials

Quality, features, schedule – pick two.

Project management? Isn't this a software development book?

Yes, but working on a larger-than-one-person development project means working on a team; and working on a team means being managed. So learning something about project management from both sides is an essential part of learning software development.

Project management is an involved and complicated set of tasks. We'll restrict ourselves to several tasks that will impact you as a developer the most. They are the following:

- Project planning

- Estimation and scheduling

- Resource management

- Project oversight

- Project reviews and presentations

- The project post-mortem

Project Planning

Project planning is forever. By that I mean that project planning continues throughout the entire duration of the project. "The Plan" is never really set in stone, because things in a typical software project are usually in constant flux. In most projects, and especially in those that are using a plan-driven process model, a project plan is an actual document that is written by the project manager, and that is approved and signed off on by the development team and by upper management. It is, in effect, a contract, albeit a rolling one, of what the team is going to do and how they are going to do it. It also says how the project will be managed, and in the extreme plan-driven cases, even states how and when the document itself will be modified.

What's in the project plan? Generally a project plan consists of the following seven parts:

- Introduction and explanation of the project

- Project organization

- Risk analysis

- Hardware, software, and human resource requirements

- Work breakdown and task estimates

- Project schedule

- Project monitoring and reporting mechanisms, collectively known as project oversight

Not all of these are necessary for all projects or project methodologies. In particular, plan-driven projects will use all of them, while agile projects may use a few on a single page.

Project plans are a great tool for setting down what you think you're doing, an outline of how it will be done, and how you plan on executing the outline. The problem with a project plan is that it's static. Once it's written and signed off on, upper management thinks the project will run exactly as stated in the plan. But the reality of the project often thwarts the plan.

Project Organization

The project organization section of the plan contains the following three things:

- How you're going to organize the team

- What process model the project will be using

- How will the project be run on a day-to-day basis

If you're working with an experienced team, all this is already known to everyone, so your project organization section can be, "We'll do what we usually do." However, this section is a necessity for brand-new projects and inexperienced teams, because the organization section gives you something to hang your hat on when you start the actual project work.

Risk Analysis

In the risk analysis section, you need to think about the bad things.[1] What can possibly go wrong with this project? What is the worst that could happen? What will we do if it does?

Some risks to watch out for are:

- *Schedule slips*: That task that you estimated would take three days has just taken three weeks. In a plan-driven project, this can be an issue if you don't have regular status meetings. Waiting three weeks to tell your boss that you're late is always worse than telling her that you'll be late as soon as you know it. In an agile project this is unlikely, because most agile projects have a daily status meeting (see the Scrum meeting section in Chapter 2).

---

[1] McConnell, S. *Rapid Development: Taming Wild Software Schedules.* (Redmond, WA: Microsoft Press, 1996.)

- *Defect rate is excessive*: Your testing is finding lots of bugs. What do you do, continue to add new features or stop to fix the bugs? Again, this can be a real issue in a project where integration builds happen according to a fixed schedule, say once a week. In a project where integrations happen every day, you can keep up with defects more easily. In either case, if you are experiencing a high defect rate, the best thing to do is to stop, take a look around, and find the root cause of the defects before adding more functionality. This can be very hard to do from a project management standpoint, but you'll thank yourself in the end.

- *Requirements misunderstood*: What you're doing isn't what the customer wanted. This classic problem is the result of the fact that customers and developers live in two different worlds. The customer lives in the application domain where he understands from a user's perspective what he wants the product to do. The developer understands from a technical perspective how the product will work. Occasionally, these worlds intersect and that's good; but lots of times they don't and that is where you get a misunderstanding of requirements. The best way to avoid this situation is to have the customer on site as often as possible and to produce deliverable products as often as possible.

- *Requirements churn*: New features, altered features, deleted features ... will the misery never end? Requirements churn is probably the largest single reason for missed delivery dates, high defect rates, and project failure. Churn happens when the customer (or your own marketing folks, or the development team itself) continues to change requirements while development is underway. It leads to massive amounts of rework in the code, retesting of baselines, and delay after delay. Managing requirements is the single most important job of the project manager. In a plan-driven process this is usually accomplished by a change control board (CCB) that examines each new requirement and decides whether to add it to the list of features to be implemented. There may be a member of the development team on the CCB, but that's not required, so the danger here is that the CCB will add new features without understanding all the scheduling and effort ramifications. In agile processes, the development team usually keeps control of the prioritized requirements list (called the product backlog in Scrum), and only adjusts the list at set points in the project – after iterations in XP, and after each sprint in Scrum.

- *Turnover.* Your most experienced developer decides to join a start-up three weeks before product delivery. The best way to reduce turnover is to (1) give your developers interesting work, (2) have them work in a pleasant environment, and (3) give them control over their own schedules. Oddly enough, money is not one of the main motivators for software developers. This doesn't mean they don't want to get paid well, but it does mean that throwing more money at them in order to get them to work harder or to keep them from leaving doesn't generally work. And if, despite your best efforts, your best developer does leave, you just have to move on. Trust me, it won't be the end of the world. The best way to mitigate the effect of turnover is to spread the knowledge of the project around all the members of the development team. Principles like *common code ownership* and techniques like *pair programming* work to invest all the team members in the product and spreads the knowledge of the code across the entire team. One of the best books on managing and keeping software developers is *Peopleware* by Tom DeMarco, published by Dorset House.[2]

Once you've got a list of the risks to your project, you need to address each one and talk about two things: *avoidance* and *mitigation.* For each risk, think about how you can avoid it. Build slack into your schedule, do constant code reviews, freeze requirements early, do frequent releases, require pair programming so you spread around the knowledge of the code, and the like. Then you need to think about what you'll do if the worst-case scenario does happen; this is *mitigation.* Remove features from a release, stop work on new features and do a bug hunt, negotiate new features into a future release, and so on. If a risk becomes a reality, you'll have to do *something* about it; it's better to have planned what you'll do beforehand.

Once you address avoidance and mitigation, you'll have a plan on how to handle your identifiable risks. This doesn't completely let you off the hook, because there are bound to be risks you miss; but the experience of addressing the risks you do think of will enable you to better handle new ones that surprise you during the project. If your project is using an iterative process model, it's a good idea to revisit your risks after every iteration and see which ones have changes, identify any new ones, and remove any that can no longer happen.

Resource Requirements

This section is a piece of cake. How many people do you need for the project? Do they all need to start at once, or can their starting dates on the project be staggered as phases are initiated? How many computers do you need? What software will you be using for development? What development environment do you need? Is everyone trained in that environment? What support software and hardware do you need? Yes, you do need a configuration management system and a stand-alone build machine – no matter what process model you're using.

Many of these resource questions are usually answered for you by the platform you're targeting and the application domain in which you are working. That's the easy part. Questions about team size, start dates, and phases of the project will likely not be able to be answered until you do a first cut at effort estimation and scheduling.

---

[2] DeMarco, T. and T. Lister. *Peopleware: Productive Projects and Teams, Second Edition.* (New York, NY: Dorset House Publishing Company, 1999.)

Work Breakdown and Task Estimates

The first step toward a project schedule is seeing what you'll be doing and how long each step will take. This is the classic chicken-egg problem. You can't really do estimation until you have a fairly detailed work breakdown into tasks. But your manager always wants effort estimates and schedule data before you start doing the design. Resist this. Make design your top priority once you've got some idea of the requirements. If you select a small set of high priority requirements, and then design a solution for that feature set, then you can do an effort estimation of that iteration. Don't worry that the requirements might change – they will. You need a detailed breakdown of features into tasks before you can do effort estimation.

Don't *ever* believe anyone who tells you, "that feature will take six months to do." That is a wild-assed guess (WAG), and bears little to no relation to reality. You just *can't* estimate something that big. The best you can do is say, "I once implemented a feature like that in six months." And even that only helps a little.

You've got to get your work broken down into tasks that are no more than about a week in duration. One or two days is a better bet. Even better, never do estimation in any unit except person-hours. That way you'll be more tempted to work with small increments of hours, and you'll break your larger tasks down into smaller ones that you may actually know how to do. Once you have a believable list of tasks, you can start doing size and then effort estimation. Size always needs to come first, because you just can't figure out how long something will take until you have an idea of how big it is.

Size can be several things, depending on your work breakdown and your development model; functional modules, number of classes, number of methods, number of function points, number of object points, or that old standby, uncommented lines of code. Actually, no matter what you initially measure size in, you'll end up with estimates in terms of KLOC – thousands of uncommented lines of code.

There are several techniques for getting effort estimates – COCOMO II [Boehm00], function point analysis, and the Delphi method are just three. All, however, depend on being able to count things in your design. The estimation mantra is size first, then effort and cost estimates, then schedule.

All other things being equal, the Delphi method is a quick and relatively efficient estimation technique. Here's one way it can work: find three of your most senior developers – these are the folks who've got the most experience, and who should therefore be able to give you a good guess. Then give them the task breakdown (assuming they weren't already involved in doing the initial breakdown – the ideal situation). Then ask them to give you three numbers for each task, the shortest amount of time it should take, the longest amount of time it should take, and the "normal" amount of time it should take, all in person-hours. Once you have these numbers, add them all up, the shortest together, the longest together, and the "normal" together and take the mean. Those are your estimates for each task. The averages of the best guess by your best developers for each task. Depending on your personality – and how hard your boss is breathing down your neck – pick one of the three values for each task as the official (for now) effort estimate and proceed to create a schedule.

Finally, you should have the right people – the developers who will do the work – do all the estimates for the project. Managers should *never* do development estimates. Even if a manager has been a developer in the past, unless one is deeply involved in the actual development work, one should not be in the business of doing development estimates.

Project Schedule

Once you have estimates of the tasks in your first release or iteration and have people resource estimates, you can create a schedule. There are several things to take into account before you can look at that spiffy Gantt chart with the nice black diamond that marks the release date. Here's a list:

- Get your developers to tell you the dependencies between tasks. There will be some tasks that can't start before others finish. There may be tasks that can start once others are half-finished. There will be some that can all start together. You need to know because the task dependencies will push out your delivery date.

- Figure out what your duty cycle is. Out of each eight-hour day, how many hours do your developers actually do development? You need to remember that reading mail, attending meetings, doing code reviews, taking breaks, going to the bathroom, all eat up time. You can't assume that an hour-hour task will be done in a single day. Realistically, out of each eight-hour day, two to four hours are eaten up with other stuff, so your duty cycle can be as low as four hours a day. Duty cycles can vary based on corporate culture, so you need to figure out what yours is before you start to schedule.

- Take weekends, vacations, sick days, training, and slack into account when you're making the schedule. If your senior developer has a task on the critical path of your project, you probably need to know that she's taking that three-week vacation in May.

- You can't schedule a developer to work on two tasks at the same time. Most project-scheduling software will not let you do this by default, but most of them will also let you override this. Don't. You will be tempted to do this so that your schedule does not push out past whatever deadline your manager or marketing team wants, but resist the temptation. You'll only have to change the schedule when you miss the date anyway.

Finally, use project-scheduling software to make your schedule. You don't have to do this, just using a simple spreadsheet technique like the one proposed in Chapter 9 of the Apress title, *Joel on Software* by Joel Spolsky.[3] can work for small projects. But using real project management software like Microsoft Project, Fast Track Scheduling, or Merlin provide lots of features that make keeping the schedule up to date much easier. The big thing that project management software can do that your spreadsheet can't is track dependencies. Joel doesn't understand how Microsoft Project is useful in this; in fact, he says, "I've found that with software, the dependencies are so obvious that it's just not worth the effort to formally keep track of them."[4] This might be true for small projects, but when your team gets to be 10 developers or larger and you're working on 100-plus tasks, knowing *something* about the dependencies of your project can help manage who's working on what, and when. Joel is right in that Project is overkill for many projects, and for those you can use a spreadsheet approach that just lists the features and tasks you can see right now (see Table 3-1); but project management software sure is handy to have around when you need it.

---

[3] Spolsky, J. *Joel on Software.* (Berkeley, CA: Apress, 2004.)
[4] Spolksy, 2004.

Table 3-1. Spolsky's Painless Schedule (with Dooley's Velocity addition)

1	2	3	4	5	6	7	8	9
Feature	Task	Priority	Orig Est	Curr Est	Elapsed	Remaining	Developer	Velocity

Spolsky's painless schedule lists the following seven columns that should be in every schedule:

- *Feature Name*

- *Tasks* within the feature

- The *Priority* of the Task

- The *Original Estimate* (in person-hours)

- The *Current Estimate* (in person-hours)

- The *Elapsed Time* worked on the task (in person-hours)

- The *Remaining Time* on the task (also in person-hours)

Joel correctly emphasizes that tasks need to be fine-grained and small in terms of effort. Otherwise, as noted previously, your estimates will most likely be wildly off. He also suggests that each developer either has a separate spreadsheet, or, as shown here, you add an eighth column with the developer assigned to the task. Having all the Tasks on the same sheet makes it more crowded, but easier to see all the tasks at once. While not exactly "painless," this method of keeping a schedule is useful for smaller projects with a fairly limited number of tasks.

I suggest adding a ninth column to measure the *velocity* of each task. Velocity is a term from XP[5] and is defined as the estimated effort of a task, divided by the actual effort. In our case, we'd use the Original Estimate of the task and the Elapsed Time. If you overestimate your task, your velocity will be greater than one (your task took less time than you originally thought); if you underestimate, it will be less than one (the task took you longer than you originally thought). Ideally, your velocity should be 1.0, but that hardly ever happens.

The reason for using velocity is to give each developer and the project manager an idea of how accurate the developer's estimates are and to help do a better job of estimating next time. Ideally, as a developer gains experience, her velocity will approach 1.0 on each task. Alternatively, if a developer's velocity jumps around a lot (one task is 0.6, another is 1.8, a third is 1.2), then a crash course in estimation techniques might be appropriate. In my experience, a new developer's velocity will start out gyrating wildly, with most values well under 1.0 – the new developer is overly optimistic. But as time goes

[5] Beck, K. *Extreme Programming Explained: Embrace Change.* (Boston, MA: Addison-Wesley 2000.)

along velocities will settle into a range centered on 1.0, maybe from 0.85 to 1.15. As a developer gains a history, the project manager can then start to depend more on their estimates, and the schedules will be more accurate.

Project Oversight

Project oversight is what happens once you've got a schedule. Once your project begins, the work needs to be managed. How this happens depends on the process you're using. But regardless of the process you need to manage the schedule, manage the developers, manage the process itself, and above all, manage your manager.

A manager's technique is critical to keeping a project on schedule. Fear is not a motivator. Appealing to professional pride is, though. If your boss doesn't support you, you're doomed.

Without creative, supportive management, you're doomed. If your people aren't happy, you don't have a hope. Treat your developers as humans, not resources. Supporting your team and keeping them insulated from distractions is your number one job. Remember, projects are cooperative, social events.[6]

Status Reviews and Presentations

Status reviews and presentations are an inescapable part of any project. The bigger the project, the more formal the review. Remember that reporting status doesn't fix problems, and that generally upper management doesn't like hearing about problems. Tough. When you give a project status report just tell 'em where your project is and where it's going during the period before the next status report. Don't embellish and don't make excuses; be honest about problems and where you are in the schedule. Just providing good news is usually bad for your reputation; something will go wrong at some point, so it is best to get it out of the way right away. You must communicate bad news about the project as soon as possible. That's the best way to mitigate the problem and get others involved in helping to find a solution.

When giving a presentation, be it a status review or a technical presentation, make sure you know your audience. Set your presentation to the level of the audience and keep the purpose of your presentation in front of you and them at all times. PowerPoint is ubiquitous in industry so learn to use it effectively. Keep your PowerPoint presentations short and to the point. Avoid cramming your slides with lots of bullet points. Do not make your bullet points complete sentences, mostly because you'll be tempted to read them. This is the kiss of death for two reasons: it takes too long and takes attention away from what you're actually saying.

It insults the audience. Surely they do know how to read?

Your bullet points should be talking points that you can then expand upon. This lets your audience focus on you, the speaker, rather than the slides. When you're constructing a PowerPoint presentation, use as few words as you can.

---

[6] Cockburn, A. "The End of Software Engineering and The Start of Economic-Cooperative Gaming." *Computer Science and Information Systems* **1**(1): 1 - 32. (2004)

Defects

Inevitably, you'll introduce defects (errors) into your program. Defects do not just appear; developers put them there. As a developer, your aim is twofold

- Introduce as few defects as possible into the code you write.

- Find as many of them as you can before releasing the code.

░ **Note:** By the way, I'm deliberately not using the word *bug* here, because it sounds both inoffensive and cute. Defects are neither. They are errors in your code that *you* put there. See Chapter 13 for a more detailed discussion on errors.

Despite your best efforts, though, you will release code with defects in it. It's just inevitable. For a program of any size, there are just too many possible paths through the program (called a *combinatorial explosion*), and too many different ways to introduce bad data for there not to be defects. Your objective is to release with as few defects as possible and to make those defects ones that don't really impact the product or its performance. To make this a reality, most development organizations have a set of defect levels they use to characterize just how bad a defect really is. One set of levels looks like the following:

1. *Fatal:* Either this defect causes the product to crash, or a fundamental piece of functionality doesn't work.

2. *Severe:* A major piece of functionality doesn't work, and there is no workaround for it that the user can perform.

3. *Serious:* A piece of functionality doesn't work, but there is a workaround for it that the customer can perform.

4. *Annoying:* A minor defect or error in the documentation that may annoy the user, but doesn't affect how the program works.

5. *New Feature Request:* This isn't a defect, but a request for the product to do something new.

Whenever you find a defect in a piece of code, you will file a defect report (to keep track of how many defects you're finding, what types they are, and how severe they are), and you'll characterize the defect by severity level. When the developers are fixing defects, they start at level 1 and work their way down.

In nearly all organizations, no product can release with known level 1 or level 2 defects in it. Most organizations also try their best to remove all the level 3 defects as well.

The Post-Mortem

Most development teams will do a post-mortem after every project. A post-mortem is an opportunity to reflect on the project just completed and answer a few questions. Typically, the questions will be like the following:

- What went right? Did our process work the way we anticipated? Did we meet our schedule? Did we implement all the features required by the customer?

- What went wrong? Why did we have so many defects? Why did we need to work 60-hour weeks for the last month of the project?

- What process issues came up? Did we follow our process? If not, what parts were problematic?

- What do we need to fix for next time? Given questions 1, 2, and 3, what do we need to fix in our process, work habits, or environment for the next project?

- Who is responsible for the fixes? Someone has to be responsible for the changes to our process; who is it? (Don't make it a manager; the development team should own the process.)

Conclusion

So where do we end up? We've gone through the general parts of managing projects and presented some alternative ways of doing project management. The most important parts are the developers should own the process and management should be supportive and listen to the developers – particularly where schedules and estimates are concerned – and be the buffer between the developers and the world. If you can work in an organization where those things are true, be a happy camper, because you'll be able to write great code.

References

Beck, K. *Extreme Programming Explained: Embrace Change.* (Boston, MA: Addison-Wesley 2000.)

Boehm, B., C. Abts, et. al. *Software Cost Estimation with COCOMO II.* (Englewood Cliffs, NJ: Prentice-Hall, 2000.)

Cockburn, A. "The End of Software Engineering and The Start of Economic-Cooperative Gaming." *Computer Science and Information Systems* 1(1): 1 - 32. (2004)

DeMarco, T. and T. Lister. *Peopleware: Productive Projects and Teams, Second Edition.* (New York, NY: Dorset House Publishing Company, 1999.)

McConnell, S. *Rapid Development: Taming Wild Software Schedules.* (Redmond, WA: Microsoft Press, 1996.)

Spolsky, J. *Joel on Software.* (Berkeley, CA: Apress, 2004.)

CHAPTER 4

Requirements

The hardest single part of building a software system is deciding <u>what to build</u>. No other part of the conceptual work is as difficult in establishing the detailed technical requirements, including the interfaces to people, to machines, and to other software systems. No other part of the work so cripples the results if done wrong. No other part is more difficult to rectify later. Therefore, the most important function that the software builder performs for the client is the iterative extraction and refinement of the product requirements.

—Fred Brooks[1]

Before you start coding – yes, *before* you start coding – you need to know what it is you're going to build. That's what requirements are: a list of stuff you have to implement in order to create your terrific program. Most developers hate requirements. Really, all we'd like to do is sit down and start coding. All of us have that super-programmer mentality; just give me the problem and I can sit down and design and code it on the fly. Not! If you want to be a productive developer and make fewer errors and come up with a good, clean design, you need requirements – the more detailed the better. A good set of requirements tells you just what the program is supposed to do. It gives you the scaffolding around which you'll hang your design. You'll do requirements anyway – it's one of those steps in a standard development lifecycle that you can't avoid, but if you don't make room for it in your project, you'll create a program that is pretty crappy. Being intentional about requirements forces you to think about the details of the program, and it also lets you listen to the users so you have a better idea of what they really want. So let's talk about requirements.

What Types of Requirements Are We Talking About Here?

We're really talking about *functional requirements*. That is, the list of features the user will see and be able to use when they fire up your program. These are the "black box" requirements that show the

---

[1]Brooks, F. P. *The Mythical Man-Month : Essays on Software Engineering, Silver Anniversary Edition.* (Boston, MA: Addison-Wesley, 1995.)

external behavior of your program. They will certainly lead to lower-level requirements that talk more about *how* your program works, rather than *what* it does. The output of this process of identifying requirements is a *functional specification* of what the software system is supposed to do.

Functional Specification?

A functional specification describes what the program will do entirely from the user's perspective. It doesn't care how the software is implemented. It talks about the features of the program and specifies screens, menus, dialogs, and the like. Think of it as a badly written user manual. A second kind of spec can be called a *technical specification*. The technical specification describes the internal implementation details of the program. That is, it talks about data structures, algorithms used, database models, choice of programming language, and so on. We're not going to talk about technical specs in this chapter, just functional specs.

"Wait," you say. "What about all those agile methodologies we talked about in Chapter 2? *They* don't write functional specs. So there! I'm off the hook." Well, in fact, agile methodologies *do* write functional specifications. They're just in a different format from the 300-page single-spaced requirements document that some plan-driven methodologies require. XP requires that together with the customer representative you write *user stories* that lay out what the program will do. That's a spec. The important part and the idea behind this entire chapter is to *write down what your program is supposed to do before you start coding.*

But I Don't Like Writing!

A standard argument made by software developers is that they can't write. Nonsense! Everyone can learn to write functional specs. But writing is work. You have to get in there and practice writing before you'll be any good at it. If you're still in school (be it undergrad or graduate school), take a course in writing, one where you've got to write essays or journal entries or stories or poetry every single week. You should also have to read other works critically; reading other people's writing, whether good or bad, is a great way to learn how to write better.

That Natural Language Thing

Functional specifications should always be written in a natural language. Why? Well, it's the Sapir-Whorf linguistic relativity hypothesis, don't you know?[2] In a nutshell, language not only determines what you *do* say, it determines what you *can* say (and think). That is, the language you use determines what kinds of thoughts you are able to have, and thus what you can think about and how you express your thoughts. If the language doesn't have room for certain kinds of thoughts, you are much less likely to think them. Natural languages are much more expressive and varied than programming languages, so you want to do your designs in natural languages and save the programming languages for implementation later. Whether you believe the Sapir-Whorf hypothesis or not, it's nearly always a good idea to develop your functional specification in a natural language so you don't get bogged down in the syntactic and semantic details of a programming language before you need to. This doesn't mean that you can't think about implementation while you're doing the functional specification (you will, trust me), but just shunt

---

[2] http://en.wikipedia.org/wiki/Linguistic_relativity retrieved, September 15, 2009.

those thoughts over into a "technical note" sidebar of your specification.[3] You might also look at Kenneth Iverson's Turing Award lecture, "Notation as a Tool of Thought," for a similar discussion.[4]

Outline of a Functional Specification

Every functional specification is different, just as every software development project is different. So take this outline with a grain of salt and just use the parts that apply to your project. Lots of the ideas here are from.[5] Every function specification should have the elements discussed in the following sections.

Overview

This is your executive summary. A paragraph or at most two of what the program is supposed to do. "This program runs your microwave oven. It interfaces to a keypad and an LCD display that provides user input and output functionality. Its functions are limited to those that a standard microwave would have, with the addition of single buttons for pizza and coffee reheating. It also will run a time of day clock and a standalone countdown timer. It doesn't control the light. It has a safety interlock that will prevent the microwave from starting if the door is open."

Disclaimer

You should always put it a statement right at the beginning that "This specification isn't done yet. If you think something is missing or wrong, just sent me an email." That helps keep all the marketing guys off your back and lets you file new feature requests in your mail trash bin. Lots of people will put a big, black DRAFT in the header or footer of the document. That can work as well, but folks tend to ignore it. Some people will use a big DRAFT watermark on their specs, so that every page has the word embedded behind the text. This doesn't stop people from yelling at you either. At some point your disclaimer should change to something like "This specification is as complete as it will be for this release. If you think something is missing or wrong, just sent an email to the author and we'll consider it for the next release."

Author's Name

Somebody needs to be responsible for the functional specification. Not a committee, not the development team, *one person*. This is usually either the development manager, the project manager, or the chief architect, depending on how your company sets up development projects. There are pros and cons to all the different organizational arrangements.

If the development manager (the person to whom the developers report) is in charge of the functional spec, then that person is usually up to speed on all the technical aspects of the project. That's good. On the other hand, if your boss writes the functional spec, it might be harder to tell her that there's something wrong with the specification, or that you don't agree with the design. Also, development

---

[3]Spolsky, J., *Joel on Software*. (Berkeley, CA: Apress, 2004.)

[4]Iverson, K. E. "Notation as a Tool of Thought." *Communications of the ACM* **23**(8): 444–465. (1980.)
[5]Spolsky, 2004.

managers were probably developers at one time and so they may not have the people skills (read: charm and schmoozing skills) necessary to talk to marketing, the customer, documentation, testing, and so on.

If your company uses project managers that are in charge of the specification, design, and schedule, but don't have developers directly reporting to them, then you run the risk of getting someone that isn't as technically astute as a former developer. On the other hand, these folks can usually charm the socks off the other teams, so negotiations are a lot smoother. Project managers need to have some technical skills and to be very good at getting all the stakeholders to reach consensus on the contents of the functional specification.

The chief architect model is like the project manager model except that the architect is a developer and so is more technically competent and is usually in charge of the functional specification and all the program design issues. This is like the chief programmer model in Brooks' *The Mythical Man-Month*. Someone else is in charge of interfacing with the other teams, the schedule, and doing all that people-interaction stuff. This can be good if the architect is disciplined and doesn't let any requirements creep get in the way of a good design.

Scenarios of Typical Usage

A great way to get customers to respond to your requirements list is to present several scenarios of typical usage of the program to them as part of the specification. This has a couple of advantages.

- First, if you write the scenarios as if they're user stories, the customer is more likely to read them.

- Second, customers are more likely to understand what you're doing and come up with ideas for things you've missed or gotten wrong. This is always a good thing, because the more customer input you get early in the process, the more likely you'll actually create something they want.

In many agile methodologies, including XP, user stories are often written like scenarios. And in XP, the customer is part of the project team, so you get constant feedback on user stories and daily program builds. In the Unified Modeling Language (UML, see www.uml.org), there is an entire notation used to create use cases (another word for scenarios). But as we discussed above, nothing beats natural language for describing usage scenarios. We'll come back to use cases later, in Chapter 8.

Detailed Screen-By-Screen Specifications

Once you've written a couple of scenarios, you will have a much better idea of how your program will flow, and what screens, dialog boxes, menus, and so on you'll need. This lets you go through each one of those screens and flesh out the details of how they're laid out, what buttons, text boxes, icons, graphics, and so on they'll have, and what other screens they connect to. Use pictures! A picture of a screen or a dialog box is worth way more than a thousand words. It gives the reader something to react to and it gets them thinking about program flow and user interface issues. Don't expect anyone to read these except for the developers who will implement them and the tech writers who will write the user manual (that no one will read).

Non-requirements

This may be the most important section of the functional specification. This tells the world what you're *not* going to do. Really, you need to put this in because after laying out what the program will do, the most important thing the functional specification does is *manage expectations*. One of the worst phrases a customer can utter at that final demo before you release is, "But I thought it was going to do ...." You need to tell all the stakeholders in a project what the program is going to do and also what it's not going to do. "This microwave software will not balance your checkbook." Well, okay, that's a little over the top, but you do need to let them know that there are requirements that won't be implemented – at least not in the current release. "Only one countdown timer may run at a time." "There will not be a defrost cycle that allows defrost modes to be selected by food type." It's likely that your customer won't read this section, but at least you can point to it when they ask.

Open Issues

When you first write the functional specification, there will be one or two (thousand) things you don't know. That's okay. Just put them in the "Open Issues" section. Then every time you meet with the customer, point to this section and try to get answers. Some of these questions will move to requirements sections and some will end up in the "Non-requirements" section, after you get those answers. By the end of the project, though, this section should be empty. If it's not, well, you've got issues that will haunt you.

Design and Feature Ideas

If you're like me, you'll be trying to design and code the program all the time you're doing your requirements gathering and analysis. That's just what developers do. So to avoid having your head explode from all these fantastic design and implementation ideas that you can't write down because you're writing requirements after all, write a separate notebook. This notebook is just a separate document – keep a text document open on your desktop for it – that contains a note for later. The two types of notes I typically create are technical notes containing design or coding ideas for developers, and marketing notes containing feature ideas for the marketing folks and the customer.

Backlog

As your project proceeds through development, new requirements will surface. Get used to it; this always happens. But if you want to keep to a schedule and deliver a working product, you just *cannot* implement everything that will come up. That's what the "Backlog" section is for, all the requirements you are going to consider for the next release of the product. Most functional specifications don't have a "Backlog" section, but if you want your functional spec to be a living document, you need a place to put all the tasks you will do later. This does a couple of good things for you. It tells the customer you haven't forgotten these features, and that by moving them to the next release you are committed to delivering the current release as close to the published schedule as possible. And it tells the developers that you're not out of control and that the project has a good shot at being done with high quality and on time. For more information on backlogs, take a look any of the Scrum agile methodology descriptions.[6]

---

[6]Schwaber, K. and M. Beedle. *Agile software development with Scrum.* (Upper Saddle River, NJ: Prentice Hall, 1980.)

One More Thing

One more thing about the functional specification – don't obsess. Chances are that you'll do a good job of picking out requirements and writing them down in the functional spec, but that it won't be as detailed as you like and it won't be complete. Don't worry, be happy. The only time a functional specification is complete is when you ship the release. Don't spend time trying to get every single detail correct, don't spend time trying to tease every requirement out of your customer. It just won't happen. Set a time limit, do your best, and let it go. You don't want to have a bunch of developers sitting around twiddling their thumbs with nothing to do waiting for the spec do you?

Types of Requirements

In a functional specification you'll usually see four different types of requirements: user requirements, domain requirements, non-functional requirements, and non-requirements.

User Requirements

User requirements are nearly always expressed in natural language. They are the details of what the user expects to see as she uses the program. They also include descriptions of screen layouts, dialog boxes, and menus. Any interaction element in the program should be described in the user requirements. For example:

> *Logging into the System*: When Gloria clicks on the Login button on the main page, a login dialog box appears in the middle of the screen. The login dialog must contain two text boxes, labeled "Username" and "Password." There must also be two buttons in the dialog box, labeled "Submit" and "Cancel." If at any time Gloria presses the Cancel button, the dialog box shall disappear and she will be taken back to the previous screen. In normal usage, she will click in the Username text box and type in her user name, and then click (or tab) in the Password text box and type in her password. The text typed in the Password text box must be hidden. Once Gloria is finished typing in her user name and password she must press the Submit button. If she has entered a correct user name/password combination she will then be taken to the main menu page. If Gloria's user name/password combination is incorrect, an "Invalid user name or password, please try again" message shall appear in the dialog box, the text boxes shall be cleared and she will be given the opportunity to login again.

As seen in this section, you can express user requirements as scenarios, and as detailed screen-by-screen descriptions. Remember to use pictures as much as you can when you're doing user requirements. If your program is web-based, do lots of quick and dirty html pages and paste them into the spec. If it's not web-based, use a drawing program to create pictures of what the user will see.

Domain Requirements

These are requirements that are imposed on you by the application domain of the program. If you're writing a new version of TurboTax®, you will be constrained by the latest IRS regulations. A general ledger program will have to abide by the latest edition of the Generally Accepted Accounting Principles (GAAP), and an AT&T-branded iPhone will need to implement the latest GSM protocols. You don't need to write down all these requirements, just refer to them. A set of detailed domain requirements give the developers information they will need during their design of the program. Domain requirements are usually considered "middle layer" software because they are the heart of the application, below the user interface and above the operating system, networking, or database software. Lots of domain requirements will get implemented as separate classes and libraries with their own APIs.

Non-functional Requirements

Non-functional requirements are constraints on the services and functions of the program and also expectations about performance. They can include target platform specifications, timing constraints, performance requirements, memory usage requirements, file access privileges, security requirements, response times, minimum number of transactions per second, and so on. These are usually requirements that may not be visible to the user, but which do effect the user experience.

Non-requirements

These are the things you're not going to do. See the previous section for a description of non-requirements.

Requirements Digging

Most software engineering texts use the phrase "requirements elicitation" to talk about the process of getting your users to tell you what they want. Hunt and Thomas, in their book *The Pragmatic Programmer* use the much more descriptive phrase "requirements digging" to emphasize the point that what you're really doing is digging for all those requirements that your customer doesn't know they want yet.[7] Hunt and Thomas also make the terrific distinction between requirements, policies, and implementations as a way to illustrate the requirements digging process.

For example, "The system must let the user choose a loan term" is a nice succinct requirement. It says that there's something you have to do. It isn't specific enough for implementation yet, but it tells the developer something concrete that must be built.

"Loan terms must be between 6 months and 30 years" is not a requirement, although it kind of looks like one. This statement is an example of a *business policy*. When statements like this are presented to developers as requirements they have a tendency to hard-code the statement in the program. Wrong, wrong, wrong. Policies like this can change, so you need to be very careful about putting business policies in your requirements. It is almost always the case that you need to implement a more general version of the business policy than is stated. The real requirement is probably something like, "Loan terms are of finite length but the length of the loan will vary by type of loan." This tells you that you probably need to build a table-driven subsystem to handle this feature. That way, the loan term for a particular type of loan can be changed by making a single change in a data table and the code doesn't need to change at all.

"The user must be able to select a loan term using a drop-down list box" isn't a requirement either, although, again, it may look like one. This is only a requirement if the customer absolutely must have a

---

[7]Hunt, A. and D. Thomas. *The Pragmatic Programmer: From Journeyman to Master.* (Boston, MA: Addison-Wesley, 2000.)

drop-down menu to choose their loan term. Otherwise, this is an example of the implementation that the customer would like to see, and it may not be a requirement. As Hunt and Thomas state in their book, "It's important to discover the underlying reason *why* users do a particular thing, rather than just *the way* they currently do it. At the end of the day, your development has to solve their *business problem*, not just meet their stated requirements. Documenting the reasons behind requirements will give your team invaluable information when making daily implementation decisions."

Why Requirements Digging Is Hard

There are several reasons why pulling requirements out of your customer is a really hard exercise. We'll look at a few.

Problems of Scope

Lots of times the actual boundaries of what your program is supposed to do are fuzzy. This can be because of several things. The program may be part of a larger system and the integration of the parts is ill-defined. The customer may not have thought through exactly what they want the program to do, so they start throwing out all sorts of ideas, many of which may not even apply to the problem at hand. Finally, the customer may have dropped into implementation-land and provides unnecessary levels of detail.

It takes lots of patience, discipline, repeatedly saying the word "no," and repeatedly asking, "why does this need to be part of the program?" in order to overcome problems of scope. Scope is directly related to requirements creep, so beware.

Problems of Understanding

Let's face it; the customer and you as the developer speak different languages. Your customer is the domain expert and they speak the domain language (accounts receivable, accounts payable, reconciliation, general ledger, and so on). You speak the design and implementation language (class, object, method, use case, recursion, activation record, and the like). This is usually worse than an American in Paris; at least there, both sides can pantomime their needs and figure things out. With problems of domain understanding, the best you can usually do is order drinks together.

There are usually two ways to overcome problems of understanding. The first is to have someone in the middle who has lived in both worlds and who can translate between the two. Some companies have folks called *system engineers* or *technical marketers* who fulfill this role. These folks have done development and have also worked the customer side of things so they can speak both languages. Good system engineers are worth their weight in use-cases. The second way to promote understanding is to have the customer as part of the development team. This is the approach taken by some agile methodologies, notably XP. When the customer is part of the development team you get to talk to them every day, ask them questions, teach them technical stuff. Both sides benefit. And because the on-site customer sees intermediate product builds as soon as they pop out of your build machine, you get immediate feedback. Win, win, win.

Problems of Volatility

Things change. This is by far the hardest part of requirements gathering and analysis and the biggest reason why schedules slip. You can't do anything about it. Get used to it. As Kent Beck says, "Embrace change." What you can do is *manage* change. Create a backlog of new features that get added as they arrive. In the Scrum methodology, new requirements are always added to the release backlog, they are not added to the current iteration; this allows the current sprint to proceed normally and the requirements are all reviewed at the end of the sprint. Another way to manage change is to push the decision onto the user; give the user a choice - "If we implement this new feature it will add 6 weeks to the schedule. Do you still want it?" Alternatively, "If you want to keep to the original schedule we can only implement and test one of A, B, or C. You pick the one you want most." This is one of the things that the agile folks mean by "courage;"[8] sometimes you have to take a stand and choose what is best for the project as a whole.

Non-technical Problems

From a developer's perspective, non-technical problems with requirements are the worst ones you will see. In fact, these are problems developers should never see; their managers should shield them from non-technical problems. Non-technical requirements problems are fundamentally political. Examples abound. One group of customers in an organization has a different view of the program requirements than another group. Or worse, one manager has a different view than another manager. The program being developed will reduce the influence of one department by automating a function that they used to be the sole source of. The program will distribute data processing across several departments where it was once centralized in a single department. The list goes on and on. The best advice for non-technical problems is to run away – quickly. Let your vice-president deal with it; that's why she is paid the big bucks.

Analyzing the Requirements

Once you've written down a set of requirements you need to make sure that these are the right requirements for the program; you need to *analyze* them. Analysis has three basic parts.

First, you *categorize* the requirements and organize them into related areas. This will help the designers a lot.

Second, you *prioritize* them based on customer input. This is critical because you won't be able to implement all the requirements in the first product release (trust me, you won't). So this prioritized list will be what you'll use to set the contents of each interim release.

Lastly, you need to *examine* each requirement in relation to all the others to make sure they fit into a coherent whole. Ask yourself a series of questions:

1. Is each requirement *consistent* with the overall project objective? If your program is supposed to sell your users books, it doesn't also have to compute their golf handicap.

2. Is this requirement *really necessary*? Have you added something that can be removed without impairing the essential functionality of the program? If your first release is supposed to allow users to buy books, then you probably don't need to also allow them to buy sailboats.

---

[8]Beck, K. *Extreme Programming Explained: Embrace Change.* (Boston, MA: Addison-Wesley, 2000.)

3. Is this requirement *testable*? This is probably the most important question when you're doing requirements analysis. If you cannot figure out how to test a requirement, then you cannot know that you've implemented it correctly or that you are finished. All requirements *must* be testable, or else they are not requirements. In most agile methodologies, the rule is to write the test first, then write the code.

4. Is this requirement *doable* in the technical environment you've got to work in? This question normally applies to those non-functional requirements mentioned previously. Are your requirements feasible given the particular target platform or set of hardware constraints you must work under for this project? For example, if your target platform is a Macintosh running OS X, a requirement that the DirectX graphics library be used is not doable because DirectX is a Windows only library.

5. Is this requirement *unambiguous*? Your requirements need to be as precise as possible (refer to the previous testable questions), because as sure as you're sitting here reading this, someone will misinterpret an ambiguous requirement and you'll discover the error the day after you ship. Your requirements should never contain the words "or" or "may."

Conclusion

Once you're done with your functional spec and the analysis of your requirements you're done with the requirements phase, right. Well, of course not. As we've said before – requirements change. So relax, don't obsess about the requirements, do the best you can to get an initial list of clear, testable requirements and then move on to design. You'll always come back here later.

References

Beck, K. *Extreme Programming Explained: Embrace Change.* (Boston, MA: Addison-Wesley, 2000.)

Brooks, F. P. *The Mythical Man-Month : Essays on Software Engineering, Silver Anniversary Edition.* (Boston, MA: Addison-Wesley, 1995.)

Hunt, A. and D. Thomas. *The Pragmatic Programmer: From Journeyman to Master.* (Boston, MA: Addison-Wesley, 2000.)

Iverson, K. E. "Notation as a Tool of Thought." *Communications of the ACM* **23**(8): 444–465. (1980.)

Schwaber, K. and M. Beedle. *Agile software development with Scrum.* (Upper Saddle River, NJ: Prentice Hall, 1980.)

Spolsky, J., *Joel on Software.* (Berkeley, CA: Apress, 2004.)Wikipedia, Sapir-Whorf Linguistic Relativity Hypothesis, http://en.wikipedia.org/wiki/Linguistic_relativity retrieved, September 15, 2009.

CHAPTER 5

Software Architecture

What do we mean by a software architecture? To me the term architecture conveys a notion of the core elements of the system, the pieces that are difficult to change. A foundation on which the rest must be built.

—Martin Fowler[1]

Once you have an idea of *what* you're going to build, then you can start thinking about *how* you're going to build it. Of course, you've already been thinking about this from the very first requirement, but now you have permission to do it. Now we begin to delve into design.

There are really two levels of software design. The level we normally think of when we're writing programs is usually called *detailed design*. What operations do we need? What data structures? What algorithms are we using? How is the database going to be organized? What does the user interface look like? What are the calling sequences? These are all very detailed questions that need to be answered before you can really get on with the detailed work of coding (well, sort of – we'll get to that later).

But there's another level of design. This kind of design is all about *style*. If you were building a house, this design level asks questions like ranch or multi-story? Tudor or Cape Cod? Which direction do the bedroom windows face? Forced-air or hot-water heat? Three bedrooms or four? Open concept floor plan or closed? These questions focus somewhat on details, but they are much more about the style of the house and how you'll be using it, rather than things like 12 or 14 gauge wire for the electrical system or the diameter of the air conditioning ductwork. This emphasis on style is what *software architecture* is all about. As Fowler says in this chapter's opening quote, you need the foundation before you can build the rest of the structure. Software architecture is a set of ideas that tells you which foundation is the right one for your program.

The idea of software architecture began as a response to the increasing size and complexity of programs. "As the size and complexity of software systems increases, the design problem goes beyond the algorithms and data structures of the computation: designing and specifying the overall system structure emerges as a new kind of problem.... This is the software architecture level of design."[2]

---

[1] "Is Design Dead?" Retrieved from http://martinfowler.com/articles/designDead.html

[2] Garlan, D. and M. Shaw (1994). An Introduction to Software Architecture. Pittsburgh, PA: Carnegie Mellon University: 49. CMU/SEI-94-TR-21. (1994)

However it is really the case that *all* programs of any size and complexity have an architecture. It's just that for larger programs you need to be more intentional about your thinking about the architecture to make sure you have the right set of architectural patterns incorporated in your system design. You need to do this. It's so much harder to change things at the architectural level once the program has been written, because architectural features are so fundamental to the structure of the program.

There are many different styles of software architecture, and in any given project you'll probably use more than one. The architectural style used for a program depends on what it is you're doing. As we'll see, different types of programs in different domains will lead us to different architectural styles; we can also call these *architectural patterns* since they have many characteristics of the *design patterns* we'll see shortly. First let's get some general vocabulary under our belts.

General Architectural Patterns

Whenever a software architect starts thinking about an architecture for a program, she usually starts by drawing pictures. Diagrams of the architecture allow people to see the structure and framework of the program much more easily than text. Software architectures are normally represented as black box *graphs* where graph nodes are *computational structures* and the graph edges are *communication conduits* between the structures. The conduits can represent data flow, object message passing, or procedure calls. Notations of this type vary and there are several standard notations, notably the United Modeling Language (UML). Visual descriptions of architectures are generally easier to understand. A particular architectural style is a pattern that can represent a set of similar structures. Let's looks at several different common architectural styles.

Pipe-and-filter Architecture

In a pipe-and-filter style architecture, the computational components are called *filters* and they act as transducers that take input, transform it according to one or more algorithms, and then output the result to a communications conduit. The input and outputs conduits are called *pipes*.

A typical pipe-and-filter architecture is linear, as in Figure 5-1.

Figure 5-1. The pipe-and-filter architecture

The filters must be independent components. That is one of the beauties of a pipe-and-filter architecture. You can join different filters in the set in different arrangements in order to get different results. The classic example of a pipe-and-filter architectural style is the Unix shell, where there are a large number of small programs that typically do a single thing and can be chained together using the Unix pipe mechanism. Here's an example that shows how a pipe-and-filter can work. This problem is from Jon Bentley's book *Programming Pearls*.[3]

---

[3] Bentley, J. *Programming Pearls, Second Edition.* (Boston, MA: Addison-Wesley, 2000.)

The Problem: Given a dictionary of words in English, find all the anagrams in the dictionary. That is, find all the words that are permutations of each other. For example, "pots," "stop," and "spot" are anagrams of each other.

So what do we know? Well, first of all, all the anagrams have the same letters and the same number of letters in each word. That gives us the clue to the method you'll use to find the anagrams. Got it yet? Don't worry; I'll wait.

Yes! If you sort each word, you'll end up with a string of characters that has all the letters in the word in alphabetical order. We call this creating a *sign* for the word. If you then sort the resulting list, all the anagrams will end up together in the sorted list because their sorted letters will be identical. If you then keep track of which words you sorted, you can then simplify the list and create a new list with, say, each set of anagrams on the same line of the output file. This is exactly how Bentley does it.

But how does this relate to a pipe-and-filter architecture, you ask? Good question. Let's break down the solution again.

1. Create a sign for each word in the list by sorting the letters in each word; keep the sign and the word together.

2. Sort the resulting list by the signs; all the anagrams should now be together.

3. Squash the list by putting each set of anagrams on the same line, removing the signs as you do.

See the pipe-and-filter now? In Unix-speak it looks like this:

```
sign <dictionary.txt | sort | squash >anagrams.txt
```

where `sign` is the filter we use to do step 1, with input file dictionary.txt. `sign` outputs a list of signs and their associated words which is piped to the Unix sort utility (we didn't need to write that one). Sort then sorts the list by the first field on each line (its default behavior), which happens to be the sign of each word. It then outputs the sorted list to the next pipe. Squash takes the sorted list from the incoming pipe and compresses it by putting all the words with the same sign on the same line, eliminating the signs as it does so. This final list is sent via one last pipe (this time a Unix I/O redirection) to the output file anagrams.txt.

Note that this example has all the features of a standard pipe-and-filter architecture: independent computational components that perform a transformation on their input data and communication conduits that transmit the data from the output of one component to the input of the next. Note also that not all applications should use the pipe-and-filter architecture. For example, it won't work so well for interactive applications or applications that respond to events or interrupts. That's why we're going to look at more architectural styles.

An Object-Oriented Architectural Pattern

The advent of object-oriented analysis, design, and programming in the early 1980s (well, it really started in the '60s, but no one was paying attention) brought with it a number of architectural and design patterns. We'll just focus on one object-oriented architectural pattern here and save discussions of the rest to the chapter on Design Patterns.

The *Model-View-Controller* (MVC) architectural pattern is a way of breaking an application, or even just a piece of an application's interface, into three parts: the model, the view, and the controller. MVC was originally developed to map the traditional input, processing, output roles of many programs into the GUI realm:

Input ➤ Processing ➤ Output

Controller ➤ Model ➤ View

The user input, the modeling of the external world, and the visual feedback to the user are separated and handled by model, view and controller *objects*, as shown in Figure 5-2.

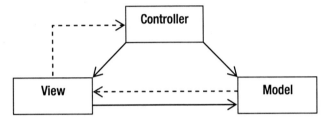

Figure 5-2. The Model-View-Controller architecture

- The *controller* interprets mouse and keyboard inputs from the user and maps these user actions into commands that are sent to the model and/or viewport to effect the appropriate change.

- The *model* manages one or more data elements, responds to queries about its state, and responds to instructions to change state. The model knows what the application is supposed to do and is the main computational structure of the architecture – it *models* the problem you're trying to solve.

- The *view* or *viewport* manages a rectangular area of the display and is responsible for presenting data to the user through a combination of graphics and text. The view doesn't know anything about what the program is actually doing; all it does is take instructions from the controller and data from the model and displays them. It communicates back to the model and controller to report status.

The flow of an MVC program typically looks like this:

1. The *user* interacts with the user interface (e.g., the user presses a button) and the controller handles the input event from the user interface, often via a registered handler or callback. The user interface is displayed by the view but controlled by the controller. Oddly enough, the controller has no direct knowledge of the view as an object; it just sends messages when it needs something on the screen updated.

2. The *controller* accesses the model, possibly updating it in a way appropriate to the user's action (e.g., controller causes the user's shopping cart to be updated by the model). This usually causes a change in the model's state as well as in its data.

3. A *view* uses the model to generate an appropriate user interface (e.g., view produces a screen listing the shopping cart contents). The view gets its own data from the model. The model has no direct knowledge of the view. It just

responds to requests for data from whomever and to requests for transforming data from the controller.

4. The controller, as the user interface manager, waits for further user interactions, which begins the cycle anew.

The main idea here is separation of concerns – and code. The objective is to separate how your program works from what it is displaying and how it gets its input data. This is classic object-oriented programming; create objects that hide their data and hide how they manipulate their data and then just present a simple interface to the world to interact with other objects. We'll see this again in Chapter 9.

An MVC Example: Let's Hunt!

A classic example of a program that uses the MVC architectural pattern is the Nifty Assignment presented by Dr. David Matuszek at the 2004 SIGCSE Technical Symposium.[4]

The Problem

The program is a simple simulation of a fox and a rabbit. The fox is trying to find the rabbit in a grid environment, and the rabbit is trying to get away. There are bushes that the rabbit can hide behind and there are some restrictions on movement.

Figure 5-3 is a typical picture of the game in action.

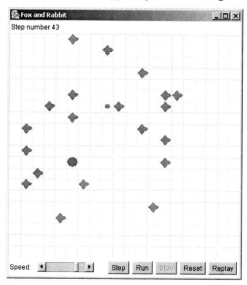

Figure 5-3. A typical fox and rabbit hunt instance

---

[4] Matuszek, David. "Rabbit Hunt," SIGCSE 2004 Technical Symposium, Nifty Assignments Session, retrieved August 17, 2009, http://nifty.stanford.edu/2004/RabbitHunt/. (2004)

The fox is the large dot, the rabbit is the small dot, and the bushes are the fat crosses.

The objective of the programming assignment is to make the rabbit smarter so it can escape from the fox. We don't really care about this; we want to look at how the program is organized. Figure 5-4 shows the organization of the program. It's a UML object diagram taken from the BlueJ IDE. The key parts of the program are the three classes, Model, View, and Controller.

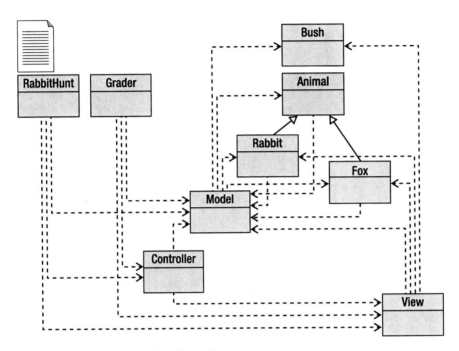

Figure 5-4. The fox and rabbit hunt class structure

Model

The model represents the rules of the game. It does all the computation, all the work of deciding whose turn it is, what happens during each turn, and whether anyone has won. The model is strictly internal and has practically nothing to do with the other parts of the program.

View

The view displays what is going on. It puts an image on the screen so the user can see what is happening. The view is completely passive; it does not affect the hunt in any way, it's just a news reporter that gives you a (partial) picture of what is happening inside the model.

Controller

The controller is the part of the program that displays the controls (the five buttons and the speed controls at the bottom of the window). It knows as little as possible about the model and view; it basically tells the model when to go and when to stop.

Model

The model part of this program is actually composed of five classes: Model (the "main" model class), Animal, Rabbit, Fox, and Bush. Rabbit and Fox are subclasses of Animal (as you can see from the solid arrows in the UML diagram). This is the part of the program that you really need to understand.

The RabbitHunt class just creates model, view, and controller objects, and turns control over to the controller object. The controller object starts the model object, and then just waits for the user to press a button. When a button is pressed, a message is sent to the model object, which decides what to do.

The model object

- places the fox, rabbit, and bushes in the field;

- gives the rabbit and the fox each a chance to move (one moves, then the other; they don't both move at the same time);

- tells the view to display the result of these two moves; and

- determines which animal won.

The advantages of breaking the program up into these separate parts are many. We can safely rewrite the GUI in the Controller object or the display in the view object without changing the model. We can make the fox and/or the rabbit smarter (or dumber!) without changing the GUI or the display. We can re-use the GUI for a different application with very little effort. The list just goes on.

In short, MVC is your friend; use it wisely and often.

The Client-Server Architectural Pattern

Moving to a more traditional architecture we go back in time. Once upon a time all programs ran on big iron and your entire program ran on a single machine. If you were lucky enough to be using a time-shared operating system, several people could be using the same program – albeit usually different copies – simultaneously. Then came personal computers and networks. And someone had the bright idea of dividing the work up between that big iron and your puny desktop machine. Thus was born the *client-server architecture.*

In a client-server architecture, your program is broken up into two different pieces that typically run on two separate computers. A server does most of the heavy lifting and computation; it provides services to its clients across a high-bandwidth network. Clients, on the other hand, mostly just handle user input, display output, and provide communication to the server. In short, the client program sends requests for services to the server program. The server program then evaluates the request, does whatever computation is necessary (including accessing a database, if needed) and responds to the client's request with an answer. The most common example of a client-server architecture today is the World Wide Web.

In the web model, your browser is the client. It presents a user interface to you, communicates with a web server, and renders the resulting web pages to your screen. The web server does a number of things. It serves web pages in HTML, but it also can serve as a database server, a file server, and a computational server – think about everything that Amazon.com does when you access that web site.

Clients and servers don't have to be on different computers, though. Two examples of programs written using a client-server architecture where both sides can reside on the same computer are *print spoolers* and the *X Windows graphical system.*

In a print spooler application, the program you are running – a word processor, a spreadsheet program, your web browser – runs as a client that makes request to a printing service that is implemented as a part of the computer's operating system. This service is typically known as a print spooler because it keeps a spool of print jobs and controls which jobs get printed and the order of their printing. So from your word processor, you'll select *Print* from a menu, set certain attributes and often pick a printer, and then click *OK* on some dialog box. This sends a print request to the print spooler on your system. The print spooler then adds your file to a queue of print jobs that it manages, contacts the printer driver and makes requests for printing to occur. The difference here is that once you've clicked the OK button, your client program (the word processor) typically does not have any more contact with the print spooler, the print *service* runs unattended.

The X Window System (see `www.xfree86.org/`) is a graphical windowing system used on all Unix and Linux based systems and also available for Apple Macintosh and Microsoft Windows systems as an add-on windowing system. The X system uses a client-server architecture where the client programs and the server typically both reside on the same computer. The X system server receives requests from client programs , processes them for the hardware that is attached to the current system, and provides an output service that displays the resulting data in bitmapped displays. Client program examples include *xterm* – a windowed terminal program that provides a command line interface to Unix, *xclock* – you guessed it – a clock, and *xdm* the X Window display manager. The X system allows hierarchical and overlapping windows, and provides the ability to configure menus, scroll bars, open and close buttons, background and foreground colors, and graphics. X can also manage a mouse and keyboards. These days the main use of the X system is as a springboard to build more sophisticated window managers, graphical environments, graphical widgets, and desktop management windowing systems like GNOME and KDE.

The Layered Approach

The layered architectural approach suggests that programs can be structured as a series of layers, much like geologic strata, with a sequence of well-defined interfaces between the layers. This has the effect of isolating each layer from the ones above and below it, so that one can change the internals of any layer without having to change any of the other layers in the program. That is, as long as your changes don't involve any changes to the interface. In a layered approach, interfaces are sacred. Two classic examples of a layered approach to programming are operating systems (OSs) and communications protocols.

An operating system's architecture has several objectives, among them to centralize control of the limited hardware resources and to protect users from each other. A layered approach to the operating system architecture does both of these things. Take a look at a pretty standard picture of an OS architecture (see Figure 5-5).

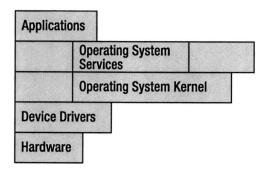

Figure 5-5. A layered architecture

In this layered model, user applications request operating system services via a system call interface. This is normally the only way for applications to access the computer's hardware. Most operating system services must make requests through the kernel and all hardware requests must go through device drivers that talk directly to the hardware devices. Each of these layers has a well-defined interface, so that, for example, a developer may add a new device driver for a new disk drive without changing any other part of the OS. This is a nice example of information hiding.

The same type of interface happens in a communications protocol. The most famous of these layered protocols is the International Standards Organization (ISO) Open Systems Interconnection (OSI) seven-layer model. This model looks like Figure 5-6.

7. Applications Layer
6. Presentation
5. Session Layer
4. Transport Layer
3. Network Layer
2. Data Link Layer
1. Physical Layer

Figure 5-6. The ISO-OSI layered architecture

In this model, each layer contains functions or services that are logically similar and are grouped together. An interface is defined between each layer and communication between layers is only allowed via the interfaces. A particular implementation need not contain all seven layers, and sometimes two or more layers are combined to make a smaller protocol stack. The OSI model defines both the seven-layer approach and all the interface protocols. The model can be downloaded as a PDF file from http://www.itu.int/rec/T-REC-X.200/en. (The ITU or International Telecommunications Union is the new name for the ISO.)

Examples of protocols that are implemented at each layer are shown in Table 5-1.

Table 5-1. Example Layered Protocols Using the ISO-OSI Architecture

Layer	Protocol
7. Application	http, ftp, telnet
6. Presentation	MIME, SSL
5. Session	Sockets
4. Transport	TCP, UDP
3. Network	IP, IPsec
2. Data Link	PPP, Ethernet, SLIP, 802.11
1. Physical	

The Main Program: Subroutine Architectural Pattern

The most traditional and oldest architectural pattern is the *main program – subroutine pattern.* While it descends from Niklaus Wirth's 1971 paper "Program Development by Stepwise Refinement,"[5] Wirth was just the first to formally define the top-down problem decomposition methodology that naturally leads to the main program – subroutine pattern.

The idea is simple. You start with a big problem, and then try to decompose the problem into several smaller problems or pieces of the original problem. For example, nearly every problem that is amenable to solution by top-down decomposition can be divided into three parts immediately – input processing, computation of the solution, and output processing.

Once you have a problem divided into several pieces, you look at each piece individually and continue dividing, ignoring all the other pieces as you go. Eventually, you'll have a very small problem where the solution is obvious; now is the time to write code. So you generally solve the problem from the top down, and write the code from the bottom up. There are many variations, however.

To quote from the conclusion to Wirth's paper:

>   1.   *Program construction consists of a sequence of refinement steps. In each step a given task is broken up into a number of subtasks. Each refinement in the description of a task may be accompanied by a refinement of the description of the data which constitute the means of communication between the subtasks...*

---

[5] Wirth, N. "Program Development by Stepwise Refinement." *Communications of the ACM* **14**(4): 221-227. (1971)

2. *The degree of modularity obtained in this way will determine the ease or difficulty with which a program can be adapted to changes or extensions of the purpose...*

3. *During the process of stepwise refinement, a notation which is natural to the problem in hand should be used as long as possible... Each refinement implies a number of design decisions based upon a set of design criteria...*

4. *The detailed elaborations on the development of even a short program form a long story, indicating that careful programming is not a trivial subject.*

Figure 5-7 gives an impression about how the main program subroutine architecture works. We'll discuss top-down decomposition of problems much more in Chapter 7.

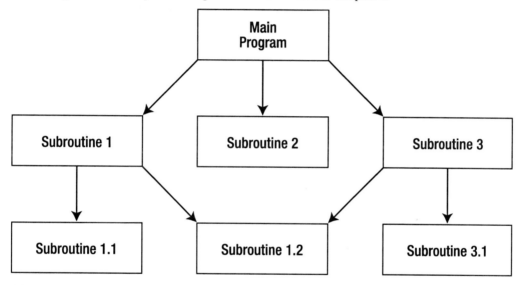

Figure 5-7. A main program – subroutine architecture

Conclusion

The software architecture is the core of your application. It is the foundation on which you build the rest of the program. It drives the rest of your design. There are many different styles of software architecture and in any given project you'll probably use more than one. The architectural style used for a program depends on what it is you're doing. That's the beauty of these styles; it may not always be true that form follows function, but for software – design follows architecture. These foundational patterns lead you down the path of design, shaping how your program will be constructed and lived in. Go out there and build a great program.

References

Bentley, J. *Programming Pearls, Second Edition.* (Boston, MA: Addison-Wesley, 2000.)

Garlan, D. and M. Shaw (1994). An Introduction to Software Architecture. Pittsburgh, PA: Carnegie Mellon University: 49. CMU/SEI-94-TR-21. (1994)

Kernighan, B. W. and R. Pike. *The Practice of Programming.* (Boston, MA: Addison-Wesley, 1999.)

Matuszek, David. "Rabbit Hunt," SIGCSE 2004 Technical Symposium, Nifty Assignments Session, retrieved August 17, 2009, `http://nifty.stanford.edu/2004/RabbitHunt/`. (2004)

McConnell, S. *Code Complete 2.* (Redmond, WA: Microsoft Press, 2004.)

Wirth, N. "Program Development by Stepwise Refinement." *Communications of the ACM* **14**(4): 221-227. (1971)

CHAPTER 6

Design Principles

There are two ways of constructing a software design. One way is to make it so simple that there are obviously no deficiencies. And the other way is to make it so complicated that there are no obvious deficiencies.

— C. A. R. Hoare

One way to look at software problems is with a model that divides the problems into two different layers:

- "Wicked" problems fall in the upper layer. These are problems that typically come from domains outside of computer science (e.g. biology, business, meteorology, sociology, political science, etc.). These types of problems tend to be open-ended, ill-defined, and large in the sense that they require much work. For example, pretty much any kind of a web commerce application is a wicked problem. Horst W. J. Rittel and Melvin M. Webber, in a 1973 paper on social policy,[1] gave a definition for and a set of characteristics used to recognize a wicked problem that we'll look at later in this chapter.

- "Tame" problems fall in the lower layer. These problems tend to cut across other problem domains; they tend to be more well defined and small. Sorting and searching are great examples of tame problems. Small and well-defined don't mean "easy" however. Tame problems can be very complicated and difficult to solve. It's just that they are clearly defined and you know when you have a solution. These are the kinds of problems that provide computer scientists with foundations in terms of data structures and algorithms for the wicked problems we solve from other problem domains.

According to Rittel and Webber, a wicked problem is one for which the requirements are completely known only after the problem is solved, or for which the requirements and solution evolve over time. It

---

[1] Rittel, H. W. J. and M. M. Webber. "Dilemmas in a General Theory of Planning." *Policy Sciences* 4(2): 155-169. (1973)

turns out this describes most of the "interesting" problems in software development. Recently, Jeff Conklin has revised Rittel and Webber's description of a wicked problem and provided a more succinct list of the characteristics of wicked problems.[2] To paraphrase:

- *A wicked problem is not understood until after the creation of a solution.* Another way of saying this is that the problem is defined and solved at the same time.[3]

- *Wicked problems have no stopping rule;* that is, you can create incremental solutions to the problem, but there's nothing that tells you that you've found the correct and final solution.

- *Solutions to wicked problems are not right or wrong;* they are better or worse, or good-enough or not-good-enough.

- *Every wicked problem is essentially novel and unique.* Because of the "wickedness" of the problem, even if you have a similar problem next week, you basically have to start over again because the requirements will be different enough and the solution will still be elusive.

- Every solution to a wicked problem is a 'one shot operation'. See number 4 above.

- *Wicked problems have no given alternative solutions.* That is, there is no small finite set of solutions from which to choose .

Wicked problems crop up all over the place. For example, creating a word processing program is a wicked problem. You may think that you know what a word processor needs to do – insert text, cut and paste, handle paragraphs, print. But this list of features is only one person's list. As soon as you "finish" your word processor and release it, you'll be inundated with new feature requests: spell checking, footnotes, multiple columns, support for different fonts, colors, styles, and the list goes on. The word processing program is essentially never done – at least not until you release the last version and end-of-life the product.

Word processing is actually a pretty obvious wicked problem. Others might include problems where you don't really know if you can solve the problem at the start. Expert systems require a user interface, an inference engine, a set of rules, and a database of domain information. For a particular domain, it's not at all certain at the beginning that you can create the rules that the inference engine will use to reach conclusions and recommendations. So you have to iterate through different rule sets, send out the next version and see how well it performs. Then you do it again, adding and modifying rules. You don't really know if the solution is correct until you're done. Now that's a wicked problem.

Conklin and Rittel and Webber say that when faced with a large, complicated problem (a wicked one), that traditional cognitive studies indicate most people will follow a linear problem solving approach, working top-down from the problem to the solution. This is equivalent to the traditional waterfall model described in Chapter 2[4]. Figure 6-1 shows this linear approach.

---

[2] Conklin, J. *Dialogue Mapping: Building Shared Understanding of Wicked Problems.* (New York, NY: John Wiley & Sons, 2005.)

[3] DeGrace, P. and L. H. Stahl *Wicked Problems, Righteous Solutions : A Catalogue of Modern Software Engineering Paradigms.* (Englewood Cliffs, NJ: Yourdon Press, 1990.)

[4] Conklin, J. *Wicked Problems and Social Complexity.* Retrieved from http://cognexus.org/wpf/wickedproblems.pdf on 8 September 2009. Paper last updated October, 2008.

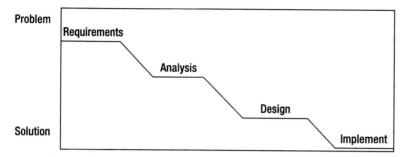

Figure 6-1. Linear problem-solving approach

Instead of this linear, waterfall approach, real wicked problem solvers tend to use an approach that swings from requirements analysis to solution modeling and back until the problem solution is good enough. Conklin calls this an *opportunity-driven* or *opportunistic* approach because the designers are looking for any opportunity to make progress toward the solution.[5] Instead of the traditional waterfall picture in Figure 601, the opportunity-driven approach looks like Figure 6-2.

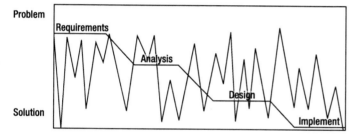

Figure 6-2. The opportunity-driven development approach

In this figure, the jagged line indicates the designer's work moving from the problem to a solution prototype and back again, slowly evolving both the requirements understanding and the solution iteration and converging on an implementation that is good enough to release. As an example, let's take a quick look at a web application.

Say that a not-for-profit organization keeps a list of activities for youth in your home county. The list is updated regularly and is distributed to libraries around the county. Currently, the list is kept on a spreadsheet and is distributed in hard copy in a three-ring binder. The not-for-profit wants to put all its data online and make it accessible over the web. It also wants to be able to update the data via the same web site. Simple, you say. It's just a web application with an HTML front-end and a database back end. Not a problem.

Ah, but this is really a wicked problem in disguise. First of all, the customer has no idea what they want the web page(s) to look like. So whatever you give them the first time will not be precisely what they want; the problem won't be understood completely until you are done. Secondly, as you develop prototypes, they will want more features – so the problem has no stopping rule. And finally, as time goes

---

[5] Conklin, J. (2008)

on the not-for-profit will want new features, so there is no "right" answer, there is only a "good enough" answer. Very wicked.

Conklin also provides a list of characteristics of "tame" problems, ones for which you can easily and reliably find a solution. "A tame problem:

- has a well-defined and stable problem statement;

- has a definite stopping point, i.e., when the solution is reached;

- has a solution which can be objectively evaluated as right or wrong;

- belongs to a class of similar problems which are all solved in the same similar way;

- has solutions which can be easily tried and abandoned; and

- comes with a limited set of alternative solutions."

A terrific example of a tame problem is sorting a list of data values.

- The problem is easily and clearly stated – sort this list into ascending order using this function to compare data elements.

- Sorting has a definite stopping point – the list is sorted.

- The result of a sort can be objectively evaluated (the list is either sorted correctly, or it isn't.)

- Sorting belongs to a class of similar problems that are all solved in the same way. Sorting integers, is similar to sorting strings, is similar to sorting database records using a key and so on.

- Sorting has solutions that can easily be tried and abandoned.

- Finally, sorting has a limited set of alternative solutions; sorting by comparison has a set of known algorithms and a theoretical lower bound.

What does this have to do with design principles, you ask? Well, realizing that most of the larger software problems we'll encounter have a certain amount of "wickedness" built into them influences how we think about design issues, how we approach the design of a solution to a large, ill-formed problem, and gives us some insight into the design process. It also lets us abandon the waterfall model with a clear conscience and pushes us to look for unifying heuristics that we can apply to design problems. In this chapter we'll discuss overall principles for design that we'll then expand upon in the chapters ahead.

The Design Process

Design is messy. Even if you completely understand the problem requirements (it's a tame problem), you typically have many alternatives to consider when you're designing a software solution. You'll also usually make lots of mistakes before you come up with a solution that works. As we saw in Figure 6-2, your design will change as you understand the problem better over time. This gives the *appearance* of messiness and disorganization, but really, you're making progress.

Design is about tradeoffs and priorities. Most software projects are time-limited, so you usually won't be able to implement all the features that the customer wants. You have to figure out the subset that will give the customer the most bang in the time you have available. So you have to prioritize the requirements and trade off one subset for another.

Design is heuristic. For the overwhelming majority of projects there is no set of cut and dried rules that says, "First we design component X using technique Y. Then we design component Z using technique W." Software just doesn't work that way. Software design is done using a set of ever-changing heuristics (rules of thumb) that each designer acquires over the course of a career. Over time good designers learn more heuristics and patterns (see Chapter 11) that allow them to quickly get through the easy bits of a design and get to the heart of the wickedness of the problem. The best thing you can do is to sit at the feet of a master designer and learn the heuristics.

Designs evolve. Finally, good designers recognize that for any problem, tame or wicked, the requirements will change over time. This will then cascade into changes in your design. And so your design will evolve over time. This is particularly true across product releases and new feature additions. The trick here is to create a software architecture (Chapter 5) that is amenable to change with limited effect on the downstream design and code.

Desirable Design Characteristics (Things Your Design Should Favor)

Regardless of the size of your project or what process you use to do your design, there are a number of desirable characteristics that every software design should have. These are the principles you should adhere to as you consider your design. Your design doesn't necessarily need to exhibit all of these characteristics, but having a majority of them will certainly make your software easier to write, understand, and use.

- *Fitness of purpose.* Your design must work, and work correctly in the sense that it must satisfy the requirements you've been given within the constraints of the platform on which your software will be running. Don't add new requirements as you go – the customer will do that for you.

- *Separation of concerns.* Related closely to modularity, this principle says you should separate out functional pieces of your design cleanly in order to facilitate ease of maintenance and simplicity. Modularity is good.

- *Simplicity.* Keep your design as simple as possible. This will let others understand what you're up to. If you find a place that can be simplified, do it! If simplifying your design means adding more modules or classes to your design, that's okay. Simplicity also applies to interfaces between modules or classes. Simple interfaces allow others to see the data and control flow in your design. In agile methodologies, this idea of simplicity is kept in front of you all the time. Most agile techniques have a rule that says if you're working on part of a program and you have an opportunity to simplify it (called *refactoring* in agile-speak) do it right then. Keep you design and your code as simple as possible at all times.

- *Ease of maintenance.* A simple, understandable design is amenable to change. The first kind of change you'll encounter is fixing errors. Errors occur at all phases of the development process, requirements, analysis, design, coding, and testing. The more coherent and easy to understand your design is, the easier it will be to isolate and fix errors.

- *Loose coupling.* When you are separating your design into either modules or in object-oriented design, into classes, the degree to which the classes depend on each other is called *coupling. Tightly coupled* modules may share data or procedures. This means that a change in one module is much more likely to lead to a required change in the other module. This increases the maintenance burden and makes the modules more likely to contain errors. *Loosely coupled* modules, on the other hand, are connected solely by their interfaces. Any data they both need must be passed between procedures or methods via an *interface.* Loosely coupled modules hide the details of how they perform operations from other modules, sharing only their interfaces. This lightens the maintenance burden because a change to how one class is implemented will not likely affect how another class operates as long as the interface is invariant. So changes are isolated and errors are much less likely to propagate.

- *High cohesion.* The complement of loose coupling is high cohesion. *Cohesion* within a module is the degree to which the module is self-contained with regards both to the data it holds and the operations that act on the data. A class that has high cohesion pretty much has all the data it needs defined within the class template and all the operations that are allowed on the data are defined within the class as well. So any object that is instantiated from the class template is very independent and just communicates with other objects via its published interface.

- *Extensibility.* An outgrowth of simplicity and coupling is the ability to add new features to the design easily. This is extensibility. One of the features of wicked software problems is that they're never really finished. So after every release of a product, the next thing that happens is the customer asks for new features. The easier it is to add new features, the cleaner your design is.

- *Portability.* While not high on the list, keeping in mind that your software may need to be ported to another platform (or two or three) is a desirable characteristic. There are a lot of issues involved with porting software, including, operating system issues, hardware architecture, and user interface issues. This is particularly true for web applications.

Design Heuristics

Speaking of heuristics, here's a short list of good, time-tested heuristics. The list is clearly not exhaustive and it's pretty idiosyncratic, but it's a list you can use time and again. Think about them and try some of them during your next design exercise. We will come back to all of these heuristics in much more detail in later chapters.

Find real world objects to model. Alan Davis[6] and Richard Fairley[7] call this "intellectual distance." It's how far your design is from a real world object. The heuristic here is to try to find real world objects that are close to things you want to model in your program. Keeping the real world object in mind as you are

---

[6] Davis, A. M. *201 Principles of Software Development.* (New York, NY: McGraw-Hill, 1995).

[7] Fairley, R. E. *Software Engineering Concepts.* (New York, NY: McGraw-Hill, 1985.)

designing your program helps keep your design closer to the problem. Fairley's advice is to minimize the intellectual distance between the real world object and your model of it .

Abstraction is key. Whether you're doing object-oriented design and you are creating interfaces and abstract classes, or whether you're doing a more traditional layered design, you want to use abstraction. Abstraction means being lazy. You put off what you need to do by pushing it higher in the design hierarchy (more abstraction) or pushing it further down (more details). Abstraction is a key element of managing the complexity of a large problem. By abstracting away the details you can see the kernel of the real problem.

Information hiding is your friend. Information hiding is the concept that you isolate information – both data and behavior – in your program so that you can isolate errors and isolate changes; you also only allow access to the information via a well-defined interface. A fundamental part of object-oriented design is encapsulation, a concept that derives from information hiding. You hide the details of a class away and only allow communication and modification of data via a public interface. This means that your implementation can change, but as long as the interface is consistent and constant, nothing else in your program need change. If you're not doing object-oriented design, think libraries for hiding behavior and structures (structs in C and C++) for hiding state.

Keep your design modular. Breaking your design up into semi-independent pieces has many advantages. It keeps the design manageable in your head; you can just think about one part at a time and leave the others as black boxes. It takes advantage of information hiding and encapsulation. It isolates changes. It helps with extensibility and maintainability. Modularity is just a good thing. Do it.

Identify the parts of your design that are likely to change. If you make the assumption that there will be changes in your requirements, then there will likely be changes in your design as well. If you identify those areas of your design that are likely to change, you can separate them, thus mitigating the impact of any changes you need to make. What things are likely to change? Well, it depends on your application, doesn't it? Business rules can change (think tax rules or accounting practices), user interfaces can change, hardware can change, and so on. The point here is to anticipate the change and to divide up your design so that the necessary changes are contained.

Use loose coupling. Use interfaces and abstract classes. Along with modularity, information hiding, and change, using loose coupling will make your design easier to understand and to change as time goes along. Loose coupling says that you should minimize the dependencies of one class (or module) on another. This is so that a change in one module won't cause changes in other modules. If the implementation of a module is hidden and only the interface exposed, you can swap out implementations as long as you keep the interface constant. So you implement loose coupling by using well-defined interfaces between modules, and in an object-oriented design, using abstract classes and interfaces to connect classes.

Use your knapsack full of common design patterns. Robert Glass[8] describes great software designers as having "...a large set of standard patterns" that they carry around with them and apply to their designs. This is what design experience is all about. Doing design over and over again and learning from the experience. In Susan Lammer's book *Programmers at Work*,[9] Butler Lampson says, "Most of the time, a new program is a refinement, extension, generalization, or improvement of an existing program. It's really unusual to do something that's completely new...." That's what design patterns are: they're descriptions of things you've already done that you can apply to a new problem. Voila!

Adhere to the Principle of One Right Place. In his book *Programming on Purpose: Essays on Software Design*, P.J. Plauger says, "My major concern here is the Principle of One Right Place – there should be

---

[8] Glass, R. L. *Software Creativity 2.0.* Atlanta, GA, developer.*. (2006)

[9] Lammers, S. *Programmers At Work.* (Redmond, WA: Microsoft Press, 1986.)

One Right Place to look for any nontrivial piece of code, and One Right Place to make a likely maintenance change."[10] Your design should adhere to the Principle of One Right Place; debugging and maintenance will be much easier.

Use diagrams as a design language. I'm a visual learner. For me, a picture really is worth a thousand or so words. As I design and code I'm constantly drawing diagrams so I can visualize how my program is going to hang together, which classes or modules will be talking to each other, what data is dependent on what function, where do the return values go, what is the sequence of events. This type of visualization can settle the design in your head and it can point out errors or possible complications in the design. Whiteboards or paper are cheap; enjoy!

Designers and Creativity

Don't think that design is cut and dried or that formal process rules can be imposed to crank out software designs. It's not like that at all. While there are formal restrictions and constraints on your design that are imposed by the problem, the problem domain, and the target platform, the process of reaching the design itself need not be formal. It is at bottom a creative activity. Bill Curtis, in a 1987 empirical study of software designers came up with a process that seems to be what most of the designers followed:[11]

1.   Understand the problem.

2.   Decompose the problem into goals and objects.

3.   Select and compose plans to solve the problem.

4.   Implement the plans.

5.   Reflect on the design product and process.

Frankly, this is a pretty general list and doesn't really tell us all we'd need for software design. Curtis, however, then went deeper in #3 on his list, "select and compose plans," and found that his designers used the following steps

6.   Build a mental model of a proposed solution.

7.   Mentally execute the model to see if it solves the problem – make up input and simulate the model in your head.

8.   If what you get is not correct, then change the model to remove the errors and go back to step 2 to simulate again.

---

[10] Plauger, P. J. *Programming on Purpose : Essays on Software Design.* Englewood Cliffs, NJ: PTR Prentice Hall, 1993.)

[11] Curtis, B., R. Guindon, et al. *Empirical Studies of the Design Process: Papers for the Second Workshop on Empirical Studies of Programmers.* Austin, TX, MCC. (1987)

9. When your sample input produces the correct output, select some more input values and go back and do steps 2 and 3 again.

10. When you've done this enough times (you'll know because you're experienced) then you've got a good model and you can stop.[12]

This deeper technique makes the cognitive and the iterative aspects of design clear and obvious. We see that design is fundamentally a function of the mind, and is idiosyncratic and depends on things about the designer that are outside the process itself.

John Nestor, in a report to the Software Engineering Institute came up with a list of what are some common characteristics of great designers.

Great designers

- have a large set of standard patterns;

- have experienced failing projects;

- have mastery of development tools;

- have an impulse towards simplicity;

- can anticipate change;

- can view things from the user's perspective; and

- can deal with complexity.[13]

Conclusion

So at the end of the chapter, what have we learned about software design?

Design is ad hoc, heuristic, and messy. It fundamentally uses a trial-and-error and heuristic process and that process is the natural one to use for software design. There are a number of well-known heuristics that any good designer should employ.

Design depends on understanding of prior design problems and solutions. Designers need some knowledge of the problem domain. More importantly, they need knowledge of design and patterns of good designs. They need to have a knapsack of these design patterns that they can use to approach new problems. The solutions are tried and true. The problems are new but they contain elements of problems that have already been solved. The patterns are malleable templates that can be applied to those elements of the new problem that match the pattern's requirements.

Design is iterative. Requirements change, and so must your design. Even if you have a stable set of requirements, your *understanding* of the requirements changes as you progress through the design activity and so you'll go back and change the design to reflect this deeper, better understanding. The iterative process clarifies and simplifies your design at each step.

Design is a cognitive activity. You're not writing code at this point, so you don't need a machine. Your head and maybe a pencil and paper or a whiteboard are all you need to do design. As Dijkstra says,

---

[12] Glass, R. L. *Software Creativity 2.0.* Atlanta, GA, developer.*. (2006)

[13] Glass, R. L. (2006)

"We must not forget that it is not our business to make programs; it is our business to design classes of computations that will display a desired behavior."[14]

Design is opportunistic. Glass sums up his discussion of design with "The unperturbed design process is opportunistic – that is, rather than proceed in an orderly process, good designers follow an erratic pattern dictated by their minds, pursuing opportunities rather than an orderly progression."[15]

All the characteristics above argue against a rigid, plan-driven design process and for a creative, flexible way of doing design. This brings us back to the first topic in this chapter – design is just wicked.

And finally:

A designer can mull over complicated designs for months. Then suddenly the simple, elegant, beautiful solution occurs to him. When it happens to you, it feels as if God is talking! And maybe He is.

—Leo Frankowski (in *The Cross-Time Engineer*)

References

Conklin, J. *Dialogue Mapping: Building Shared Understanding of Wicked Problems.* (New York, NY: John Wiley & Sons, 2005.)

Conklin, J. *Wicked Problems and Social Complexity.* Retrieved from `http://cognexus.org/wpf/wickedproblems.pdf` on 8 September 2009. Paper last updated October, 2008.

Curtis, B., R. Guindon, et al. Empirical Studies of the Design Process: Papers for the Second Workshop on Empirical Studies of Programmers. Austin, TX, MCC. (1987)

Davis, A. M. *201 Principles of Software Development.* (New York, NY: McGraw-Hill, 1995).

DeGrace, P. and L. H. Stahl *Wicked Problems, Righteous Solutions : A Catalogue of Modern Software Engineering Paradigms.* (Englewood Cliffs, NJ: Yourdon Press, 1990.)

Dijkstra, E. "The Humble Programmer." CACM 15(10): 859-866. (1972)

Fairley, R. E. *Software Engineering Concepts.* (New York, NY: McGraw-Hill, 1985.)

Glass, R. L. *Software Creativity 2.0.* Atlanta, GA, developer.*. (2006)

Lammers, S. *Programmers At Work.* (Redmond, WA: Microsoft Press, 1986.)

McConnell, S. *Code Complete 2.* (Redmond, WA: Microsoft Press, 2004.)

---

[14] Dijkstra, E. "The Humble Programmer." CACM 15(10): 859-866. (1972)
[15] Glass, R. L. (2006)

Parnas, D. "On the Criteria to be Used in Decomposing Systems into Modules." *CACM* **15**(12): 1053-1058. (1972)

Plauger, P. J. *Programming on Purpose : Essays on Software Design.* Englewood Cliffs, NJ: PTR Prentice Hall, 1993.)

Rittel, H. W. J. and M. M. Webber. "Dilemmas in a General Theory of Planning." *Policy Sciences* **4**(2): 155-169. (1973)

CHAPTER 7

Structured Design

Invest in the abstraction, not the implementation. Abstractions can survive the barrage of changes from different implementations and new technologies"

—Andy Hunt and Dave Thomas[1]

Structured Programming

Structured design has its genesis in Edsger Dijkstra's famous 1968 letter to the *Communications of the ACM*, "Go To Statement Considered Harmful." Dijkstra's paper concludes with

> *The **go to** statement as it stands is just too primitive; it is too much an invitation to make a mess of one's program. One can regard and appreciate the clauses considered (ed. if-then-else, switch, while-do, and do-while) as bridling its use. I do not claim that the clauses mentioned are exhaustive in the sense that they will satisfy all needs, but whatever clauses are suggested (e.g. abortion clauses) they should satisfy the requirement that a programmer independent coordinate system can be maintained to describe the process in a helpful and manageable way.[2]*

Programming languages created from this point onward, while not eliminating the goto statement (except for Java, which has none), certainly downplayed its use, and courses that taught programming encouraged students to avoid it. Instead, problem-solving was taught in a top-down structured manner, where one begins with the problem statement and attempts to break the problem down into a set of solvable sub-problems. The process continues until each sub-problem is small enough to be either trivial or very easy to solve. This technique is called *structured programming*. Before the advent and acceptance of object-oriented programming in the mid-80s, this was the standard approach to problem solving and programming. It is still one of the best ways to approach a large class of problems.

---

[1] Hunt, A. and D. Thomas. *The Pragmatic Programmer: From Journeyman to Master.* (Boston, MA: Addison-Wesley, 2000.)

[2] Dijkstra, E. "GoTo Statement Considered Harmful." *Communications of the ACM* 11(3): 147-148. (1968)

Stepwise Refinement

Niklaus Wirth formalized the technique in his 1971 paper, "Program Development by Stepwise Refinement."[3] *Stepwise refinement* contends that designing programs consists of a set of refinement steps. In each step, a given task is broken up into a number of subtasks. Each refinement of a task must be accompanied by a refinement of the data description and the interface. The degree of modularity obtained will determine the ease or difficulty with which a program can be adapted to changes in requirements or environment.

During refinement, you use a notation that is natural to the problem space. Avoid using a programming language for description as long as possible. Each refinement implies a number of design decisions based on a set of design criteria. These criteria include efficiency of time and space, clarity, and regularity of structure (simplicity).

Refinement can proceed in two ways, top-down or bottom-up. Top-down refinement is characterized by moving from a general description of the problem to detailed statements of what individual modules or routines do. The guiding principle behind stepwise refinement is that humans can concentrate on only a few things at a time; Miller's famous 7 +/- 2 chunks of data rule.[4] One works by

- analyzing the problem and trying to identify the outlines of a solution and the pros and cons of each possibility;

- then, designing the top levels first;

- steering clear of language-specific details;

- pushing down the details until you get to the lower levels;

- formalizing each level;

- verifying each level; and

- moving to the next lower level to make the next set of refinements. (That is, repeat.)

One continues to refine the solution until it seems as if it would be easier to code than to decompose; we'll see an example of this process later in this chapter.

That is, you work until you become impatient at how obvious and easy the design becomes. The down-side here is that you really have no good metric on "when to stop." It just takes practice.

If you can't get started at the top, then start at the bottom.

- Ask yourself, "What do I know that the system needs to do?" This usually involves lower level I/O operations, other low-level operations on data structures, and so on.

- Identify as many low-level functions and components as you can from that question.

---

[3] Wirth, N. "Program Development by Stepwise Refinement." *CACM* **14**(4): 221-227. (1971)

[4] Miller, G. A. "The magical number seven, plus or minus two: Some limits on our capacity for processing information." *Psychological Review* **63**: 81-97. (1956)

- Identify common aspects of the low-level components and group them together.

- Continue with the next level up, or go back to the top and try again to work down.

Bottom-up assessment usually results in early identification of utility routines, which can lead to a more compact design. It also helps promote reuse – because you are reusing the lower level routines. On the downside, bottom-up assessment is hard to use exclusively – you nearly always end up switching to a top down approach at some point, sometimes you find you just can't put a larger piece together from the bottom-up. This isn't really stepwise refinement, but it can help get you started. Most real step-wise refinements involve alternating between top-down and bottom-up design elements. Fortunately, top-down and bottom-up design methodologies can be very complementary.

Example of Stepwise Refinement: The Eight-Queens Problem

The eight queens problem is familiar to most students. The problem is to find a placement of eight queens on a standard 8 × 8 chess board in such a way that no queen can be attacked by any other. One possible solution to the problem is shown in Figure 7-1.

Figure 7-1. One solution to the eight-queens problem

Remember that queens can move any number of spaces horizontally, vertically, or diagonally. It turns out that no one has yet found an analytical solution to this problem, and it's likely one does not exist. So how would you approach this problem? Go ahead, think about it; I'll wait.

…

…

Done? Okay. Let's see one way to decompose this problem.

Proposed Solution 1

The first thing we need to do is to look at the problem and tease out the requirements and the outline of a solution. This will start us down the road of answering the question of what the top-level decomposition should be.

First you could think of solving the problem using brute force; just try all the possible arrangements of queens and pick the ones that work. With 8 queens and 64 possible squares there are

$$\frac{n!}{k!(n-k)!} = \frac{64!}{56! \times 8!} = 2^{32}$$

possible board configurations, where n is the number of squares on the board and k is the number of queens, which is only 4,426,165,368 (a bit over 4 billion configurations). These days, that's not very many, so brute force might be the way to go.

So if we generate a set A of all the possible board combinations, we can create a test called *q(x)* that returns a *true* if the board configuration x is a solution, and returns *false* if x is not a solution. Then we can create a program that looks like the following:

> Generate the set A of all board configurations;
>
> *while* there are still untested configurations in A *do*
>
> > x = the next configuration from A
> >
> > *if* (q(x) == true) *then* print the solution x and stop
> >
> > *go back* to the top and do it again.

Notice that all the work is getting done in two steps – generating the set A and performing the test *q(x)*. The generation of A only happens once, but performing the test *q(x)* happens once for every configuration in A until you find a solution. While this decomposition will surely work, it's not terribly efficient. So let's just say that we'd rather reduce the number of combinations. Efficiency is a good thing, after all.

Proposed Solution 2

Again, we need to start at the top level. But this time we've done some analysis, so we have a clearer idea of what has to happen. We've eliminated brute-force, but we see that we can think in terms of board configurations. In order to reduce the number of total possible configurations and then come up with a more efficient algorithm, we need to think about the problem. The first thing to notice is that you can never have more than one queen in a column, in fact, you must have *exactly* one queen per column. That reduces the number of possible combinations to 2^{24} or just 16 million. Although this is good, it doesn't really change the algorithm. Our proposed solution would now look like:

> Generate the set B of restricted board configurations;
>
> *while* there are still untested configurations in B *do*
>
> > x = the next configuration from B
> >
> > *if* (q(x) == true) *then* print the solution x and stop
> >
> > *go back* to the top and do it again.

This version requires generating the set, B, of board positions with one queen in each column and still requires visiting up to 16 million possible board positions. Generating B is now more complicated than generating A because we now have to test to see if a proposed board position meets the one queen per column restriction. There must be a better way.

Proposed Solution 3

Well, of course there is. We just need to be more intelligent about generating board configurations and evaluate board positions while we're generating them. Instead of generating a complete board configuration and then testing it, why not generate and test *partial solutions?* If we can stop as soon as we know we don't have a valid solution, then things should go faster. Also, if we can back up from a bad solution to the last good partial solution, we can eliminate bad configurations more quickly.

Now we're at the point where we can do that top-level design, formalize it, and move down to the next refinement level.

Refinement 1

Here's the idea.

1. Put down a queen on the next row in the next available column.

2. Test the queen to see if she can attack any other queen. (That's a variation on the $q(x)$ test above.)

3. If she can attack, pick her back up, back up to the previous trial solution and try again.

4. If she can't attack, leave her alone and go back to the top and try the next queen.

With this method, we're guaranteed that the trial solution at column j is correct. We then attempt to generate a new solution by adding a queen in column j+1. If this fails, we just need to back up to our previous correct trial solution at column j and try again. This technique of creating and testing partial solutions is called a *stepwise construction of trial solutions* by Wirth. And the backing up technique is, of course, called *backtracking.* Here's more formal pseudo-code to find a single solution:

```
do {
        while ((row < 8) && (col < 8))  {
            if (the current queen is safe) then
                advance: keep the queen on the board and advance to the next col.
            else
                the queen is not safe, so move up to the next row.
        }
        if (we've exhausted all the rows in this column) then
            regress: retreat a column, move its queen up a row, and start again.

    } while ((col < 8) && (col >= 0));
    if (we've reached column 8) then
      we have a solution, print it.
```

This solution tests only a single queen at a time. One implication of this is that, at any given time, there are only j queens on the board and so only j queens need to be tested each time through the outer loop. (One only needs to test the queens up through column j.) That reduces the amount of work in the testing routine.

This algorithm is our first formal view of the solution. Notice in the method described above that we're using pseudo-code rather than a real programming language. This is because we want to push language details further down the refinement levels. Also, while we've got a general outline of the method, there are a lot of details still to be considered. These details have been pushed down in the hierarchy of control we're creating, and we'll get to them in the next refinement iteration. This is also a function of the stepwise refinement.

Now that we have a description of the algorithm, we can also work to verify it. The final verification will, of course, be watching the program produce a correct solution but we're not at that point yet. However, we can surely take a chess board (or a piece of paper) and walk through this algorithm by hand to verify that we can generate a placement of queens on the board that is a solution to the problem.

At this point we've got a more formal top-level description, we've done what verification we can, and we're ready to expand those fuzzy steps we see above.

Refinement 2

Now that we've got a first cut at the program, we need to examine each of the steps in the program and see what they are made of. The steps we're interested in are

1. Check to see if the current queen is safe.

2. Keep a safe queen on the board and advance to the next column.

3. Advance an unsafe queen up a row.

4. Retreat a column and reset the queen in that column.

Checking to see if the current queen is safe means that we need to check that there are no other queens on either of the diagonals (the up or down diagonals) or the row that the current queen is on. The row check is easy, one just checks all the other squares in the same row. To check the up and down diagonals, remember that if the current queen is at column j, that we only need to check columns 1 through j-1. If you think about it for a minute, you'll see that the difference between the row and column indexes of all the squares on the up diagonal (those that go from lower-left to upper-right) are a constant. Similarly, the sum of the row and column indexes of all the squares on the down diagonal (those that go from upper-left to lower-right) are also a constant. This makes it easier to figure out which cells are on the diagonal of a queen and how to check them.

Now we're ready to start considering data structures. Where did this come from, you ask? Well, stepwise refinement is mostly about describing the control flow of the program. But at some point you need to decide on exactly what the data will look like. For each problem you try to solve, this will happen at a different place in your refinement process. For this problem we're at a place where in the next refinement we should be writing more detailed pseudo-code. That is pretty much forcing us to think about data structures now, so we can do the pseudo-code.

In particular now we need to ask ourselves, how are we going to represent the board and the queens on the board? How are we going to represent the empty cells? We need a data structure that will allow us to efficiently represent queens and check whether they can be attacked. A first cut at this might be an 8×8 two-dimensional array where we place queens at the appropriate row and column intersections. Because we don't need to do any computation on this matrix – all we need is to indicate the presence or absence of a queen – we can save space by making it a boolean array. This data structure also allows us to quickly check the rows, and the up and down diagonals for queens that can attack the current queen. So we should use a 2D boolean array, right?

Well, not so fast. This isn't the only way to think about the data representation for queens. In fact, if we think about the data structure and the operations we need to perform during the safety check we might be able to simplify things a bit.

First of all, since we know that there can only be one queen in each column and one queen in each row, why not combine that information? Instead of a 2D array, why not just use a 1D boolean array, say

```
boolean column[8];
```

where column[i] = true means that the ith column is still free. For the diagonals, we can use the property about the constant difference or sum of up and down diagonals to create two other arrays

```
boolean up[-7..+7], down[0..14];
```

that will indicate which diagonal squares are free. With this arrangement, the test for a queen being safe is

```
(column[i] and up[row-col] and down[row+col])⁵
```

All right. This seems simple enough , so we're finally done with this, right?

Well, no. There's yet another way to think about this. Going back to using a 1D array, but this time using an integer array

```
int board[8];
```

where each *index* into the array represents a column (0 through 7 in the eight-queens case), and each *value* stored in the array represents the row on which a queen is deposited (also 0 through 7 in the eight-queens case). Because we now have data on the exact location (rows and columns) of each queen, we don't need separate arrays for the up and down diagonals. The test for safety is a bit more difficult, but still simple. This might be the time for some more code. At this point it seems appropriate to move from pseudo-code to a real language. You'll have to make that move at some point in the refinement process. Just like deciding when to define your data structures, exactly when to insert language-specific features depends on the problem and what how detailed the refinement is at this point. A Java method to test for safety might look like:

```
public boolean isSafe (int[ ] board) {
        boolean safe = true;
        for (int i = 0; i < col; i++) {
                if ( ( ( board[i] + i) == (row + col) ) ||       // down diagonal test
                        ( ( board[i] - i) == (row - col) ) ||     // up diagonal test
                        ( board[i]   == row) )                    // row test
                        safe = false;
        }
        return safe;
}
```

Remember that, because we're creating partial solutions by adding one queen to a column at a time, we only need to test the first *col* columns each time.

---

⁵ Dahl, O. J., E. Dijkstra, et al. (1972). *Structured Programming.* (London, UK: Academic Press, 1972.)

CHAPTER 7 ▪ STRUCTURED DESIGN

Now that we have the safety procedure out of the way and we've decided on a simple data structure to represent the current board configuration, we can proceed to the remaining procedures in the decomposition. The remaining procedures are

5. Keep a safe queen on the board and advance to the next column;

6. Advance an unsafe queen up a row; and

7. Retreat a column and reset the queen in that column.

These are all simple enough to just write without further decomposition. This is a key point of structured programming – keep doing the decompositions until a procedure becomes obvious, then you can code. These three methods then look like the following when written in code:

```
/*
 * keep a safe queen on the board and advance to the next column
 * the queen at (row, col) is safe, so we have a partial solution.
 * advance to the next column
 */
public void advance (int[] board) {
    board[col] = row;        // put the queen at (row, col) on the board
    col++;                   // move to the next column
    row = 0;                 // and start at the beginning of the column
}
```

For *advance an unsafe queen up a row* we don't even need a method. The test in the main program for safety moves the queen up a row if the isSafe() method determines that the current (row, col) position is unsafe. The code for this is:

```
        if (isSafe(board))
            advance(board);
        else
            row++;
```

Finally, we have:

```
/**
 * retreat a column and reset the queen in that column
 * we could not find a safe row in current col
 * so back up one col and move that queen
 * up a row so we can start looking again
 */
public void retreat (int[] board) {
    col--;
    row = board[col] + 1;
}
```

The complete Java program is in the Appendix.

Modular Decomposition

In 1972, David Parnas published a paper titled "On the Criteria to Be Used in Decomposing Systems into Modules" that proposed that one could design programs using a technique called *modularity*.[6] Parnas' paper was also one of the first papers to describe a decomposition based on *information hiding*, one of the key techniques in object-oriented programming. In his paper, Parnas highlighted the differences between a top-down decomposition of a problem based on the *flow of control* of a problem solution and a decomposition of the problem that used *encapsulation* and *information hiding* to isolate data definitions and their operations from each other. His paper is a clear precursor to object-oriented analysis and design (OOA&D), which we'll see in the next chapter.

While Parnas' paper pre-dates the idea, he was really talking about a concept called *separation of concerns*. "In computer science, *separation of concerns* is the process of separating a computer program into distinct features that overlap in functionality as little as possible. A concern is any piece of interest or focus in a program. Typically, concerns are synonymous with features or behaviors. Progress towards separation of concerns is traditionally achieved through modularity of programming and encapsulation (or "transparency" of operation), with the help of information hiding."[7] Traditionally, separation of concerns was all about separating functionality of the program. Parnas added the idea of separating the data as well, so that individual modules would control data as well as the operations that acted on the data and the data would be visible only through well-defined interfaces.

There are three characteristics of modularity that are key to creating modular programs:

- Encapsulation

- Loose coupling (how closely do modules relate to each other)

- Information hiding

In a nutshell, *encapsulation* means to bundle a group of services defined by their data and behaviors together as a module, and keep them together. This group of services should be coherent and clearly belong together. (Like a function, a module should do just one thing.) The module then presents an *interface* to the user and that interface is ideally the only way to access the services and data in the module. An objective of encapsulating services and data is high cohesion. This means that your module should do one thing and all the functions inside the module should work towards making that one thing happen. The closer you are to this goal, the higher the cohesion in your module. This is a good thing.

The complement of encapsulation is *loose coupling*. Loose coupling describes how strongly two modules are related to each other. This means we want to minimize the dependence any one module has on another. We separate modules to minimize interactions and make all interactions between modules through the module interface. The goal is to create modules with internal integrity (strong cohesion) and small, few, direct, visible, and flexible connections to other modules (loose coupling). Good coupling between modules is loose enough that one module can easily be called by others.

---

[6] Parnas, D. "On the Criteria to be Used in Decomposing Systems into Modules." *Communications of the ACM* 15(12): 1053-1058. (1972)

[7] Wikipedia. *Separation of Concerns.* 2009. http://en.wikipedia.org/wiki/Separation_of_concerns. Retrieved on December 7, 2009.

Coupling falls into four broad categories that go from good to awful:

- *Simple data coupling:* Where non-structured data is passed via parameter lists. This is the best kind of coupling, because it lets the receiving module structure the data as it sees fit and it allows the receiving module to decide what to do with the data.

- *Structured data coupling:* Where structured data is passed via parameter lists. This is also a good kind of coupling, because the sending module keeps control of the data formats and the receiving module gets to do what it wants to with the data.

- *Control coupling:* Where data from module A is passed to module B and the content of the data tells module B what to do. This is not a good form of coupling; A and B are too closely coupled in this case because module A is controlling how functions in module B will execute.

- *Global-data coupling:* Where the two modules make use of the same global data. This is just awful. It violates a basic tenet of encapsulation by having the modules share data. This invites unwanted side effects and ensures that at any given moment during the execution of the program that neither module A nor module B will know precisely what is in the globally shared data. And what the heck are you doing using global variables anyway? Bad programmer!

Information hiding is often confused with encapsulation, but they are not the same thing. Encapsulation describes a process of wrapping both data and behaviors into a single entity – in our case, a module. Data can be publicly visible from within a module, and thus not hidden. Information hiding, on the other hand, says that the data and behaviors in a module should be controlled and visible only to the operations that act on the data within the module, so it's invisible to other, external, modules. This is an important feature of modules (and later of objects as well) because it leaves control of data in the module that understands best how to manipulate the data and it protects the data from side effects that can arise from other modules reaching in and tweaking the data.

Parnas was not just talking about hiding data in modules. His definition of information hiding was even more concerned with hiding design decisions in the module definition. "We propose … that one begins with a list of difficult design decisions or design decisions which are likely to change. Each module is then designed to hide such a decision from the others."[8] Hiding information in this manner allows clients of a module to use the module successfully without needing to know any of the design decisions that went into constructing the module. It also allows developers to change the implementation of the module without affecting how the client uses the module.

Example: Keyword in Context: Indexes for You and Me

Back in the day, when Unix was young and the world was new, the Unix documentation was divided into eight (8) different sections and the entire manual started with a permuted index. The problem with Unix is not the command line interface, it's not the inverted tree file system structure. No, the problem with Unix is that the three guys who developed it Kernighan, Ritchie, and Thompson, are the three laziest

---

[8] Parnas, 1972.

guys on the planet. How do I know? Where's my proof? Well, the proof is in practically every Unix command- `ls`, `cat`, `cp`, `mv`, `mkdir`, `ps`, `cc`, `as`, `ld`, `m4` ... I could go on. Unix has to have the most cryptic command line set of any operating system on the planet. The cardinal rule for creating Unix command line tools was apparently, "why use three characters when two will do?"

So finding anything in any of the 8 sections of Unix documentation could have been a real trial. Enter the permuted index. Every Unix man page starts with a header line that contains the name of the command, and a short description of what the command does. For example, the cat(1) man page begins

> cat -- concatenate and print files

The problem is, what if I don't know the name of a command, but I do know what it does? The permuted index solves this problem by making most of the words in the description (the articles were ignored) of the command part of the index itself. So that *cat* could be found under "cat" and also "concatenate", "print" and "files." This is known as a **Keyword in Context** (KWIC) index. It works just dandy.

So our problem is to take as input two files, the first of which contains words to ignore, the second of which contains lines of text to index, and create a KWIC index for them. For example, say that we're ignoring the articles for, the, and, et.c, and the second file looks like

> The Sun also Rises
>
> For Whom the Bell Tolls
>
> The Old Man and the Sea

Our KWIC index would look like:

```
                the sun ALSO rises
            for whom the BELL tolls
             the old MAN and the sea
                 the OLD man and the sea
              the sun also RISES
        the old man and the SEA
                 the SUN also rises
          for whom the bell TOLLS
                for WHOM the bell tolls
```

Note that each keyword is in all caps, each input line appears once for every index word in the line, and the keywords are sorted alphabetically. Each line of text has its keywords made visible by circularly shifting the words in the line. In the case of a tie (two lines of text have the same index word and so should appear together in the output), the lines of text should appear in the same order in which they appeared in the text input file. So the question we have to answer is is, how do we create the KWIC index? A secondary question we'll need to answer almost immediately is, how do we store the data?

Top-Down Decomposition

We'll start by designing the problem solution using a top-down decomposition. Top-down decompositions, as we've seen with the eight queens problem earlier in this chapter, are all about *control flow*. We want to figure out how to sequentially solve the problem, making progress with each step we take. It is assumed that the data are stored separately from the routines and each subroutine in the control flow can access the data it needs. The alternative is to pass the data along to each subroutine as we call it; this can be cumbersome and time consuming because the data usually has to be copied each time you pass it to a routine. A first decomposition of this problem might look like:

1. Input the words to ignore and the text.

2. Create a data structure containing the circularly shifted lines of text, keeping track of which word in the line is the index word for this line.

3. Sort the circularly shifted lines of text by the index words.

4. Format the output lines.

5. Output the text.

Note that these five steps can easily become five subroutines that are all called in sequence from a main program. The data structure used for the input text could be an array of characters for each line, a String for each line, or an array of Strings for the entire input file. One could also use a map data structure that uses each index word as the key and a String containing the input text line as the value of the map element. There are certainly other possible data structures to be used. Sorting can be done by any of the stable sorting algorithms and which algorithm to use would depend on the data structure chosen and on the expected size of the input text. Your sort must be stable because of the requirement that identical index words sort their respective lines in the same order that they appear in the input text file. Depending on the programming language you use and the data structure you choose, sorting might be done automatically for you. The data structure you choose will affect how the circular shifts are done and how the output routine does the work of formatting each output line.

Now that we've got a feel for how a top-down decomposition might proceed, let's move on and consider a modular decomposition.

Modular Decomposition of KWIC

A modular decomposition of the KWIC problem can be based on information hiding in the sense that we will hide both data structures and design decisions. The modules we create will not necessarily be the sequential list we have above, but will be modules that can cooperate with each other and are called when needed. One list of modules for KWIC is:

*   A Line module (for lines of input text)

*   A Keyword-Line pair module

*   A KWICIndex module to create the indexed list itself

*   A Circular Shift module

*   A module to format and print the output

*   A master control module

The Line module will use the Keyword-Line module to create a map data structure where each Line is a keyword and a list of lines that contain that keyword. The KWICIndex module will use the Line module to create the indexed list. The Circular Shift module will use the KWICIndex module (and recursively, the Line and Keyword-Line modules) and create the circularly shifted set of keyword-line pairs. Sorting will be taken care of internally in the KWICIndex module; ideally the index will be created as a sorted list and any additions to the list will maintain the ordering of the index. The format and print module will organize the keyword-lines so that the keywords are printed in all caps and centered on the output line. Finally, the master control module will read the input, create the KWICIndex and cause it to print correctly.

The key of these modules is that one can describe the modules and their interactions without needing the details of how each module is implemented and how the data is stored. That is hidden in the module description itself. Other designs are also possible. For example, it might be better to subsume the circular shift operations inside the Line module, allowing it to store the input lines and their shifts. Regardless, the next step in the design is to create the interface for each module and to coordinate the interfaces so that each module can communicate with every other module regardless of the internal implementation.

We'll continue this discussion in way more detail in the next chapter on object-oriented design.

Conclusion

Structured design describes a set of classic design methodologies. These design ideas work for a large class of problems. The original structured design idea, stepwise refinement, has you decompose the problem from the top-down, focusing on the control flow of the solution. It also relates closely to some of the architectures mentioned in Chapter 5, particularly the main program-subroutine and pipe-and-filter architectures. Modular decomposition is the immediate precursor to the modern object-oriented methodologies, and introduced the ideas of encapsulation and information hiding. These ideas are the fundamentals of your design toolbox.

References

Dahl, O. J., E. Dijkstra, et al. (1972). *Structured Programming*. (London, UK: Academic Press, 1972.)

Dijkstra, E. "GoTo Statement Considered Harmful." *Communications of the ACM* 11(3): 147-148. (1968)

Hunt, A. and D. Thomas. *The Pragmatic Programmer: From Journeyman to Master*. (Boston, MA: Addison-Wesley, 2000.)

McConnell, S. *Code Complete 2*. (Redmond, WA: Microsoft Press, 2004.)

Miller, G. A. "The magical number seven, plus or minus two: Some limits on our capacity for processing information." *Psychological Review* 63: 81-97. (1956)

Parnas, D. "On the Criteria to be Used in Decomposing Systems into Modules." *Communications of the ACM* 15(12): 1053-1058. (1972)

Wikipedia. *Separation of Concerns*. 2009. http://en.wikipedia.org/wiki/Separation_of_concerns. Retrieved on December 7, 2009.

Wirth, N. "Program Development by Stepwise Refinement." *CACM* 14(4): 221-227. (1971)

Appendix: The Complete Non-Recursive Eight-Queens Program

```java
/*
 *  NQueens.java
 *  8-Queens Program
 *  A non-recursive version for a single solution
 *  jfd
 */

import java.util.*;

public class NQueens
{

        static int totalcount = 0;
        static int row = 0;
        static int col = 0;

    /*
     *  the queen at (row, col) is safe,
     *  so we have a partial solution.
     *  advance to the next column
     */
    public void advance (int[] board) {
        board[col] = row;
        col++;
        row = 0;
    }

    /*
     *  could not find a safe row in current col
     *  so back up one col and move that queen
     *  up a row
     */
    public void retreat (int[] board) {
        col--;
        row = board[col] + 1;
    }

    /*
     *   check to see if queen at (row, col)  can be
     *   attacked
     */
    public boolean isSafe (int[] board) {
        boolean safe = true;
        totalcount++;
        /*
         *  check diagonals and row for attacks
         *  since we're just checking partial solutions
         *  only need to go up to current col
         */
```

```
        */
      for (int i=0; i<col; i++)  {
        if (( (board[i] + i) == (row + col) ) ||   // up diagonal
            ( (board[i] - i) == (row - col) ) ||   // down diagonal
            (board[i]   == row) ) {
            safe = false;
              }
      }
      return safe;
}

public static void main(String args[]) {
    int N = 8;       // default board size

    System.out.print("Enter the size of the board: ");
    Scanner stdin = new Scanner(System.in);
    N = stdin.nextInt();
    System.out.println();

    NQueens queen = new NQueens();
    /*
     *   index into board is a column number
     *   value stored in board is a row number
     *   so board[2] = 3; says put a queen on col 2, row 3
     */
    int[] board = new int [N];        /*
     *   simple algorithm to build partial solutions
     *   for N-queens problem. Place a queen in the
     *   next available column, test to see if it
     *   can be attacked. If not, then move to the next
     *   column. If it can be attacked, move the queen
     *   up a row and try again.
     *   If we exhaust all the rows in a column, back up
     *   reset the previous column and try again.
     */
    do {
        while ((row < N) && (col < N))  {
            if (queen.isSafe(board)) {
                queen.advance(board);
            } else {
                row++;
            }
        }
        if (row == N) {
            queen.retreat(board);
        }

    } while ((col < N) && (col >= 0));

    /* If we've placed all N queens, we've got a solution */
    if (col == N) {
        for (int i = 0; i < N; i++) {
```

```
                System.out.print(board[i] + " ");
            }
        } else {
            System.out.println("No solution. ");
            }

        System.out.println();

        System.out.println("after trying " + totalcount +
                        " board positions.");
    }
}
```

CHAPTER 8

Object-Oriented Analysis and Design

Object-oriented programming is an exceptionally bad idea, which could only have originated in California.

—Edsger Dijkstra

The object has three properties, which makes it a simple, yet powerful model building block. It has state so it can model memory. It has behavior, so that it can model dynamic processes. And it is encapsulated, so that it can hide complexity.

—Trygve Reenskaug, *Working With Objects*

Well, yes, we've all learned about the object-oriented programming paradigm before. But it never hurts to go over some basic definitions so that we're all on the same page for our discussion about object-oriented analysis and design.

First of all, objects are *things*. They have an *identity* (i.e., a name), a *state* (i.e., a set of attributes that describes the current data stored inside the object), and a defined set of *operations* that operate on that state. A stack is an object, as is an Automobile, a Bank Account, a Window, or a Button in a graphical user interface. In an object-oriented program, a set of cooperating objects pass messages among themselves. The messages make requests of the destination objects to invoke methods that either perform operations on their data (thus changing the state of the object), or to report on the current state of the object. Eventually work gets done. Objects use *encapsulation* and *information hiding* (remember, they're different) to isolate data and operations from other objects in the program. Shared data areas are (usually) eliminated. Objects are members of *classes* that define attribute types and operations.

Classes are *templates* for objects. Classes can also be thought of as factories that generate objects. So an Automobile class will generate instances of autos, a Stack class will create a new stack object, and a Queue class will create a new queue. Classes may inherit attributes and behaviors from other classes. Classes may be arranged in a class hierarchy where one class (a *super class* or *base class*) is a generalization of one or more other classes (*sub-classes*). A sub-class inherits the attributes and operations from its super class and may add new methods or attributes of its own. In this sense a sub-class is more specific and detailed than its super class; hence, we say that a sub-class extends a superclass. For example, a priority queue is a more specific version of a queue; it has all the attributes and operations of a queue, but it adds the idea that some queue elements are more important that others. In Java this feature is called *inheritance* while in UML it's called *generalization.*[1] Go figure.

There are a number of advantages to inheritance. It is an *abstraction mechanism* which may be used to classify entities. It is a *reuse mechanism* at both the design and the programming level. The inheritance graph is a source of organizational knowledge about domains and systems.

And, of course, there are problems with inheritance, as well. It makes object classes that are not self-contained; sub-classes cannot be understood without reference to their super classes. Inheritance introduces complexity and this is undesirable, especially in critical systems. Inheritance also usually allows overloading of operators (methods in Java) which can be good (polymorphism) or bad (screening useful methods in the superclass).

Object-oriented programming (OOP) has a number of advantages, among them easier maintenance, because objects can be understood as stand-alone entities. Objects are also appropriate as reusable components. But, for some problems there may be no mapping from real-world objects to system objects, meaning that OOP is not appropriate for all problems.

An Object-Oriented Analysis and Design Process

Object-oriented analysis (OOA), design (OOD) and programming (OOP) are related but distinct. OOA is concerned with developing an *object model of the application domain.* So, for example, you take the problem statement, generate a set of features and (possibly) use cases,[2] tease out the objects and some of the methods within those objects that you'll need to satisfy the use case, and you put together an architecture of how the solution will hang together. That's object-oriented analysis.

OOD is concerned with developing an *object-oriented system model* to satisfy requirements. You take the objects generated from your OOA, figure out whether to use inheritance, aggregation, composition, abstract classes, interfaces, and so on, in order to create a coherent and efficient model, draw the class diagrams, and flesh out the details of what each attribute is and what each method does, and describe the interfaces. That's the design.

Some people like object-oriented analysis, design, and programming[3] and some people don't.[4]

So object-oriented analysis allows you to take a problem model and re-cast it in terms of objects and classes and object-oriented design allows you to take your analyzed requirements and connect the dots between the objects you've proposed and to fill in the details with respect to object attributes and methods. But how do you really do all this? Well, here is a proposed process that starts to fill in some of the details.[5] We'll figure out the rest as we go along.

[1] Fowler, M. *UML Distilled.* (Boston, MA: Addison-Wesley, 2000.)

[2] Cockburn, A. *Writing Effective Use Cases.* (Boston, MA: Addison-Wesley, 2000.)

[3] Beck, K., and B. Boehm. "Agility through Discipline: A Debate." *IEEE Computer* 36 (6):44-46. (2003)

[4] Graham, Paul. "Why Arc isn't Especially Object Oriented," retrieved from www.paulgraham.com/noop.html on October 12, 2009.

[5] McLaughlin, Brett D., et. al. *Head First Object-Oriented Analysis & Design.* (O'Reilly Media, Inc. Sebastopol, CA: 2007.)

1. Write (or receive) the problem statement. Use this to generate an initial set of features.

2. Create the feature list. The feature list is the set of program features that you derive from the problem statement; it contains your initial set of requirements.

3. Write up use cases. This helps to refine the features and to dig out new requirements and to expose problems with the features you just created. We'll also see that we can use user stories for this step.

4. Break the problem into subsystems or modules or whatever you want to call them as long as they're smaller, self-contained bits usually related to functionality.

5. Map your features, subsystems, and use cases to domain objects; create abstractions.

6. Identify the program's objects, methods, and algorithms.

7. Implement this iteration.

8. Test the iteration.

9. If you've not finished the feature list and you still have time and/or money left, go back to step 4 and do another iteration, otherwise…

10. Do final acceptance testing and release.

Note that this process leaves out a lot of details like the length of iteration. How many features end up in an iteration? How and when do we add new features to the feature list? How exactly do we identify objects and operations? How do we abstract objects into classes? Where do we fix bugs that are found in testing? Do we do reviews of code and other project work products?

Leaving out steps here is okay. We're mostly concerned with the analysis and design elements of the process. We'll discuss ideas on the rest of the process below and some of the answers are also in Chapter 3 on project management.

How do the process steps above fit into the software development life cycle? Well, I'm glad you asked. Recall that the basic development life cycle has four steps:

1. Requirements Gathering and Analysis;

2. Design;

3. Implementation and Testing; and

4. Release, Maintenance, and Evolution.

We can easily assign the previous ten steps into four buckets, as follows:

Requirements Gathering and Analysis

1. Problem statement.

2. Feature list creation.

3. Use case generation.

Design

1. Break up the problem.

2. Map features and use cases to domain objects.

3. Identify objects, methods, and algorithms.

Implementation and Testing

1. Implement this iteration.

2. Test the iteration.

3. If you've not finished with the feature list or out of time, go back to step 4, otherwise…

Release/Maintenance/Evolution

1. Do final acceptance testing and release.

Once again we can ignore the details of each process step for now. These details really depend on the process methodology you choose for your development project. The description of the process above uses an iterative methodology and can easily be fitted into an agile process, or a more traditional staged release process.

Note also, that you'll need to revisit the requirements whenever you get to step 4, because you're likely to have uncovered or generated new requirements during each iteration. Also, whenever your customer sees a new iteration, they'll ask for more stuff (yes, they will, trust me). This means you'll be updating the feature list (and re-prioritizing) at the beginning of each new iteration. BEWARE!

Doing the Process

Let's continue by working through an extended example, seeing where the problem statement leads us and how we can tease out requirements and begin our object oriented analysis.

The Problem Statement

Burt, the proud owner of Birds by Burt, has created the ultimate in bird feeders. Burt's Bird Buffet and Bath (B^4), is an integrated bird feeder and bird bath. It comes in 12 different colors (including camo) and 1, 3, and 5 lb capacities. It will hold up to one gallon of water in the attached bird bath, it has a built-in hanger so you can hang it from a tree branch or from a pole, and the B^4 is just flying off the shelves. Alice and Bob are desperate for a B^4, but they'd like a few changes. Alice is a techno-nerd and a fanatic songbird watcher. She knows that her favorite songbirds only feed during the day, so she wants a custom B^4 that allows the feeding doors to open automatically at sunrise and close automatically at sunset. Burt, ever the accommodating owner, has agreed and the hardware division of Birds by Burt is hard at work designing the B^4++ for Alice. Your job is to write the software to make the hardware work.

The Feature List

The first thing we need to do is figure out what the B^4++ will actually *do*. This version seems simple enough. We can almost immediately write down three requirements:

- The feeding doors must all open and close simultaneously.

- The feeding doors should open automatically at sunrise.

- The feeding doors should close automatically at sunset.

So this doesn't seem so bad. The requirements are simple and there is no user interaction required. The next step is to create a use case so we can see just what the bird feeder is really going to do.

Use Cases

A *use case* is a description of what a program does in a particular situation. It's the detailed set of steps that the program executes when a user asks for something. Use cases always have an *actor* – some outside agent that gets the ball rolling, and a *goal* – what the use case is supposed to have done by the end. The use case describes what it takes to get from some initial state to the goal from the user's perspective.[6] Here's a quick example of a use case for the B^4++:

1. The sensor detects sunlight at a 40% brightness level.

2. The feeding doors open.

3. Birds arrive, eat, and drink.

4. Birds leave.

5. The sensor detects a decrease in sunlight to a 25% brightness level.

6. The feeding doors close.

Given the simplicity of the B4++, that's about all we can expect out of a use case. In fact, steps 3 and 4 aren't technically part of the use case, because they aren't part of the program – but they're good to have so that we can get a more complete picture of how the B^4++ is operating. Use cases are very useful in requirements analysis because they give you an idea – in English – of what the program needs to do in a particular situation and because they nearly always will help you uncover new requirements. Note that in the use case we don't talk about *how* a program does something, we only concentrate on *what* the program has to do to reach the goal. Use cases are generated during the Requirements Gathering and Analysis phase of the software life cycle, so we're not so much concerned with the details yet, we just treat the program as a black box and let the use case talk about the *external behavior* of the program. Most times there will be several use cases for every program you write. We've only got one because this version of the B^4++ is so simple.

Decompose the Problem

So now that we've got our use case we can probably just decompose the problem and identify the objects in the program. You go ahead, I'll wait....

---

[6] Cockburn, 2000.

Done? Okay. This problem is quite simple; if you look at the use case above and pick out the nouns, you see that we can identify several objects. Each of these objects has certain characteristics and contributes to reaching the goal of getting the birds fed. (Yes, I know, "birds" is a noun in the use case, but they are the actors in this little play so for the purposes of describing the objects we ignore them – they're not part of the program.) The other two nouns of interest are "sensor" and "doors." These are the critical pieces of the B^4++, because the use case indicates that they are the parts that accomplish the goal of opening and closing the feeding doors at sunrise and sunset. So it's logical that they are objects in our design. Here are the objects I came up with for this first version of the B^4++ and a short description:

> *BirdFeeder.* The top-level object. The bird feeder has one or more feeding doors at which the birds will gather, and a sensor to detect sunrise and sunset. The *BirdFeeder* class needs to control the querying of the light sensor and the opening and closing of the feeding doors.

> *Sensor.* There will be a hardware light sensor that detects different light levels. We'll need to ask it about light levels.

> *FeedingDoor.* There will be several feeding doors on the bird feeder. They have to open and close.

That's probably about it for classes at this point. Now what do they all do? To describe classes and their components we can use another UML feature, *class diagrams.*

Class Diagrams

A *class diagram* allows you to describe the attributes and the methods of a class. A set of class diagrams will describe all the objects in a program and the relationships between the objects. We draw arrows of different types between class diagrams to describe the relationships. Class diagrams give you a visual description of the object model that you've created for your program. We saw a set of class diagrams for the Fox and Rabbit program we described in Chapter 5.

Class diagrams have three sections:

- **Name**: The name of the class
- **Attributes**: The instance data fields and their types used by the class
- **Methods**: The set of methods used by the class and their visibility.

We can see an example of a class diagram for our BirdFeeder class in Figure 8-1.

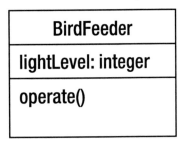

Figure 8-1. The BirdFeeder class

The diagram shows that the *BirdFeeder* class has a single integer attribute, *lightLevel*, and a single method, *operate()*. By themselves class diagrams aren't terribly interesting, but when you put several of them together and show the relationships between them, then you can get some interesting information about your program. So what else do we need in the way of class diagrams? In our program the *BirdFeeder* class uses the *FeedingDoor* and *Sensor* classes, but they don't know (or care) about each other. In fact, while *BirdFeeder* knows about *FeedingDoor* and *Sensor* and uses them, they don't know they are being used. Ah, the beauty of object-oriented programming. This relationship can be expressed in the class diagram of all three classes shown in Figure 8-2.

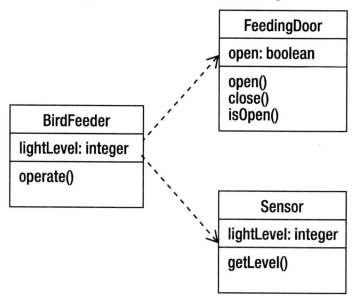

Figure 8-2. BirdFeeder uses FeedingDoor and Sensor

In UML, the dotted line with the open arrow at the end indicates that one class (in our case BirdFeeder) is *associated* with another class (in our case either FeedingDoor or Sensor) by *using* it.

Code Anyone?

Now that we've got the class diagrams and know the attributes, the methods, and the association between the classes it's time to flesh out our program with some code.

In the BirdFeeder object, the operate() method needs to check the light levels and open or close the feeding doors depending on the current light level reported by the Sensor object, and does nothing if the current light level is above or below the threshold values..

In the Sensor object, the getLevel() method just reports back the current level from the hardware sensor.

In the FeedingDoor object, the open() method checks to see if the doors are closed. If they are, it opens them and sets a boolean to indicate that they're open. The close() method does the reverse.

Here's the code for each of the classes described.

```
/**
 * class BirdFeeder
 *
 * @author John F. Dooley
 * @version 1.0
 */

import java.util.ArrayList;
import java.util.Iterator;

public class BirdFeeder
{
    /* instance variables */
    private static final int ON_THRESHOLD = 40;
    private static final int OFF_THRESHOLD = 25;
    private int lightLevel;
    private Sensor s1;
    private ArrayList<FeedingDoor> doors = null;

    /*
     * Default Constructor for objects of class BirdFeeder
     */
    public BirdFeeder()
    {
        doors = new ArrayList<FeedingDoor>();
        /* initialize lightLevel */
        lightLevel = 0;
         s1 = new Sensor();
        /* by default we have a feeder with just one door */
        doors.add(new FeedingDoor());

    }
    /*
     * The operate() method operates the birdfeeder.
     * It gets the current lightLevel from the Sensor and
     * checks to see if we should open or close the doors
     */
    public void operate()
    {
        lightLevel = s1.getLevel();

        if (lightLevel > ON_THRESHOLD) {
            Iterator door_iter = doors.iterator();
            while (door_iter.hasNext()) {
                FeedingDoor a = (FeedingDoor) door_iter.next();
                a.open();
                System.out.println("The door has opened.");
            }
        } else if (lightLevel < OFF_THRESHOLD) {
            Iterator door_iter = doors.iterator();
            while (door_iter.hasNext()) {
```

```java
                FeedingDoor a = (FeedingDoor) door_iter.next();
                a.close();
                System.out.println("The door has closed.");
            }
        }
    }
}


/**
 * class FeedingDoor
 *
 * @author John Dooley
 * @version 1.0
 */
public class FeedingDoor
{
    /* instance variables */
    private boolean doorOpen;

    /*
     * Default constructor for objects of class FeedingDoors
     */
    public FeedingDoor()
    {
        /* initialize instance variables */
        doorOpen = false;
    }

    /*
     * open the feeding doors
     * if they are already open, do nothing
     */
    public void open( )
    {
        /** if the door is closed, open it */
        if (doorOpen == false) {
            doorOpen = true;
        }
    }

    /*
     * close the doors
     * if they are already closed, do nothing
     */
    public void close( )
    {
        /* if the door is open, close it */
        if (doorOpen == true) {
            doorOpen = false;
        }
    }
```

```
    /*
     * report whether the doors are open or not
     */
    public boolean isOpen()
    {
        return doorOpen;
    }
}

/**
 * class Sensor
 *
 * @author John Dooley
 * @version 1.0
 */
public class Sensor
{
    /* instance variables */
    private int lightLevel;

    /*
     * Default constructor for objects of class Sensor
     */
    public Sensor()
    {
        /** initialize instance variable */
        lightLevel = 0;
    }

    /**
     * getLevel - return a light level
     *
     * @return the value of the light level
     * that is returned by the hardware sensor
     */
    public int getLevel( )
    {
        /* till we get a hardware light sensor, we just fake it */
        lightLevel = (int) (Math.random() * 100);
        return lightLevel;
    }
}
```

Finally, we have a BirdFeederTester class that operates the B[4]++.

```
/**
 * The class that tests the BirdFeeder, Sensor, and
 * FeedingDoor classes.
 *
 * @version 0.1
```

```java
    */
public class BirdFeederTester
{
    private BirdFeeder feeder;

    /*
     * Constructor for objects of class BirdFeederTest
     */
    public BirdFeederTester()
    {
        this.feeder = new BirdFeeder();
    }

    public static void main(String [] args)
    {
        BirdFeederTester bfTest = new BirdFeederTester();

        for (int i = 0; i < 10; i++) {
            System.out.println("Testing the bird feeder");
            bfTest.feeder.operate();
            try {
                Thread.currentThread().sleep(2000);
            } catch (InterruptedException e) {
                System.out.println("Sleep interrupted" + e.getMessage());
                System.exit(1);
            }
        }
    }
}
```

When Alice and Bob take delivery of the B^4++ they are thrilled. The doors automatically open and close, the birds arrive and eat their fill. Birdsong fills the air. What else could they possibly want?

Conclusion

Object-oriented design is a methodology that works for a very wide range of problems. The real world is easily characterized as groups of cooperating objects. This single simple idea promotes simplicity of design, reuse of both designs and code, and the ideas of encapsulation and information hiding that Parnas advocated in his paper on modular decomposition. It's not the right way to solve some problems, including problems like communications protocol implementations, but it opens up a world of new and better solutions for many others and it closes the "intellectual distance" between the real-world description of a problem and the resulting code. Onward!

References

Beck, K., and B. Boehm. "Agility through Discipline: A Debate." *IEEE Computer* 36 (6):44-46. (2003)

Cockburn, A. *Writing Effective Use Cases.* (Boston, MA: Addison-Wesley, 2000.)

Fowler, M. *UML Distilled.* (Boston, MA: Addison-Wesley, 2000.)

Graham, Paul. "Why Arc isn't Especially Object Oriented," retrieved from `www.paulgraham.com/noop.html` on October 12, 2009.

McLaughlin, Brett D., et. al. *Head First Object-Oriented Analysis & Design.* (O'Reilly Media, Inc. Sebastopol, CA: 2007.)

Wirfs-Brock, R. and A. McKean. *Object Design: Roles Responsibilities, and Collaborations.* (Boston, MA: Addison-Wesley, 2003.)

CHAPTER 9

Object-Oriented Analysis and Design

A Play in Several Acts

When doing analysis you are trying to understand the problem. To my mind this is not just listing requirements in use cases. ... Analysis also involves looking behind the surface requirements to come up with a mental model of what is going on in the problem. ... Some kind of conceptual model is a necessary part of software development, and even the most uncontrolled hacker does it.

—-Martin Fowler[1]

Object-oriented design is, in its simplest form, based on a seemingly elementary idea. Computing systems perform certain actions on certain objects; to obtain flexible and reusable systems, it is better to base the structure of software on the objects than on the actions.

Once you have said this, you have not really provided a definition, but rather posed a set of problems: What precisely is an object? How do you find and describe the objects? How should programs manipulate objects? What are the possible relations between objects? How does one explore the commonalities that may exist between various kinds of objects? How do these ideas relate to classical software engineering concerns such as correctness, ease of use, efficiency?

Answers to these issues rely on an impressive array of techniques for efficiently producing reusable, extendible and reliable software: inheritance, both in its linear (single) and multiple forms; dynamic binding and polymorphism; a new view of types and type checking; genericity; information hiding; use of assertions; programming by contract; safe exception handling.

—Bertrand Meyer[2]

---

[1] Martin, Robert, Single Responsibility Principle. www.butunclebob.com/ArticleS .UncleBob.PrinciplesOfOod. Retrieved on December 10, 2009.

PRELUDE: In Which We Set the Scene

When defining object-oriented analysis and design, it's best to keep in mind your objectives. In both of these process phases we're producing a *work product* that is closer to the code that is your end goal. In *analysis*, you're refining the feature list you've created and producing a model of what the customer wants. In design you're taking that model and creating the classes that will end up being code.

In analysis you want to end up with a description of what the program is supposed to do, its *essential features*. This end product takes the form of a *conceptual model* of the problem domain and its solution. The model is made up of a number of things, including use cases, user stories, preliminary class diagrams, user interface storyboards, and possibly some class interface descriptions.

In *design* you want to end up with a description of how the program will implement the conceptual model and do what the customer wants. This end product takes the form of an *object model* of the solution. This model is made up of groups of related class diagrams, their associations and descriptions of how they interact with each other. This includes the programming interface for each class. From here you should be able to get to coding pretty quickly.

ACT ONE, Scene 1: In Which We Enquire into Analysis

So what is object-oriented analysis? Well, it depends on who you talk to. For our purposes, we'll define *object-oriented analysis* as a method of studying the nature of a problem and *determining its essential features and their relations to each other.*[3] Your objective is to end up with a conceptual model of the problem solution that you can then use to create an object model – your design. This model doesn't take into account any implementation details or any constraints on the target system. It looks at the domain that the problem is in and tries to create a set of features, objects and relations that describe a solution in that domain. What makes a feature essential? Typically, a feature is essential if it's a feature the customer has said they must have, if it's a non-functional requirement that the program won't run without, or if it's a core program element that other parts of the program depend on.

The conceptual model describes *what* the solution will do and will typically include use cases,[4] user stories,[5] and UML sequence diagrams.[6] It can also include a description of the user interface and a preliminary set of UML class diagrams (but that, of course, is shading over into design).

So how do you create this conceptual model? Just like all the other methodologies in software development there is exactly one correct way to create a conceptual model – *not*! Really, just like with all the other methodologies we've talked about, the correct answer is: it depends.

---

[2] Meyer, Bertrand. *Object-Oriented Software Construction.* (Upper Saddle River , NJ: Prentice Hall, 1988).

[3] McLaughlin, Brett D., et. al. *Head First Object-Oriented Analysis & Design.* (Sebastopol, CA: O'Reilly Media, Inc., 2007).

[4] Cockburn, A. (2000). *Writing Effective Use Cases.* (Boston, MA: Addison-Wesley, 2000).

[5] Beck, K. *Extreme Programming Explained: Embrace Change.* (Boston, MA: Addison-Wesley, 2000).

[6] Fowler, M. *UML Distilled.* (Boston, MA: Addison-Wesley, 2000).

It depends on understanding the problem domain, on understanding the feature list you've already come up with, and it depends on understanding how the customer reacts to each of the program iterations they'll see. As we'll see, change is constant.

The key part of object-oriented analysis is the creation of *use cases*. With use cases you create a walkthrough of a scenario from the user's perspective and that walkthrough gives you an understanding of what the program is supposed to do from the outside. A program of any size will normally have several use cases associated with it. In fact, a single use case may have alternative paths through the scenario. More on this later.

Once you get a few use cases created how do you get to the class diagrams? There are several methods suggested, but we'll just go over one now and save the rest for later. The first method we'll look at is called *textual analysis*. With textual analysis, you take your uses cases and examine the text for clues about classes in your programs. Remember that the object-oriented paradigm is all about objects and the behavior of those objects, so those are the two things to pluck out of your use cases.

In textual analysis, you pluck potential objects out of the text by picking out the nouns in your use case. Because nouns are things and objects are (usually) things, the nouns stand a good chance of being objects in your program. In terms of behavior, you look at the verbs in the use case. Verbs provide you with action words that describe changes in state or actions that report state. This usually isn't the end, but it gives you your first cut at method names and parameter lists for the methods.

Let's go back to Burt's Bird Buffet and Bath, the B^4++. When last we left the B^4++ it automatically opened the feeding doors at sunrise and closed them at sunset. The B^4++ was a hit and Alice and Bob were thrilled with its performance. Once again the B^4 models were flying off the shelves.

Then one day Burt gets a call from Alice. It seems she has an issue. While the B^4++ works just fine, Alice has noticed that she's getting unwanted birds at her bird feeder. Recall that Alice is a songbird fanatic and she's thrilled when cardinals, painted buntings, scarlet tanagers, American goldfinches, and tufted titmice show up at the feeder. But she's not so thrilled when grackles, blue jays, and starlings drive away the songbirds and have their own feast. So Alice wants to be able to close the B^4++ feeding doors when the bad birds show up and open them again when the songbirds come back. And you're just the guy to do it.

The first obvious question you ask Alice is, "How do you want to open and close the feeding doors?" "Well," she says, "how about a remote control? That way I can stay inside the house and just open and close the doors when the birds arrive." And so the game begins again.

Just like last time we can take this sketchy problem statement and try to put together a use case. Our previous use case looked like:

1. The sensor detects sunlight at a 40% brightness level.

2. The feeding doors open.

3. The birds arrive, eat, and drink.

4. The birds leave.

5. The sensor detects a decrease in sunlight to a 25% brightness level.

6. The feeding doors close.

So the first thing we need to decide is whether our new problem is an alternate path in this use case, or whether we need an entirely new use case.

Let's try a new use case. Why? Well, using the remote control doesn't really fit into the sensor use case, does it? The remote can be activated at any time and it requires a user interaction, neither of which fits with our sensor. So let's see what we can come up with for a remote control use case:

1. Alice hears or sees birds at the bird feeder.

2. Alice determines that they are *not* songbirds

3. Alice presses the remote control button.

4. The feeding doors close.

5. The birds give up and fly away.

6. Alice presses the remote control button.

7. The feeding doors open again.

Does this cover all the situations? Are there any we've missed? There are two things to think of. First, in step #1 we have "Alice hears or sees birds." The question is should the "or" matter to us? In this case the answer is no, because Alice is the one deciding and she's the actor in this use case. We can't control the actor; we can only respond to something the actor wants to do and make available options for the actor to exercise. In our case, our program will need to wait for the signal from the remote control and then do the right thing. (Not to get ahead of ourselves, but look at our program now as an event-driven system and the program has to wait (aka listen) for an event before it does something.)

Secondly, what are the steps in the use case that will help us identify new objects? This is where our textual analysis comes in. In our previous version of this application, we've already got *BirdFeeder*, *Sensor*, and *FeedingDoor* objects. These are identified in the use case easily. So what is new now? The only new object here is the remote control. So what does the remote control do? How many buttons does it have? What does the program do when the remote control button(s) is(are) pressed?

In our example, the remote control seems relatively simple. Opening and closing the feeding doors is a toggle operation. The doors open if they are closed, and close if they are open. Those are the only options. So the remote really just needs a single button to implement the toggle function.

So at the end of the day we've got a new use case and a new class for the B⁴++ program (see Figure 9-1).

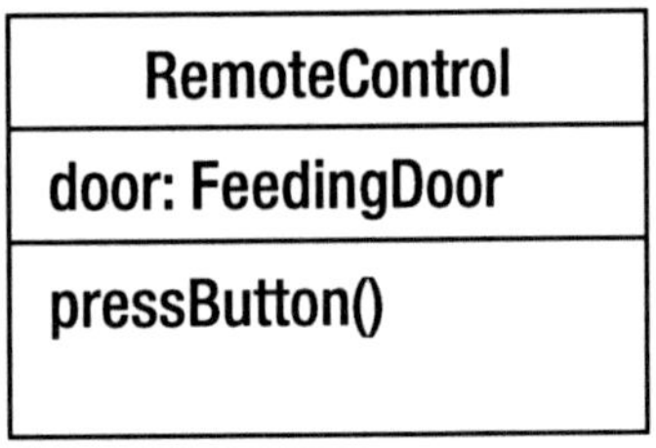

RemoteControl
door: FeedingDoor
pressButton()

Figure 9-1. The new RemoteControl class

And that, I think, is all the analysis we need for this version of the program.

This exercise provides us with a couple of guidelines we can use for analysis.

- First, make *simple classes that work together* by sending and responding to messages. In our example, the simple classes *FeedingDoor* and *Sensor* encapsulate knowledge about the current state of the *BirdFeeder* and allow us to control the bird feeder with simple messages. This simplicity allows us to easily add a new way of controlling the bird feeder with the *RemoteControl* class.

- Second, we say that *classes should have one responsibility*. Not only are the FeedingDoor and Sensor simple and easy to control, but they each only do one thing. That makes them easier to change later and easier to reuse.

ACT ONE, Scene 2: In Which We Deign to Design

Now what about design? Assuming you've got a conceptual model from your analysis in the form of a few use cases and a few class diagrams, your design should follow from this. In object-oriented design, you now need to firm up the class designs, decide on the methods your classes will contain, determine the relationships between the classes, and figure out how each of the methods will do what it's supposed to do.

In our current example, we've decided on four classes, *BirdFeeder*, *FeedingDoor*, *Sensor*, and *RemoteControl*. The first three classes we've already developed, so the question here is do we need to change any of these classes in order to integrate the *RemoteControl* class into the program? Figure 9-2 shows what we've got right now.

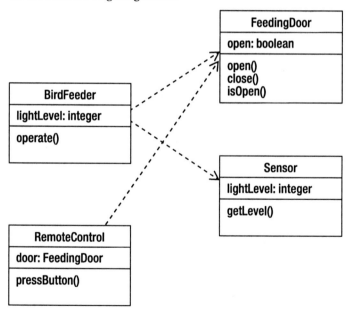

Figure 9-2. How to integrate the RemoteControl class?

Thinking about it, it seems that nothing in *FeedingDoor* nor *Sensor* should have to change. Why?

Well, it's because the *BirdFeeder* class uses those two classes, and they don't need to use or inherit anything from any other class; they are pretty self sufficient (ya gotta love encapsulation). If you recall, it's the *operate()* method in the *BirdFeeder* class that does all the hard work. It has to check the light level from the *Sensor* and if appropriate, send a signal to the doors to open or close. So it seems that maybe the *RemoteControl* class will work the same way. So the question for our design is: does the *BirdFeeder* class also use the *RemoteControl* class, or does the *RemoteControl* class stand alone and just wait for an "event" to happen?

Let's take a look at the code for the operate() method again:

```
public void operate()
    {
        lightLevel = s1.getLevel();

        if (lightLevel > ON_THRESHOLD) {
            Iterator door_iter = doors.iterator();
            while (door_iter.hasNext()) {
                FeedingDoor a = (FeedingDoor) door_iter.next();
                a.open();
            }
        } else if (lightLevel < OFF_THRESHOLD) {
            Iterator door_iter = doors.iterator();
            while (door_iter.hasNext()) {
                FeedingDoor a = (FeedingDoor) door_iter.next();
                a.close();
            }
        }
    }
```

In this method, we check the light level from the *Sensor* object and if it's above a certain level (the sun has risen), then we ask the doors to open. It's the doors themselves that check to see if they are already open or not. Regardless, when the open() method returns, each door is open. The same thing happens with the close() method. Regardless of how they start out, when each invocation of close() returns its door is closed. It seems as if this is just the behavior we want from the *RemoteControl* object, except that instead of a light threshold, it responds to a button press. So the pseudo-code for *pressButton()* will look like:

```
pressButton()
        while (there are still doors left to process) do
                if (the door is open) then
                        door.close()
                else
                        door.open()
                end-if
        end-while
end-method.
```

And from here you can just write the code.

ACT TWO, Scene 1: Change in the Right Direction

A key element of the last two sections is that object-oriented analysis and design are *all about change*. Analysis is about understanding behavior and *anticipation of change*, while design is about implementing the model and *managing change*. In a typical process methodology, analysis and design are iterative. As you begin to create a new program you uncover new requirements; as the user begins to use your prototypes they discover new ideas, things that don't work for them, and new features they hadn't mentioned previously. All of these things require you to go back and re-think what you already know about the problem and what you have designed. In order to avoid what's known as "analysis paralysis" you need to manage this never-ending flow of new ideas and requirements.

There are a number of techniques that can be used to see and deal with change. The first we'll look at is recognizing what might change in your design. So let's look at the B⁴++ again. Right now, our B⁴++ will open and close the bird feeder's doors at sunrise and sunset in response to the light levels returned by the sensor. It will also open and close the feeding doors in response to a button push from the remote control. What might change here?

Well, the hardware might change. If the sensor changes that might affect the Sensor class or it might cause your boss to re-think how the Sensor class should work. You might also get new hardware. This is just like the remote control addition we made above. And just like the remote control example new hardware can result in the appearance of new use cases or changes to existing use cases. These changes can consequently ripple down through your class hierarchy.

The requirements might change. Most likely new requirements would crop up. A requirement change can lead to alternate paths through use cases. This implies that behavior will change requirements, which then leads to design changes. Design change happens because requirements change.

By thinking about what things can change in your program and design, you can begin to anticipate change. *Anticipating change* can lead you to be careful about encapsulation, inheritance, dependencies of one class on another, and so on.

Songbirds Forever

While we're talking about change, let's look back at B⁴++ again. It's several weeks now since Alice and Bob received delivery of their new and improved B⁴++ with remote control. Alice loves it. She can watch the birds out her kitchen window and when the grackles swoop in she just hits the remote control button and the doors shut. The grackles leave disappointed and she hits the button again, the doors open. The new version works like a charm and does everything they had asked for.

There's just one little thing....

Alice has discovered that sometimes she has to run errands, or go to the bathroom, or watch her favorite nature show on The Discovery Channel. When she does this, she can't close the door with the remote and the grackles can come and feed to their hearts content, chasing away all the songbirds. Bummer.

So Alice would like yet another small, insignificant change to the B⁴++; hardly worth mentioning, really. She wants the B⁴++ to detect the pesky birds and close the doors automatically. How to do this? I'll wait....

So the new requirement is that "The B⁴++ must be able to detect the unwanted birds and close the doors automatically." Is this a complete requirement? It doesn't seem so because it begs the obvious question – when do the doors open again? So it seems we have at least a couple of things to decide.

1.   How does the bird feeder detect the birds?

2.   How do we distinguish between the unwanted birds and the songbirds?

3.   When does the bird feeder open the doors again after they've been closed?

Luckily for us, our sensor supplier, SensorsRUs, has just come out with a programmable audio sensor that will let us identify birdsong. So if we integrate that hardware into the B⁴++ that takes care of item #1 above. It also turns out that the pesky birds have way different songs from the songbirds we want to attract, so that the audio sensor can be programmed via firmware to distinguish between the different bird species. Whew! So much for issue #2. So what about issue #3, getting the closed doors open again?

It seems as if there are two ways you can get the B⁴++ to open the doors again. We can have a timer that keeps the doors shut for a specific amount of time and then opens them again. This has the advantage of simplicity, but it's also a pretty stupid bit of programming. Stupid in the sense that the timer program just implements a countdown timer with no information about the *context* in which it operates. It could easily open the door while there are still a bunch of unwanted birds around. Another way we could implement the bird identifier is to have it only open the door when it hears one of our songbirds. If you reason that the songbirds won't be around if the pesky birds are still there, then the only time you'll hear songbirds singing is if there are no pesky birds around. If that's the case then it's safe to open the feeding doors.

So let's do a use case. Because opening and closing the feeding doors with the song identifier is a lot like using the remote control, let's start with the `RemoteControl` use case and add to it.

1.   Alice hears or sees birds at the bird feeder.

   a. 1.1   The songbird identifier hears birdsong.

2.   Alice determines that they are *not* songbirds.

   b. 2.1   The songbird identifier recognizes the song as from an unwanted bird.

3.   Alice presses the remote control button.

   c. 3.1   The songbird identifier sends a message to the feeding doors to close.

4.   The feeding doors close.

5.   The birds give up and fly away.

   d. 5.1   The songbird identifier hears birdsong.

   e. 5.2   The songbird identifier recognizes the song as from a songbird.

6.   Alice presses the remote control button.

   f. 6.1   The songbird identifier sends a message to the feeding doors to open.

7.   The feeding doors open again.

What we've created here is an *alternate path* in the use case. This use case looks pretty awkward now, because the sub-cases look like they flow from the upper cases when, in fact, one or the other of them should be done. We can rewrite the use case to look like Table 9-1.

Table 9-1. The Song Identifier Use Case and Its Alternate

Main Path	Alternate Path
1. Alice hears or sees birds at the bird feeder.	1.1 The songbird identifier hears birdsong.
2. Alice determines that they are *not* songbirds.	2.1 The songbird identifier recognizes the song as from an unwanted bird.
3. Alice presses the remote control button.	3.1 The songbird identifier sends a message to the feeding doors to close.
4. The feeding doors close.	
5. The birds give up and fly away.	5.1 The songbird identifier hears birdsong.
	5.2 The songbird identifier recognizes the song as from a songbird.
6. Alice presses the remote control button.	6.1 The songbird identifier sends a message to the feeding doors to open.
7. The feeding doors open again.	

These two paths aren't exactly the same. For instance, in the Main Path, Alice sees the birds give up and fly away before she presses the remote control button. In the alternate path, the bird song identifier must wait until it hears birdsong before it can consider opening the feeding doors again. So we could easily make these two different use cases. It depends on *you*. Use cases are there to illustrate different scenarios in the use of the program so you can represent them in any way you want. If you want to break this use case up into two different ones, feel free. Just be consistent. You're still managing change.

ACT TWO, Scene 2: In Which the Design Will also Change, for the Better

As we've said before, it is difficult to separate analysis and design. The temptation for every programmer, particularly beginning programmers, is to start writing code *now*. That temptation bleeds over into doing analysis, design, and coding all at once and thinking about all three phases together. Unless your program is just about 10 lines long, this is usually a *bad idea*. It's nearly always better to abstract out requirements and architectural ideas from your low-level design and coding. Chapters 5 and 6 talked about this separation more.

Separating object-oriented analysis and design is a particularly difficult task. In analysis we are trying to understand the problem and the problem domain from an object-oriented point of view. That means we start thinking about objects and their interactions with each other *very* early in the process.

Even our use cases are littered with loaded object words. Analysis and design are nearly inseparable, when you are "doing analysis" you can't help but "think design" as well. So what should you do when you really want to start thinking about design?

Your design must produce, at minimum, the classes in your system, their public interfaces, and their relationships to other classes, especially base or super classes. If your design methodology produces more than that, ask yourself if all the pieces produced by that methodology have value over the lifetime of the program. If they do not, maintaining them will cost you. Members of development teams tend not to maintain anything that does not contribute to their productivity; this is a fact of life that many design methods don't account for.

All software design problems can be simplified by introducing an extra level of conceptual indirection. This one idea is the basis of abstraction, the primary feature of object-oriented programming. This is why in UML, what we call inheritance in Java is called generalization. The idea is to identify common features in two or more classes and abstract those features out into a higher level, more general class, that the lower level classes then inherit from.

When designing, make your classes as atomic as possible; that is, give each class a single, clear purpose. This is the *Single Responsibility Principle* that we'll talk more about in the next chapter on design principles.[7] If your classes or your system design grows too complicated, break complex classes into simpler ones. The most obvious indicator of this is sheer size: if a class is big, chances are it's doing too much and should be broken up.

You also need to look for and separate things that change from things that stay the same. That is, search for the elements in a program that you might want to change without forcing a redesign, then encapsulate those elements in classes.

All of these guidelines are key to managing the changes in your design. In the end you want a clean, understandable design that is easy to maintain.

ACT THREE, Scene 1: In Which We Do Design

Your goal is to invent and arrange objects in a pleasing fashion. Your application will be divided into neighborhoods where clusters of objects work toward a common goal. Your design will be shaped by the number and quality of abstractions and by how well they complement one another. Composition, form, and focus are everything.

—Rebecca Wirfs-Brock and Alan McKean[8]

Identifying objects (or object classes) is a difficult part of object-oriented design. There is no 'magic formula' for object identification. It relies on the skill, experience and domain knowledge of system designers (that would be you). Object identification is an iterative process. You are not likely to get it right the first time.

You begin finding objects by looking for real-world analogues in your requirements. That gets you started, but it's only the first step. Other objects hide in the abstraction layers of your domain. Where to find these hidden objects? You can look to your own knowledge of the application domain, you can look

---

[7] Martin, 2009.

[8] Wirfs-Brock, R. and A. McKean. *Object Design: Roles Responsibilities, and Collaborations.* (Boston, MA, Addison-Wesley, 2003).

for operations that crop up in your requirements and in your architectural concepts of the system. You can even look to your own past experience designing other systems.

Steps to finding candidate objects in your system:

1. *Write a set of use cases* describing how the application will work for a number of different scenarios. remember, each use case must have a goal. Remember that a scenario is a path through a use case. If you have use cases with alternate paths as we saw above, your use case may represent several scenarios.

2. *Identify the actors* in each use case, the operations they need to perform, and the other things they need to use in performing their actions.

3. *Name and describe each candidate object.* Base the identification on tangible things in the application domain (like nouns). Use a behavioral approach and identify objects based on what participates in what behavior (use verbs).

4. Objects can manifest themselves in a number of ways. They can be

   - External entities that produce or consume information.

   - Things that are part of the information domain (reports, displays, and the like).

   - Occurrences or events that occur within the system.

   - Internal producers (objects that make something).

   - Internal consumers (objects that consume what producers make).

   - Places (remote systems, databases, and so on).

   - Structures (windows, frames).

   - People (well people are objects, right? We have state and behavior, no?)

   - Things that are owned or used by other objects (like bank accounts, or automobile parts).

   - Things that are lists of other objects (like parts lists, any kind of collection, and so on).

8. *Organize the candidate objects into groups.* Each group represents a cluster of objects that work together to solve a common problem in your application. Each object will have several characteristics:

   - *Required information:* The object has information that must be remembered so the system can function.

   - *Needed services:* The object must provide services relating to the system goals.

   - *Common attributes:* The attributes defined for the object must be common to all instances of the object.

   - *Common operations:* The operations defined for the object must be common to all instances of the object.

9. Look at the groups you've created and *see if they represent good abstractions for objects* and that work in the application. Good abstractions will help make your application easier to re-work when you inevitably need to change some feature or relationship in the application.

ACT FOUR, Scene 1: In Which We Philosophize on Abstraction

Let's change tack here and talk about a different example. Alice and Bob (remember them?) have just moved to a new city and they need to transfer their old Second City Bank and Trust bank accounts to First Galactic Bank. Alice and Bob are typically middle class and have several bank accounts they need to transfer: a checking account, a passbook savings account, and an investment account. (Luckily for them, First Galactic also handles investments – shares in Venusian Mining are particularly hot this year.)

Nobody actually opens a "bank account;" they open different types of accounts that each have different characteristics. You can write checks on a checking account, but you can't write checks on a passbook savings account. You can earn interest on a savings account, but you normally don't earn interest on a checking account; you pay a monthly service fee instead. But, all different types of bank accounts have some things in common. All of them use your personal information (name, social security number, address, city, state, ZIP), all of them allow you to deposit money and withdraw money.

So when putting together a program that handles "bank accounts" you may realize that there will be common attributes and behaviors among several classes. Let's look at some classes for a bank account example, shall we?

Since we know that checking accounts, savings accounts, and investment accounts are all different, let's first create three different classes and see what we've got (see Figure 9-3).

CheckingAcct	SavingsAcct	InvestmentAcct
LastName: string FirstName: string Address: string City: string State: string Zip: integer AcctNumber: integer SSN: integer Balance: real SvcCharge: real	LastName: string FirstName: string Address: string City: string State: string Zip: integer AcctNumber: integer SSN: integer Balance: real InterestRate: real	LastName: string FirstName: string Address: string City: string State: string Zip: integer AcctNumber: integer SSN: integer Balance: real SvcCharge: real InterestRate: real
deposit(amt) withdraw(amt) applySvcCharge() getBalance()	deposit(amt) withdraw(amt) computeInterest() getBalance()	deposit(amt) withdraw(amt) applySvcCharge() computeInterest() getBalance()

Figure 9-3. Bank Accounts with a lot in common

Notice that all three classes have a lot in common. One of the things we always try to do, no matter what design or coding techniques we're using is to avoid duplication of design and code. This is what abstraction is all about! If we abstract out all the common elements of these three classes, we can create a new (super) class, BankAccount, that incorporates all of them. The CheckingAcct, SavingsAcct, and InvestmentAcct classes can then inherit from BankAccount.

So here's BankAccount, in Figure 9-4.

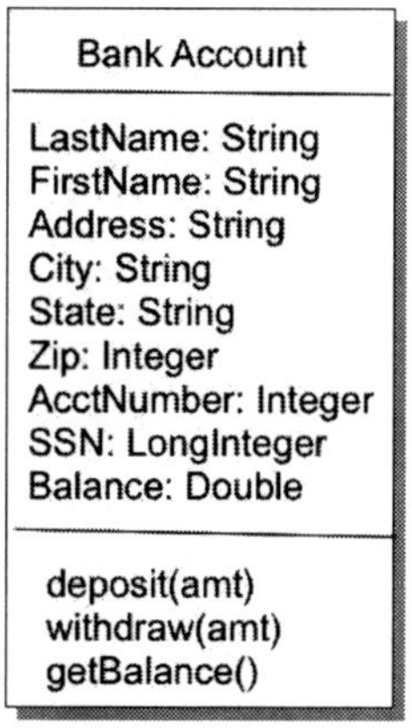

Bank Account

LastName: String
FirstName: String
Address: String
City: String
State: String
Zip: Integer
AcctNumber: Integer
SSN: LongInteger
Balance: Double

deposit(amt)
withdraw(amt)
getBalance()

Figure 9-4. A cleaner BankAccount class

But wait! Is the BankAccount class one that we would want to instantiate? If you look, you'll see that each of the other classes is much more specific than the BankAccount class is. So there isn't enough information in the BankAccount class for us to use. This means we'll always be inheriting from it, but never instantiating it. It's a perfect *abstract class*. (Note the little bit of UML below – class diagrams of abstract classes put the class name in *italics*.) See Figure 9-5.

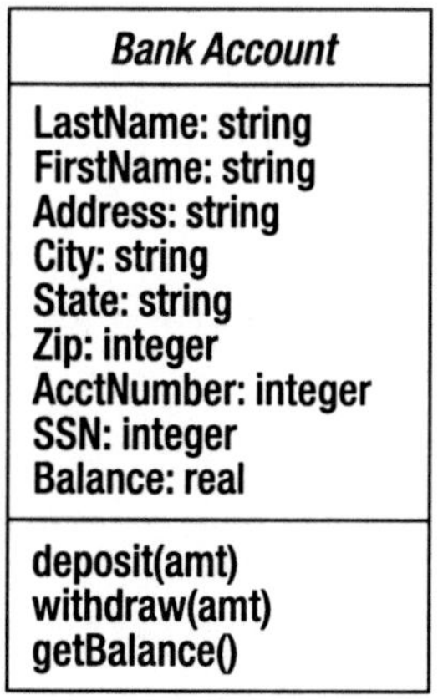

Bank Account

LastName: string
FirstName: string
Address: string
City: string
State: string
Zip: integer
AcctNumber: integer
SSN: integer
Balance: real

deposit(amt)
withdraw(amt)
getBalance()

Figure 9-5. The BankAccount as an abstract class

Abstract classes are templates for actual concrete classes. They encapsulate shared behavior and define the protocol for all subclasses. The abstract class defines behavior and sets a common state, and then concrete subclasses inherit and implement that behavior. You can't instantiate an abstract class; a new concrete class must be created that extends the abstract class. Whenever you find common behavior in two or more places, you should look to abstract that behavior into a class and then reuse that behavior in the common concrete classes.

Here's what we end up with after abstracting out all the personal data and common behavior into the *BankAccount* abstract class. Notice one more little bit of UML here – the new UML arrow types – open arrow ends. These open arrows indicate *inheritance;* so the CheckingAcct class inherits all the attributes and methods from the BankAccount abstract class. UML calls it *generalization* because the super class generalizes the subclasses. That's why the arrows point up to the super class. See Figure 9-6.

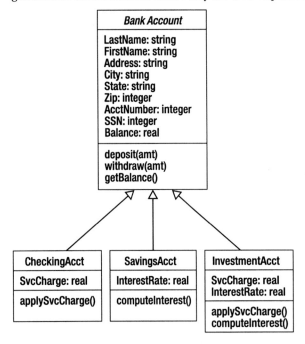

Figure 9-6. The concrete account classes inherit from BankAccount

Now let's move on to explain in detail a number of object-oriented design principles that we've just hinted at so far.

Conclusion

In object-oriented analysis and design it's best to keep in mind your objectives. In analysis you're refining the feature list you've created and producing a model of what the customer wants. You want to end up with a description of what the program is supposed to do, its essential features. This creates a conceptual model of the problem domain and its solution. The model is made up of a number of things, including use cases, user stories, preliminary class diagrams, user interface storyboards, and possibly some class interface descriptions.

In design you're taking that conceptual model and creating the classes that will end up being code. You want to end up with a description of how the program will implement the conceptual model and do what the customer wants. This is an object model of the solution. This model is made up of groups of related class diagrams, their associations and descriptions of how they interact with each other. This includes the programming interface for each class. This design is an abstraction of the class details and code you'll create later. From here you should be able to get to coding pretty quickly.

References

Beck, K. *Extreme Programming Explained: Embrace Change.* (Boston, MA: Addison-Wesley, 2000).

Cockburn, A. (2000). *Writing Effective Use Cases.* (Boston, MA: Addison-Wesley, 2000).

Fowler, M. *UML Distilled.* (Boston, MA: Addison-Wesley, 2000).

McLaughlin, Brett D., et. al. *Head First Object-Oriented Analysis & Design.* (Sebastopol, CA: O'Reilly Media, Inc., 2007).

Meyer, Bertrand. *Object-Oriented Software Construction.* (Upper Saddle River , NJ: Prentice Hall, 1988).

Martin, Robert, Single Responsibility Principle. `www.butunclebob.com/ArticleS .UncleBob.PrinciplesOfOod`. Retrieved on December 10, 2009.

Wirfs-Brock, R. and A. McKean. *Object Design: Roles Responsibilities, and Collaborations.* (Boston, MA, Addison-Wesley, 2003).

CHAPTER 10

Object-Oriented Design Principles

Devotion to the facts will always give the pleasures of recognition; adherence to the rules of design, the pleasures of order and certainty.

—Kenneth Clark

How can I qualify my faith in the inviolability of the design principles? Their virtue is demonstrated. They work.

—Edgar Whitney

Now that we've spent some time looking at object-oriented analysis and design, let's recapitulate some of what we've already seen and add some more pithy prose. First, let's talk about some *common design characteristics.*

First, designs have a purpose. They describe how something will work in a context, using the requirements (lists of features, user stories, and use cases) to define the context. Second, designs must have enough information in them so that someone can implement them. You need enough details in the design so that someone can come after you and implement the program correctly. Next, there are different styles of design, just like there are different types of house architectures. The type of design you want depends on what it is you're being required to build. It depends on the context (see, we're back to context); if you're an architect, you'll design a different kind of house at the sea shore than you will in the mountains. Finally, designs can be expressed at different levels of detail. When building a house, the framing carpenter needs one level of detail, the electrician and plumber another, and the finish carpenter yet another.

There are a number of rules of thumb about object-oriented design that have evolved over the last few decades. These *design principles* act as guidelines for you the designer to abide by so that your design ends up being a good one, easy to implement, easy to maintain, and one that does just what your customer wants. We've looked at several of them already in previous chapters, and here I've pulled out ten fundamental design principles of object-oriented design that are likely to be the most useful to you as you become that designer extraordinaire. I'll list them here and then explain them and give examples in the rest of the chapter.

Our List of Fundamental Object-Oriented Design Principles

Here are the ten fundamental principles:

1. Encapsulate things in your design that are likely to change.

2. *Code to an interface* rather than to an implementation.

3. The *Open-Closed Principle (OCP)*: Classes should be open for extension and closed for modification.

4. The *Don't Repeat Yourself Principle (DRY)*: Avoid duplicate code. Whenever you find common behavior in two or more places, look to *abstract that behavior* into a class *and then reuse* that behavior in the common concrete classes. Satisfy one requirement in one place in your code.

5. The *Single Responsibility Principle (SRP)*: Every object in your system should have a single responsibility, and all the objects services should be focused on carrying out that responsibility. Another way of saying this is that a *cohesive* class does one thing well and doesn't try to do anything else. This implies that higher cohesion is better. It also means that each class in your program should have *only one reason to change*.

6. The *Liskov Substitution Principle (LSP)*: Subtypes must be substitutable for their base types. (in other words, inheritance should be well designed and well behaved.)

7. The *Dependency Inversion Principle (DIP)*: Don't depend on concrete classes; depend on abstractions.

8. The *Interface Segregation Principle (ISP)*: Clients shouldn't have to depend on interfaces they don't use.

9. The *Principle of Least Knowledge (PLK)* (also known as the *Law of Demeter*): Talk only to your immediate friends.

10. The *Principle of Loose Coupling*: Objects that interact should be loosely coupled with well-defined interfaces.

As you probably notice, there's some overlap here, and one or more of the design principles may depend on others. That's okay. It's the fundamentals that count. Let's go through these one at a time.

Encapsulate Things in Your Design That Are Likely to Change

This first principle means to protect your classes from unnecessary change by separating the features and methods of a class that remain relatively constant throughout the program from those that will change. By separating the two types of features, we isolate the parts that will change a lot into a separate class (or classes) that we can depend on changing, and we increase our flexibility and ease of change. We also leave the stable parts of our design alone, so that we just need to implement them once and test them once. (Well, you hope.) This protects the stable parts of the design from any unnecessary changes.

Let's create a very simple class Violinist. Figure 10-1 is a class diagram for the Violinist class.

Violinist
setUpMusic() tuneInstrument() play()

Figure 10-1. *A Violinist*

Notice that the setUpMusic() and tuneInstrument() methods are pretty stable. But what about the play() method? It turns out that there are several different types of playing styles for violins – classical, bluegrass, and Celtic, just to name three. So that means that the play() method will vary, depending on the playing style. Because we have a behavior that will change depending on the playing style, maybe we should abstract that behavior out and encapsulate it in another class? If we do that, then we get something like Figure 10-2.

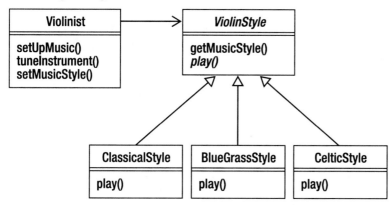

Figure 10-2. *Violinist and playing styles*

Notice that we're using association between the Violinist class and the ViolinStyle abstract class. This allows Violinist to use the concrete classes that inherit the abstract method from the abstract ViolinStyle class. We've abstracted out and encapsulated the play() method – which will vary – in a separate class so that we can isolate any changes we want to make to the playing style from the other stable behaviors in Violinist.

Code to an Interface Rather Than to an Implementation

The normal response to this design principle is, "Huh? What does that mean?" Well, here's the idea. This principle – like many of the principles in this chapter - has to do with inheritance and how you use it in your program. Say you have a program that will model different types of geometric shapes in two dimensions. We'll have a class `Point` that will represent a single point in 2D, and we'll have an interface named `Shape` that will abstract out a couple of things that all shapes have in common – areas and perimeters. (okay, circles and ellipses call it circumference; bear with me.) So here's what we've got (see Figure 10-3).

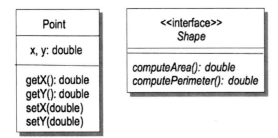

Figure 10-3. A simple Point class and the common Shape Interface

If we want to create concrete classes of some different shapes, we'll *implement* the Shape interface. This means that the concrete classes must implement each of the abstract methods in the Shape interface. See Figure 10-4.

Rectangle	Circle	Triangle
width: double height: double	center: Point radius: double	v1, v2, v3: Point
computeArea(): double computePerimeter(): double	computeArea(): double computePerimeter(): double	computeArea(): double computePerimeter(): double

Figure 10-4. Rectangle, Circle, and Triangle all implement Shape

So now we've got a number of classes that represent different geometric shapes. How do we use them? Say we're writing an application that will manipulate a geometric shape. We can do this in two different ways. First, we can write a separate application for each geometric shape. See Figure 10-5.

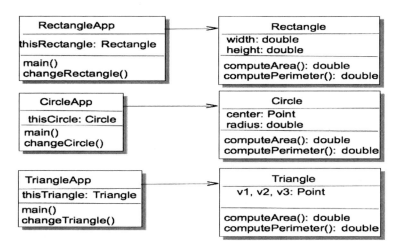

Figure 10-5. Using the geometric objects.

What's wrong with these apps? Well, we've got three different applications doing the same thing. If we want to add another shape, say a rhombus, we'd have to write two new classes, the Rhombus class, which implements the Shape interface, and a new RhombusApp class. Yuk! This is inefficient. We've coded to the implementation of the geometric shape rather than coding to the interface itself.

So how do we fix this? The thing to realize is that the interface is the top of a class hierarchy of all the classes that implement the interface. As such it's a class type and we can use it to help us implement polymorphism in our program. In this case, since we have some number of geometric shapes that implement the Shape interface we can create an array of Shapes that we can fill up with different types of shapes and then iterate through. In Java we'll use the *List* collection type to hold our shapes:

```
import java.util.*;

/**
 * ShapeTest - test the Shape interface implementations.
 *
 * @author fred
 * @version 1.0
 */
public class ShapeTest
{
    public static void main(String [] args)
    {
        List<Shape> figures = new ArrayList<Shape>();

        figures.add(new Rectangle(10, 20));
        figures.add(new Circle(10));
        Point p1 = new Point(0.0, 0.0);
```

```
        Point p2 = new Point(5.0, 1.0);
        Point p3 = new Point(2.0, 8.0);
        figures.add(new Triangle(p1, p2, p3));

        Iterator<Shape> iter = figures.iterator();

        while (iter.hasNext()) {
            Shape nxt = iter.next();
            System.out.printf("area = %8.4f perimeter = %8.4f\n",
                nxt.computeArea(), nxt.computePerimeter());
        }
    }
}
```

So when you code to the interface, your program becomes easier to extend and modify. Your program will work with all the interface's subclasses seamlessly.

As an aside, the principles above let you know that you should be constantly reviewing your design. Changing your design will force your code to change because of the need to *refactor*. Your design is iterative. Pride kills good design; don't be afraid to revisit your design decisions. (Hey! Maybe that's another design principle!)

The Open-Closed Principle (OCP)

Classes should be open for extension and closed for modification.[1]

Find the behavior that does not vary and abstract that behavior up into a super/base class. That locks the base code away from modification but all subclasses will inherit that behavior. You are encapsulating the behavior that varies in the subclasses (those classes that extend the base class) and closing the base class from modification. The bottom line here is that in your well-designed code, you add new features not by modifying existing code (it's closed for modification), but by adding new code (it's open for extension).

The *BankAccount* class example that we did in the previous chapter is a classic example of the Open-Closed Principle at work. In that example, we abstracted all the personal information into the abstract *BankAccount* class, closed it from modification and then extended that class into the different types of bank accounts. In this situation it is very easy to add new types of bank accounts just by extending the *BankAccount* class again. We avoid duplication of code, and we preserve the integrity of the *BankAccount* properties. See Figure 10-6.

---

[1] Larman, C. "Protected Variation: The Importance of Being Closed." *IEEE Software* **18**(3): 89-91. 2001.

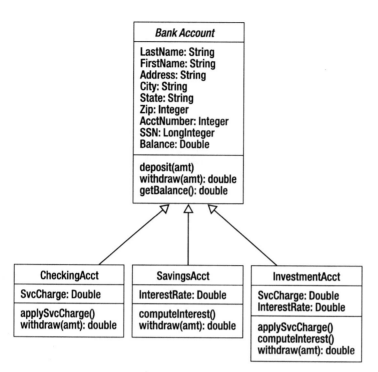

Figure 10-6. The classic BankAccount example for OCP

For example, in the `BankAccount` class we define the `withdraw()` method that allows a customer to withdraw funds from an account. But the way in which withdrawals occur can differ in each of the extended account classes. While the `withdraw()` method is closed for modification in the `BankAccount` class it can be overridden in the subclasses to implement the specific rules for that type of account and thus extend the power of the method. It's closed for modification but open for extension.

The Open-Closed Principle doesn't have to be limited to inheritance either. If you have several private methods in a class, those methods are closed for modification, but if you then create one or more public methods that use the private methods, you've opened up the possibility of extending those private methods by adding functionality in the public methods. Think outside the box – er, class.

Don't Repeat Yourself Principle (DRY)

Avoid duplicate code by abstracting out things that are common and placing those things in a single location.[2]

DRY is the motherhood and apple pie design principle. It's been handed down ever since developers started thinking about better ways to write programs. Go back and look at Chapters 6 and 7 if you don't

---

[2] Hunt, A. and D. Thomas. *The Pragmatic Programmer: From Journeyman to Master.* (Boston, MA: Addison-Wesley, 2000.)

believe me. With DRY you have each piece of information and each behavior in a single place in the design. Ideally you have one requirement in one place. This means that you should create your design so that there is one logical place where a requirement is implemented. Then if you have to change the requirement you have only one place to look to make the change. You also remove duplicate code and replace it with method calls. If you are duplicating code, you are duplicating behavior.

DRY doesn't have to apply just to your code either. It's always a good idea to comb your feature list and requirements for duplications. Rewriting requirements to avoid duplicating features in the code will make your code much easier to maintain.

Consider the final version of the B^4++ bird feeder that we discussed in the last chapter. The last thing we worked on was adding a song identifier to the feeder so that the feeding doors would open and close automatically. But let's look at the two use cases we ended up with (see Table 10-1).

Table 10-1. The Song Identifier Use Case and Its Alternate

Main Path	Alternate Path
1. Alice hears or sees birds at the bird feeder.	1.1 The songbird identifier hears birdsong.
2. Alice determines that they are *not* songbirds.	2.1 The songbird identifier recognizes the song as from an unwanted bird.
3. Alice presses the remote control button.	3.1 The song bird identifier sends a message to the feeding doors to close.
4. The feeding doors close.	
5. The birds give up and fly away.	5.1 The songbird identifier hears birdsong.
	5.2 The songbird identifier recognizes the song as from a songbird.
6. Alice presses the remote control button.	6.1 The songbird identifier sends a message to the feeding doors to open.
7. The feeding doors open again.	

Notice that we're opening and closing the feeding doors in two different places, via the remote control and via the song identifier. But if you think about it, regardless of where we request the doors to be open or closed, they always open and close in the same way. So this is a classic opportunity to abstract out the open and close door behavior and put them in a single place, say the FeedingDoor class. DRY at work!

The Single Responsibility Principle (SRP)

This principle says that a class should have one, and only one, reason to change.[3]

Here's an example of the overlap between these design principles that was mentioned above: SRP, the first principle about encapsulation, and DRY all say similar, but slightly different things. Encapsulation is about abstracting behavior and putting things in your design that are likely to change in the same place. DRY is about avoiding duplicating code by putting identical behaviors in the same place. SRP is about designing your classes so that each does just one thing, and does it very well.

Every object should have a single responsibility and all the object's services are targeted towards carrying out that responsibility. *Each class should have only one reason to change.* Put simply, this means to beware of having your class try to do too many things.

As an example, let's say we're writing the embedded code for a mobile phone. After months (really) of discussions with the marketing folks, our first cut at a MobilePhone class looks like Figure 10-7.

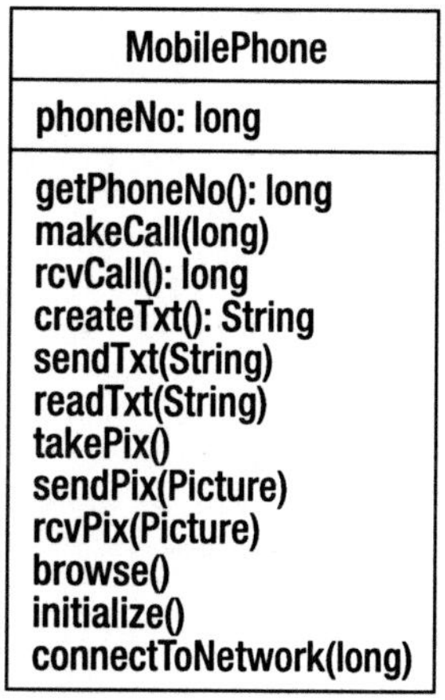

MobilePhone
phoneNo: long
getPhoneNo(): long makeCall(long) rcvCall(): long createTxt(): String sendTxt(String) readTxt(String) takePix() sendPix(Picture) rcvPix(Picture) browse() initialize() connectToNetwork(long)

Figure 10-7. A very busy MobilePhone class

This class seems to incorporate a lot of what we would want a mobile phone to do, but it violates the SRP in several different ways. This class is not trying to do a single thing, it is trying to do way too many things – make and receive phone calls (who does that, anyway?), create, send, and receive text messages, create, send and receive pictures, browse the Internet. The class doesn't have a *single responsibility*. It has many. But we don't want a single class to be impacted by these completely different forces. We don't want to modify the MobilePhone class every time the picture format is changed, or every time the browser changes. Rather, we want to separate these functions out into different classes so that they can change independently of each other. So how do we recognize the things that should move out of this class, and how do we recognize the things that should stay? Have a look at Figure 10-8.

---

[3] McLaughlin, Brett D., et. al., *Head First Object-Oriented Analysis & Design.* (Sebastopol, CA: O'Reilly Media, Inc., 2007.)

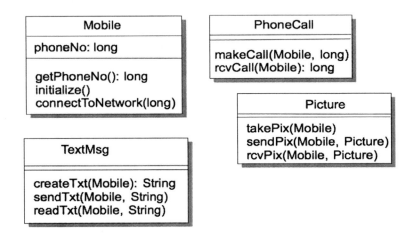

Figure 10-8. Mobile phone classes each with a single responsibility

In this example, we ask the question, "What does the mobile phone do (to itself)?" as opposed to, "What services are offered by the mobile phone?" By asking questions like this, we can start to separate out the responsibilities of the objects in the design. In this case, we can see that the phone itself can get its own phone number, initialize itself, and connect itself to the mobile phone network. The services offered, on the other hand, are really independent of the actual mobile phone, and so can be separated out into PhoneCall, TextMsg, and Picture classes. So we divide up the initial one class into four separate classes, each with a single responsibility. This way we can change any of the four classes without affecting the others. We've simplified the design (although we've got more classes), and made it easier to extend and modify. Is that a great principle, or what?

Liskov Substitution Principle (LSP)

Subclasses must be substitutable for their base class..[4] This principle says that inheritance should be well designed and well behaved. In any case a user should be able to instantiate an object as a subclass and use all the base class functionality invisibly.

In order to illustrate the LSP, most books give an example that violates the Substitution Principle and say, "don't do that." Why should we be any different? One of the best and canonical examples of violating the Liskov Substitution Principle is the Rectangle/Square example. The example itself is all over the Internet; Robert Martin gives a great variation on this example in his book *Agile Software*

---

[4] Wintour, Damien. "The Liskov Substitution Principle." 1988. Downloaded on September 14, 2010 from www.necessaryandsufficient.net/2008/09/design-guidelines-part3-the-liskov-substitution-principle/.

Development, Principles, Patterns, and Practices,[5] and we'll follow his version of the example. Here it is in Java.

Say you have a class Rectangle that represents the geometric shape of a rectangle:

```java
/**
 * class Rectangle.
 */
public class Rectangle
{
    private double width;
    private double height;

    /**
     * Constructor for objects of class Rectangle
     */
    public Rectangle(double width, double height) {
        this.width = width;
        this.height = height;
    }

    public void setWidth(double width) {
        this.width = width;
    }

    public void setHeight(double height) {
        this.height = height;
    }

    public double getHeight() {
        return this.height;
    }

    public double getWidth() {
        return this.width;
    }
}
```

And, of course, one of your users wants to have the ability to manipulate squares as well as rectangles. You, being the bright math student you are, already know that squares are just a special case of rectangles; in other words a Square IS-A Rectangle. Being a great object-oriented designer as well, you know all about inheritance. So you create a Square class that inherits from Rectangle.

```java
/**
 * class Square
 */
public class Square extends Rectangle
```

---

[5] Martin, R. C. *Agile Software Development: Principles, Patterns, and Practices.* (Upper Saddle River, NJ: Prentice Hall, 2003.)

```
{
    /**
     * Constructor for objects of class Square
     */
    public Square(double side) {
        super(side, side);
    }

    public void setSide(double side) {
        super.setWidth(side);
        super.setHeight(side);
    }

    public double getSide() {
        return super.getWidth();
    }
}
```

Well, this seems to be okay. Notice that because the width and height of a Square are the same, we couldn't run the risk of changing them individually, so setSide() uses setWidth() and setHeight() to set both for the sides of a Square. No big deal, right?

Well, if we have a function like:

```
void myFunc(Rectangle r, double newWidth) {
        r.setWidth(newWidth);
}
```

and we pass myFunc() a Rectangle object, it works just fine, changing the width of the Rectangle. But what if we pass myFunc() a Square object? Well, it turns out that in Java the same thing happens as before, but that's *wrong*. It violates the integrity of the Square object by just changing its width without changing its height as well. So we've violated the LSP here and the Square can not substitute for a Rectangle without changing the behavior of the Square. The LSP says that the subclass (Square) should be able to substitute for the superclass (Rectangle), but it doesn't in this case.

Now we can get around this. We can override the Rectangle class' setWidth() and setHeight() methods in Square like this:

```
public void setWidth(double w) {
        super.setWidth(w);
        super.setHeight(w);
}

    public void setHeight(double h) {
        super.setWidth(h);
        super.setHeight(h);
}
```

These will both work and we'll get the right answers and preserve the invariants of the Square object, but where's the point in that? If we have to override a bunch of methods we've inherited, then what's the point of using inheritance to begin with? That's what the LSP is all about: getting the *behavior* of derived classes right and thus getting inheritance right. If we think of the base class as being a contract that we adhere to (remember the Open-Closed Principle?), then the LSP is saying that you must adhere to the contract even for derived classes. Oh, by the way, this works in Java because Java public methods are all *virtual methods*, and are thus able to be overridden. If we had defined setWidth() and setHeight() in Rectangle with a *final* keyword or if they had been *private*, then we couldn't have overridden them.

In this example, while a square is mathematically a specialized type of rectangle and one where the invariants related to rectangles still hold, that mathematical definition just doesn't work in Java. In this case you don't want to have Square be a subclass of Rectangle; inheritance doesn't work for you in this case, because you think about rectangles having two different kinds of sides – length and width - and squares having only one kind of side. So if a Square class inherits from a Rectangle class the image of what a Square is versus what a Rectangle is gets in the way of the code. Inheritance is just the wrong thing to use here.

How can you tell when you're likely to be violating the Liskov Substitution Principle? Indications that you're violating LSP include:

- A subclass doesn't keep all the external observable behavior of its super class.

- A subclass modifies, rather than extends, the external observable behavior of its super class.

- A subclass throws exceptions in an effort to hide certain behavior defined in its super class.

- A subclass that overrides a virtual method defined in its super class using an empty implementation in order to hide certain behavior defined in its super class.

- Method overriding in derived classes is the biggest cause of LSP violations.[6]

Sometimes inheritance just isn't the right thing to do. Luckily, you're not screwed here. You've got options.

It turns out there are other ways to share the behavior and attributes of other classes. The three most common are delegation, composition, and aggregation.

Delegation – it's what every manager should do. Give away work and let someone else do it. If you want to use the behaviors in another class but you don't want to change that behavior consider using delegation instead of inheritance. Delegation says to give responsibility for the behavior to another class; this creates an association between the classes. Association in this sense means that the classes are related to each other, usually through an attribute or a set of related methods. Delegation has a great side benefit. It shields your objects from any implementation changes in other objects in your program; you're not using inheritance, so encapsulation protects you.[7] Let's show a bit of how delegation works with an example.

When last we left Alice and Bob and their B^4++, Alice was tired of using the remote to open and close the feeding doors to keep away the non-song birds. So they'd requested yet another new feature – an automatic song identifier. With the song identifier the B^4++ itself would recognize songbird songs and open the doors, and keep them closed for all other birds. We can think of this in a couple of ways.

The BirdFeeder class, because of the Single Responsibility Principle, shouldn't do the identification of bird songs, but it should know what songs are allowed. We'll need a new class, SongIdentifier, that will do the actual song identification. We'll also need a Song object that contains a birdsong. Figure 10-9 shows what we've got so far.

---

[6] Wintour, 1998.
[7] Mclaughlin, 2007.

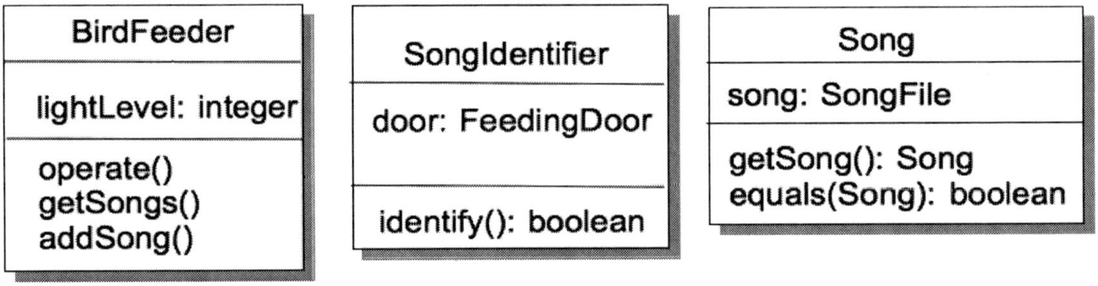

Figure 10-9. A first cut at the song identifier feature

Now, the BirdFeeder knows about birdsong and keeps a list of the allowed songs for the feeder. The SongIdentifier has the single job of identifying a given song. Now, there are two ways that this can happen. The first is that the SongIdentifier class can do the work itself in the identify() method. That would mean that SongIdentifier would need an equals() method in order to do the comparison between two songs (the allowed song from the door, and the song that the new B⁴++ hardware just sent to us). The second way of identifying songs is for the Song class to do it itself, using its own equals() method. Which should we choose?

Well, if we do all the identification in the SongIdentifier class, that means that any time anything changes in a Song, that we'll have to change both the Song class *and* the SongIdentifier class. This doesn't sound optimal. But! If we delegate the song comparison work to the Song class, then the SongIdentifier's identify() method could just take a Song as an input parameter and call that method and we've isolated any Song changes to just the Song class. Figure 10-10 shows the revised class diagrams.

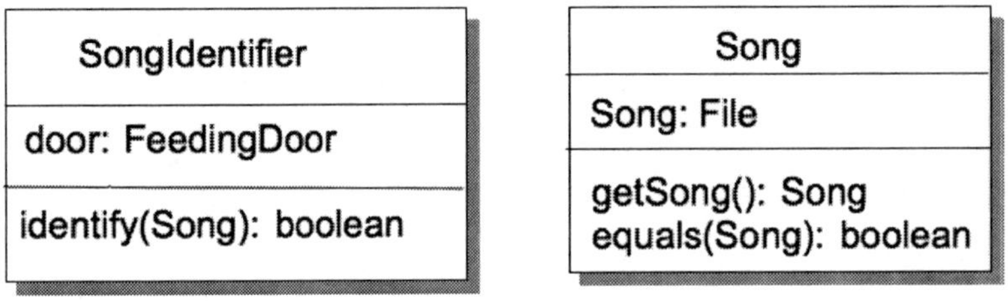

Figure 10-10. Simplifying SongIdentifier and Song

And our corresponding code might look like:

```
public class SongIdentifier {
  private BirdFeeder feeder;
  private FeedingDoor door;
  public SongIdentifier(BirdFeeder feeder) {
    this.door = feeder.getDoor();
  }
  public void identify(Song song) {
  List<Song> songs = feeder.getSongs();
  Iterator<Song> song_iter = songs.iterator();
```

```
    while (song_iter.hasNext()) {
        Song nxtSong = song_iter.next();
        if (nxtSong.equals(song)) {
            door.open();
            return;
        }
    }
    door.close();
  }
}

public class Song {
  private File song;
  public Song(File song) {
    this.song = song;
  }
  public File getSong() {
    return this.song;
  }
  public boolean equals(Object newSong) {
    if (newSong instanceof Song) {
      Song newSong2 = (Song) newSong;
      if (this.song.equals(newSong2.song)) {
        return true;
      }
    }
    return false;
  }
}
```

In this implementation, if we change anything with regards to a Song , then the only changes we make will be in the Song class, and SongIdentifier is insulated from those changes. The *behavior* of the Song class doesn't change, although how it *implements* that behavior might. SongIdentifier doesn't care how the behavior is implemented, as long as it is always the same behavior. BirdFeeder has delegated the work of handling birdsong to the SongIdentifier class and SongIdentifier has delegated the work of comparing songs to the Song class, all without using inheritance. What a concept.

Delegation allows you to give away the responsibility for a behavior to another class and not have to worry about changing the behavior in your class. You can count on the behavior in the delegated class not changing. But sometimes you will want to use an entire set of behaviors simultaneously, and delegation doesn't work for that. Instead, if you want to have your program use that set of behaviors you need to use composition. We use *composition* to assemble behaviors from other classes.

Say that you're putting together a space-based role playing game (RPG), *Space Rangers*. One of the things you'll model in your game is the spaceships themselves. Spaceships will have lots of different characteristics. For example, there are different types of ships, shuttles, traders, fighters, freighters, capital ships. Each ship will also have different characteristics, weapons, shields, cargo capacity, number of crew, and so on. But what will all the ships have in common?

Well, if you want to create a generic Ship class, it will be hard to gather all these things together in a single Ship superclass so you can create subclasses for things like Shuttle, Fighter, Freighter, and the like. They are all just too different. This seems to imply that inheritance isn't the way to go here. So back to our question – what do all the ships have in common?

We can say that all the Ships in Space Rangers have just two things in common – a ship type, and a set of properties that relate to that ship type. This gets us to our first class diagram, shown in Figure 10-11.

SpaceShip
shipType: String properties: Map
getType(): String setType(String) getProperty(String): Object setProperty(String, Object)

Figure 10-11. What do all Spaceships have in common?

This allows us to store the space ship type and a map of the various properties for an instance of a ship. It means we can then develop the properties independently from the ships and then different ships can share similar properties. For example, all ships can have weapons, but they can have different ones with different characteristics. This leads us to develop a weapons interface that we can then use to implement particular classes. We get to use these weapons in our SpaceShip by using composition. Remember that composition allows us to use an entire family of behaviors that we can be guaranteed won't change. See Figure 10-12.

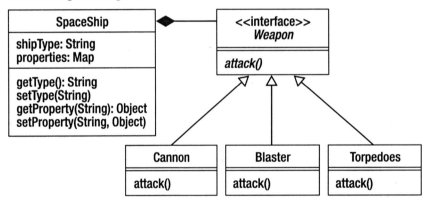

Figure 10-12. Using composition to allow the SpaceShip to use Weapons

Remember that the open triangle in the UML diagram means inheritance (or in the case of an interface, it means implements). The closed diamond in UML means composition. So in this design we can add several weapons to our properties Map and each weapon can have different characteristics, but all of them exhibit the same behavior. Isn't *composition* grand?

You should also note that in composition the component objects (Weapons) become part of a larger object (SpaceShip) and when the larger object goes away (you get blown up), so do the components. The object that is composed of other behaviors owns those behaviors. When that object is destroyed, so are all of its behaviors. The behaviors in a composition don't exist outside of the composition itself. When your SpaceShip is blown up, so are all your weapons.

Of course, sometimes you want to put together a set of objects and behaviors in such a way that when one of them is removed, the others continue in existence. That's what *aggregation* is all about. If the behaviors need to persist, then you must aggregate. Aggregation is when one class is used as a part of another class, but still exists outside of that other class. If the object does make sense existing on its own, then use aggregation, otherwise use composition. For example, a library is an example of aggregation. Each book makes sense on its own, but the aggregation of them all is a library. The key is to show an instance where it makes sense to use a component outside a composition implying that it should have a separate existence.

In *Space Rangers,* we can have `Pilot` objects in addition to `SpaceShip` objects. A `Pilot` can also carry weapons. Different ones, of course; `Pilots` probably don't carry `Cannon` objects with them! Say a `Pilot` is carrying around a `HandBlaster`, so in object-oriented speak he's using the behaviors of the `HandBlaster`. If the `Pilot` is accidentally crushed by a mad `SpaceCow`, is the weapon destroyed along with the `Pilot`? Probably not, hence the need for a mechanism where the `HandBlaster` can be used by a `Pilot` but has an existence outside of the `Pilot` class. Ta, da! Aggregation!

So we've seen three different mechanisms that allow objects to use the behaviors of other objects, none of which require inheritance. As it's said in OOA&D, "If you favor delegation, composition, and aggregation over inheritance your software will usually be more flexible and easier to maintain, extend and reuse."[8]

The Dependency Inversion Principle (DIP)

Robert C. Martin introduced the Dependency Inversion Principle in his C++ Report and later in his classic book "Agile Software Development."[9] In his book, Martin defined the DIP as

> a. *High-level modules should not depend on low-level modules. Both should depend on abstraction.*

> b. *Abstractions should not depend on details. Details should depend on abstractions.*

The simple version of this is: don't depend on concrete classes; depend on abstractions. Martin's contention is that object-oriented design is the inverse of traditional structured design. In structured design as we saw in Chapter 7, one either works from the top-down, pushing details and design decisions as low in the hierarchy of software layers as possible. Or one works from the bottom-up, designing low-level details first, and later putting together a set of low-level functions into a single higher-level abstraction. In both these cases, the higher level software depends on decisions that are made at the lower levels, including interface and behavioral decisions.

Martin contends that for object-oriented design that this is backward. The Dependency Inversion Principle implies that higher-level (more abstract) design levels should create an interface that lower (more concrete) levels should code to. This will mean that as long as the lower level – concrete – classes *code to the interface* of the upper level abstraction that the upper level classes are safe. As Martin puts it, "The modules that contain the high-level business rules should take precedence over, and be

---

[8] McLaughlin, 2007.
[9] Martin, 2003.

independent of, the modules that contain the implementation details. High-level modules simply should not depend on low-level modules in any way."

Here's a simple example. Traditionally, in structured design we write many programs with the general format of:

11. Get input data from somewhere.

12. Process the data.

13. Write the data to somewhere else.

In this example, the Processor uses the Collector to get data, it then packages the data and uses the Writer to write the data to, say, a database. If we draw this out, we get something that looks like Figure 10-13.

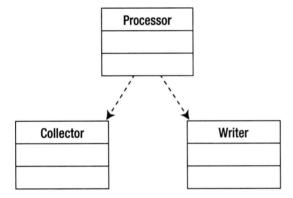

Figure 10-13. A traditional input-process-output model

One problem with this implementation is that the Processor must create and use the Writer whose interface and parameter types it must know in order to write correctly. This means that the Processor must be written to a concrete implementation of a Writer and so must be re-written if we want to change what kind of Writer we want. Say the first implementation writes to a File, if we then want to write to a printer, or a database, we need to change Processor every time. This is not very reusable. So the Dependency Inversion Principle says that the Processor should be coded to an interface (we abstract Processor) and then the interface is implemented in separate concrete classes for each type of Writer destination. The resulting design looks like Figure 10-14.

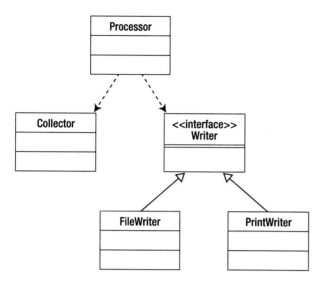

Figure 10-14. *Using an interface to allow different writer implementations*

In this way, different writers can be added and as long as they adhere to the interface, Processor never needs to change. Note that the DIP is closely related to Principle #2, Code to an Interface.

The Interface Segregation Principle (ISP)

Clients shouldn't have to depend on interfaces they don't use. In particular, they shouldn't have to depend on *methods* they don't use.[10]

We've talked a lot about interfaces in this chapter. Coding to interfaces, using interfaces to abstract out common details, and so on. We use interfaces to make our code more flexible and maintainable. So overall, interfaces are a great thing, right? Well, young Skywalker, you must beware of interfaces as well.

One of the greatest temptations with respect to interfaces is to make them bigger. If an interface is good, then a bigger interface must be better, right? After all, you can then use the interface is way more objects and *the user just has to not implement certain methods that they don't need.* Ack! By doing that you are ruining the *cohesion* of your interface. By "generalizing" an interface too much you are moving away from that single lightning bolt of a set of methods that are all closely related to each other to a jumble of methods that say hello to each other in passing. Remember **cohesion is good**. Your applications should be cohesive and the classes and interfaces they depend on should also be cohesive.

You make your interfaces less cohesive, and begin to violate the Interface Segregation Principle when you start adding new methods to your interface because one of the subclasses that implements the interface needs it – *and others do not.* So what's the answer here? How do we keep our interfaces cohesive and still make them useful for a range of objects?

The answer is: make more interfaces. The Interface Segregation Principle implies that instead of adding new methods that are only appropriate to one or a few implementation classes, that you *make a new interface.* You divide your bloated interface into two or more smaller, *more cohesive* interfaces. That

---

[10] Martin, 2003.

way, new classes can just implement the interfaces that they need and not implement ones that they don't.

The Principle of Least Knowledge (PLK)

(Also known as the *Law of Demeter*). Talk only to your immediate friends.[11]

The complement to strong cohesion in an application is *loose coupling*. That's what the Principle of Least Knowledge is all about. It says that classes should collaborate *indirectly* with as few other classes as possible.[12] Here's an example.

You've got a computer system in your car – we all do these days. Say you're writing an application that graphs temperature data in the car. There are a number of sensors that provide temperature data and that are part of a family of sensors in the car's engine. Your program should select a sensor, gather and plot its temperature data. (This example is derived from one found in Hunt).[13] Part of your program might look like:

```
public void plotTemperature(Sensor theSensor) {
        double temp = theSensor.getSensorData().getOilData().getTemp();
        ...
}
```

This will likely work – once. But now you've coupled your temperature plotting method to the *Sensor*, *SensorData*, and *OilSensor* classes. Which means that a change to *any one of them* could affect your plotTemperature() method and cause you to have to refactor your code. Not good.

This is what the PLK urges you to avoid. Instead of linking your method to a hierarchy and having to traverse the hierarchy to get the service you're looking for, just ask for the data directly

```
public void plotTemperature(double theSensor) {
        ...
}
...
plotTemperature(aSensor.getTemp());
```

Yup, we had to add a method to the Sensor class to get the temperature for us, but that's a small price to pay for cleaning up the mess (and the possible errors) above. Now your class is just collaborating directly with *one* class, and letting that class take care of the others. Of course, your Sensor class will do the same thing with SensorData, and so on.

This leads us to a corollary to the PLK – *keep dependencies to a minimum*. This is the crux of loose coupling. By interacting with only a few other classes, you make your class more flexible and less likely to contain errors.

---

[11] Martin, 2003.

.[12] Lieberherr, K., I. Holland, et al. *Object-Oriented Programming: An Objective Sense of Style.* OOPSLA '88, Association for Computing Machinery, 1988.

[13] Hunt, 2000.

Class Design Guidelines for Fun and Enjoyment

Finally, just so we shouldn't exit the chapter without yet another list, we present a list of 24 class design guidelines. These guidelines are somewhat more specific than the general design guidelines that we have described above, but they are handy to have around. Cut them out and burn them into your brain.

These 24 class design guidelines are taken from Davis[14] and McConnell.[15]

1. Present a *consistent level of abstraction* in the class interface.

2. Be sure you understand what abstraction the class is implementing.

3. Move unrelated information to a different class (ISP).

4. Beware of erosion of the class's interface when you are making changes. (ISP).

5. Don't add public members that are inconsistent with the interface abstraction.

6. Minimize accessibility of classes and members (OCP).

7. Don't expose member data in public.

8. Avoid putting private implementation details into the class's interface.

9. Avoid putting methods into the public interface.

10. Watch for coupling that's too tight (PLK).

11. Try to implement "has a" relations through containment within a class (SRP).

12. Implement "is a" relations through inheritance (LSP).

13. Only inherit if the derived class is a more specific version of the base class.

14. Be sure to inherit only what you want to inherit (LSP).

15. Move common interfaces, data, and operations as high in the inheritance hierarchy as possible (DRY).

16. Be suspicious of classes of which there is only one instance.

17. Be suspicious of base classes that only have a single derived class.

18. Avoid deep inheritance trees (LSP).

19. Keep the number of methods in a class as small as possible.

20. Minimize indirect method calls to other classes (PLK).

21. Initialize all member data in all constructors, if possible.

22. Eliminate data-only classes.

---

[14] Davis, A. M. *201 Principles of Software Development.* (New York, NY: McGraw-Hill, Inc., 1995.)

[15] McConnell, Steve, *Code Complete, 2nd Edition.* (Redmond, WA: Microsoft Press, 2004.)

23. Eliminate operation-only classes.

24. Oh, and be careful out there.... (OK, I added this one.)

Conclusion

In this chapter we examined a number of rules of thumb about object-oriented design that have evolved over the last few decades. These design principles act as guidelines for you the designer to abide by so that your design ends up being a good one, easy to implement, easy to maintain, and one that does just what your customer wants. Importantly, these design principles give guidance when you're feeling your way from features to design. They talk about ways to examine and implement the important object-oriented principles of inheritance, encapsulation, polymorphism, and abstraction. They also reinforce basic design principles like cohesion and coupling. Burn these principles into your brain, OO designer.

References

Davis, A. M. *201 Principles of Software Development.* (New York, NY: McGraw-Hill, Inc., 1995.)

Hunt, A. and D. Thomas. *The Pragmatic Programmer: From Journeyman to Master.* (Boston, MA: Addison-Wesley, 2000.)

Larman, C. "Protected Variation: The Importance of Being Closed." *IEEE Software* **18**(3): 89-91. 2001.

Lieberherr, K., I. Holland, et al. *Object-Oriented Programming: An Objective Sense of Style.* OOPSLA '88, Association for Computing Machinery, 1988.

Martin, R. C. *Agile Software Development: Principles, Patterns, and Practices.* (Upper Saddle River, NJ: Prentice Hall, 2003.)

McConnell, Steve, *Code Complete, 2ⁿᵈ Edition.* (Redmond, WA: Microsoft Press, 2004.)

McLaughlin, Brett D., et. al., *Head First Object-Oriented Analysis & Design.* (Sebastopol, CA: O'Reilly Media, Inc., 2007.)

Wintour, Damien. "The Liskov Substitution Principle." 1988. Downloaded on September 14, 2010 from `www.necessaryandsufficient.net/2008/09/design-guidelines-part3-the-liskov-substitution-principle/`.

CHAPTER 11

Design Patterns

Each pattern describes a problem which occurs over and over again in our environment, and then describes the core of the solution to that problem, in such a way that you can use this solution a million times over, without ever doing it the same way twice.

— Christopher Alexander[1]

Do you reinvent the wheel each time you write code? Do you have to re-learn how to iterate through an array every time you write a program? Do you have to re-invent how to fix a dangling else in every function you write? Do you need to relearn insertion sort or binary search every time you want to use them? Of course not!

Over the time you've spent writing programs you've learned a *set of idioms* that you employ whenever you're writing code. For example, if you need to iterate through all the elements of an array in Java you're likely to do the following:

```
for (int i = 0; i < myArray.length; i++) {
        System.out.printf(" %d ", myArray[i]);
}
```

or

```
for (int nextElement: myArray) {
        System.out.printf(" %d ", nextElement);
}
```

and the code just flows out of your fingertips as you type. These *code patterns* are sets of rules and templates for code that you accumulate as you gain more experience writing programs.

Design patterns are the same thing – but for your design. The famous architect Christopher Alexander, in his book *A Pattern Language*, defined patterns for design in architecture. The same ideas

---

[1] Alexander, C., S. Ishikawa, et al. *A Pattern Language: Towns, Buildings, Construction.* (Oxford, UK: Oxford University Press, 1977.)

carry over into software design. If you go back and read the Alexander quote at the top of this chapter, you'll see the following three key elements in Alexander's definition of design pattern:

- *Recurring*: The problem that evokes the design pattern must be a common one.

- *Core solution*: The pattern provides a template for the solution; it tries to extract out the essence of the solution.

- *Reuse*: The pattern must be easily reusable when the same problem appears in different domains.

In fact, you've already seen at least one design pattern so far in this book: the *Model-View-Controller* pattern (MVC) that we discussed in Chapter 5 is one of the earliest published examples of a software design pattern.[2] The MVC design pattern is used with programs that use graphical user interfaces. It divides the program into three parts: the *Model* that contains the processing rules for the program, the *View* that presents the data and the interface to the user, and the *Controller* that mediates communication between the *Model* and the *View*. In a typical object-oriented implementation, each of these abstractions becomes a separate object.

The *Gang of Four* (Gamma, Helm, Johnson, and Vlissides), in their seminal book on design patterns, *Design Patterns: Elements of Reusable Object-Oriented Software*,[3] define a design pattern as something that "names, abstracts, and identifies the key aspects of a common design structure that makes it useful for creating a reusable object-oriented design." In other words, a design pattern is a *named abstraction* from a *concrete example* that represents a *recurring solution* to a *particular, but common, problem* – recurring, core solution, reuse.

But why do we need design patterns in the first place? Why can't we just get along with the object-oriented design principles we studied in Chapter 10 and with our old favorites, abstraction, inheritance, polymorphism, and encapsulation?

Well, it turns out that design is hard. That's why. Design for re-use is even harder. Design is also much more of an art than a science or an engineering discipline. Experienced software designers rarely start from first principles; they look for similarities in the current problem to problems they've solved in the past. And they bring to the design table the set of design idioms that they've learned over time. Design patterns provide a *shared vocabulary* that makes this expert knowledge available to everyone.

Design Patterns and the Gang of Four

In their book, the Gang of Four describe design patterns as having four essential features:

- *The Pattern Name*: "… a handle we can use to describe a design problem, its solution, and consequences in a word or two. Naming a pattern immediately increases our design vocabulary."

- *The Problem*: Describes when to use the pattern. "It explains the problem and its context."

---

[2]Krasner, G. E. and S. T. Pope. "A cookbook for using the Model-View-Controller user interface paradigm in Smalltalk-80." *Journal of Object-Oriented Programming* 1(3): 26-49. 1988.

[3]Gamma, E., Helm, R., Johnson, R., Vlissides. *Design Patterns: Elements of Reusable Object-Oriented Software*. (Boston, MA: Addison-Wesley, 1995.)

- *The Solution:* "… describes the elements that make up the design, their relationships, responsibilities, and collaborations…the pattern provides an abstract description of a design problem and how a general arrangement of elements solves it."

- *The Consequences:* The results and trade-offs of applying the pattern to a problem. These include time and space trade-offs, but also flexibility, extensibility, and portability, among others.[4]

Design patterns are classified using two criteria, *scope* and *purpose*. Scope deals with the relationships between classes and objects. Static relationships between classes are fixed at compile time, whereas, dynamic relationships apply to objects and these relationships can change at run-time. Purpose, of course, deals with what the pattern does with respect to classes and objects. Patterns can deal with object creation, composition of classes or objects, or the ways in which objects interact and distribute responsibilities in the program.

The Gang of Four describe 23 different design patterns in their book, dividing them into three different classes of patterns: *creational, structural,* and *behavioral.*

- *Creational design patterns* are those that deal with when and how objects are created. These patterns typically create objects for you, relieving you of the need to instantiate those objects directly.

- *Structural design patterns* are those that describe how objects are composed into larger groups,

- *Behavioral design patterns* generally talk about how responsibilities are distributed in the design and how communication happens between objects.

The list is not meant to be complete, and over the 15 years since the publication of the Gang of Four's *Design Patterns* book, many more patterns have been added to this original list by developers everywhere. A recent Google search for the phrase "design patterns" yielded 2.5 million hits, so lots of object-oriented developers have jumped on the design patterns bandwagon.

The Classic Design Patterns

The 23 (classic) design patterns described by the Gang of Four are (in the remainder of this chapter we'll go over the six design patterns that are in italics):

Creational Patterns

1. Abstract factory
2. Builder
3. *Factory Method*

---

[4]Gamma et. al, 1995.

4. Prototype

5. *Singleton*

Structural Patterns

6. *Adapter*

7. Bridge

8. Composite

9. Decorator

10. Façade

11. Flyweight

12. Proxy

Behavioral Patterns

13. Chain of responsibility

14. Command

15. Interpreter

16. *Iterator*

17. Mediator

18. Memento

19. *Observer*

20. State

21. *Strategy*

22. Template method

23. Visitor

Patterns We Can Use

The six patterns in this section are a representative sample of the classic design patterns, and are six that you'll find the most useful right away.

Creational Patterns

Creational Patterns all have to do with creating objects. If we think about class definitions as templates for producing objects, then these patterns are all about how to create those templates. The two patterns we'll look at next, Singleton and Factory show us two different ways of thinking about creating objects.

The Singleton Pattern

Singleton[5] is almost certainly the easiest of the Design Patterns to understand and to code. The idea is simple. You are writing a program and you have a need for one – *and only one* – instance of a class. And you need to enforce that "and only one" requirement. Examples of programs that would use a Singleton pattern are things like print spoolers, window managers, device drivers, and the like.

So what are the implications of the "one, and only one" requirement? Well, first, it means your program can only say "**new** Singleton()" once, right? But what's to stop other objects in your program (or objects in the program that you didn't write) from issuing another "**new** Singleton()"? The answer is – nothing! As long as your class can be instantiated once, other objects should be able to instantiate it again and again. Well, bummer.

So what we need to do is to create a class that can be instantiated once and only once and which *doesn't use* **new** to do the instantiation. Huh?

You heard me right: we need a class that can be instantiated without using **new**. Go ahead, think about it.

Here's what we'll do. The method that gets called when an object is instantiated is the constructor. In Java you can say **new** Singleton() because the Singleton() constructor is **public** – it's visible from outside the class definition. If we want to keep the constructor so we can make instances of Singleton objects, but we don't want anyone to be able to use **new** to do that, we must make the constructor **private**. "But wait!" you cry, "if the constructor is private then we can't instantiate the object at all!" *Au contraire*, dear reader. If the constructor is private, then it can only be accessed from inside the class definition, so it's entirely possible to instantiate the object from within the class definition itself!

"But wait again!" you say. "How do we get to the constructor from *outside* the class definition?" Well, in Java is there a way to access a method inside a class without having to have an instantiation of the class? (Think the Math class.)

Aha! Class methods! If you create a **public** method that is **static** (a class method) then that method is visible outside the class definition without having the object actually instantiated. So, if we create a class with a private constructor and then use a **static** method to create an instance of the class, you can control how many instances of the class you create. Here's the code:

```
public class Singleton {
        // this is the instance that will hang around
        private static Singleton uniqueInstance;
        // the private constructor - can't be accessed from outside
        private Singleton() {
                // do stuff here to initialize the instance
        }
        // here's the static method we'll use to create the instance
        public static Singleton getInstance() {
                if (uniqueInstance == null) {
                        uniqueInstance = new Singleton();
                }
                return uniqueInstance;
        }
        // Other methods - after all Singleton is a real class
}
```

and in order to use the Singleton class we'd do something like:

---

[5]Gamma et. al, 1995

```
public class SingletonTest {

        public static void main(String [] args) {
                Singleton mySingle;
                mySingle = Singleton.getInstance();
                // and we do other stuff here
        }
}
```

When we instantiate the Singleton instance by calling the getInstance() method, it will test to see if we've done this before. If not, it creates the instance using the private constructor in the Singleton class. If the instance already exists (the uniqueInstance variable is not **null**) then we just return the reference to the object. Told you it was simple.

This version of the Singleton pattern isn't without its problems; for one thing, it can fail if you are writing a multi-threaded Java program. The solution above is not "thread safe." It's possible that in between the test for the existing of a Singleton instance and the actual creation of an instance that your program could be swapped out while another thread executes. When it swaps back in, it could erroneously create another instance of the Singleton. There are relatively easy solutions to this.

The simplest way to make your Singleton pattern thread-safe is to make the getInstance() method a synchronized method. That way it will execute to completion and not be swapped out. Here's a version of the getInstance() method that is thread safe:

```
public synchronized static Singleton getInstance() {
        if (uniqueInstance == null) {
                uniqueInstance = new Singleton();
        }
        return uniqueInstance;
}
```

Notice that the only difference is the inclusion of the synchronized keyword in the method signature.

On to the next pattern.

The Factory Pattern

Say you've got a small company and your company is making ice cream. Because you're a small company, your factory can only make one type of ice cream at a time, so you have to tell the workers on any given day what kind of ice cream they're making that day. Of course, you don't change the different ice cream recipes every day, and you don't change the basic makeup of the factory every day, but you do change which ice cream is being manufactured, packaged, and shipped each day. And, of course, you have a program to model your factory. So the question is, how do you write the program in such a way that you don't have to change it every day? And how do you write it so you don't need to change (most) of it when you add a new ice cream flavor? That's where the Factory design pattern comes in.

A *Factory* pattern (also called a *Factory Method* pattern)[6] creates objects for you. You use it when you need to create several types of objects that are usually related to each other – they usually have the same abstract parent class - but are different. You ask the factory to create an object of type X and it creates one; you ask it to create an object of type Y and it creates one. This forces the creation of concrete classes

---

[6]Gamma, et. al, 1995.

142

to be relegated to subclasses of an interface that knows how to create concrete classes, and keeps your other classes closed for modification. All without changing X or Y or the factory. In our example we can create Vanilla, Chocolate, or Strawberry ice cream objects, using an IceCreamFactory class to generate the different types of ice cream. The Factory pattern allows you to define an interface for creating a family of objects, and it allows subclasses to decide which members of the family to instantiate. It defers instantiation down into the subclasses.

In our example, we'll have several classes:

> *IceCream*: An interface that defines our ice cream objects

> VanillaIceCream: A concrete class that inherits from *IceCream*

> ChocolateIceCream: A concrete class that inherits from *IceCream*

> StrawberryIceCream: A concrete class that inherits from *IceCream*

> *Factory*: An interface that defines the methods used to make *IceCream* objects

> IceCreamFactory: Our concrete implementation of the Factory interface that makes different *IceCream* objects

> IceCreamStore: A driver class that lets us make and sell ice cream

Our IceCream interface could look like:

```
public interface IceCream {
        public  void yummy();
        // plus other methods
}
```

and our ice cream flavors end up as concrete classes:

```
public class VanillaIceCream implements IceCream {
        public void yummy() {
                System.out.println("Vanilla!");
        }
}

public class ChocolateIceCream implements IceCream {
        public void yummy() {
                System.out.println("Chocolate!");
        }
}

public class StrawberryIceCream implements IceCream {
        public void yummy() {
                System.out.println("Strawberry!");
        }
}
```

The Factory pattern depends on defining an interface for the factory and then allowing subclasses that implement that interface to actually create the objects; our Factory interface will look something like the following:

```
public interface Factory {
        public  IceCream makeIceCream(String type);
```

```
        // and other methods here to sell, package and transport
        // the ice cream
}
```

And finally, our concrete *IceCreamFactory* which will implement the *makeIceCream()* method from the *Factory* interface and actually make an IceCream object looks like this:

```
public class IceCreamFactory implements Factory {
        public IceCream makeIceCream(String type) {
                IceCream newIceCream = null;
                if (type.equals("Vanilla")) {
                        newIceCream = new VanillaIceCream();
                } else if (type.equals("Chocolate")) {
                        newIceCream = new ChocolateIceCream();
                } else if (type.equals("Strawberry")) {
                        newIceCream = new StrawberryIceCream();
                }
                return newIceCream;
        }
}
```

In order to test our factory we create a driver – our ice cream store!

```
public class IceCreamStore {
        public static void main (String [] args) {
                IceCreamFactory myStore = new IceCreamFactory();
                IceCream vanilla = myStore.makeIceCream("Vanilla");
                vanilla.yummy();
                IceCream choco = myStore.makeIceCream("Chocolate");
                choco.yummy();
                IceCream straw = myStore.makeIceCream("Strawberry");
                straw.yummy();
        }
}
```

Figure 11-1 shows what these look like in a version of UML.

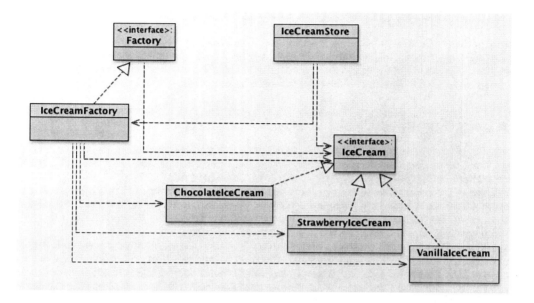

Figure 11-1. The Ice Cream Store using an IceCreamFactory

What to notice about this Factory pattern example? Well, how about the following:

- The factory method (*makeIceCream()*) encapsulates the creation of the IceCream object. Our driver just tells the factory which ice cream to make.

- The *Factory* interface provides the interface for the subclasses to create the actual objects.

- The IceCreamFactory concrete class actually creates the objects by implementing the makeIceCream() method. This also implies that other concrete classes that implement Factory could do the same.

- This leaves the *IceCream* classes alone, and makes it easier for the IceCreamStore to create new objects.

- Notice also that the IceCreamStore class only deals with *IceCream* objects. It doesn't have to know anything about particular types of ice cream. The concrete *IceCream* objects implement the methods from the *IceCream* interface and the IceCreamStore just uses them regardless of which type of *IceCream* you've created.

- It also means that you can change the implementation of a particular type of *IceCream* without changing either the interface or the IceCreamStore. What a concept!

Structural Patterns

Structural patterns help you put objects together so you can use them more easily. They are all about grouping objects together and providing ways for objects to coordinate to get work done. Remember, composition, aggregation, delegation, and inheritance are all about structure and coordination. The Structural pattern we'll look at here – the Adapter – is all about getting classes to work together.

The Adapter Pattern

So here's the problem. You've got a client program Foo that wants to access another class or library or package, Bar. The problem is, Foo is expecting a particular interface and that interface is different from the public interface that Bar presents to the world. What are you to do?

Well, you could rewrite Foo to change the interface it expects to conform to the interface that Bar is presenting. But if Foo is large, or if it's being used by other classes, that may not be a viable possibility. Or you could rewrite Bar, so it presents the interface that Foo is expecting. But maybe Bar is a commercial package and you don't have the source code?

That's where the Adapter design pattern comes in.[7] You use the Adapter pattern to create an intermediate class that wraps the Bar interface inside a set of methods that presents the interface that Foo is looking for. Here's the idea: the Adapter can interface with Foo on one side and with Bar on the other. So the interface to Bar doesn't have to change, and Foo users gets the interface they expects. Everyone is happy! By the way, the Adapter design pattern is also called the *Wrapper* pattern because it wraps an interface.[8] See Figure 11-2.

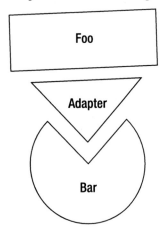

Figure 11-2. The Adapter lets Foo use Bar

There are two ways to implement adapters: *class adapters*, where the adapter will inherit from the target class, and *object adapters* that use delegation to create the adapter. Note the difference: a c*lass*

---

[7]Gamma et. al, 1995.
[8]Gamma et. al, 1995.

adapter subclasses an existing class and implements a target interface. An *object adapter* subclasses a target class and delegates to an existing class. Figure 11-3 is the UML for a generic class adapter.

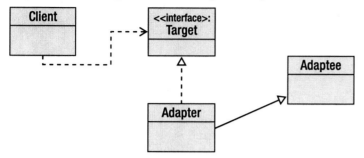

Figure 11-3. A class adapter example

Note that the Adapter class inherits from the Adaptee class and implements the same Target interface that the Client class uses. Here's the code for this example:

```java
public class Client
{
    public static void main(String [] args) {
        Target myTarget = new Adapter();

        System.out.println(myTarget.sampleMethod(12));
    }
}

public interface Target
{
    int sampleMethod(int y);
}

public class Adapter extends Adaptee implements Target
{
    public int sampleMethod(int y) {
        return myMethod(y);
    }
}

public class Adaptee
{
    public Adaptee() {
    }

    public int myMethod(int y) {
        return y * y;
    }
}
```

The object adapter, on the other hand still implements the Target interface, but uses composition with the Adaptee class in order to accomplish the wrapping; it will look like:

```
public class Adapter implements Target
{
    Adaptee myAdaptee = new Adaptee();

    public int sampleMethod(int y) {
        return myAdaptee.myMethod(y);
    }
}
```

In both cases, the Client doesn't have to change! That's the beauty of Adapter. You can change which Adaptee you're using, by changing the Adapter and not the Client.

Behavioral Patterns

Where creational patterns are all about how to create new objects, and structural patterns are all about getting objects to communicate and cooperate, behavioral patterns are all about getting objects to do things. They examine how responsibilities are distributed in the design and how communication happens between objects. The three patterns we'll look at here all describe how to assign behavioral responsibilities to classes. The Iterator pattern is about how to traverse a collection of objects. The Observer pattern tells us how to manage push and pull state changes. The Strategy pattern lets us select different behaviors behind a single interface.

The Iterator Pattern

If you've programmed in Java, you have seen iterators. We'll get to that, but let's start at the beginning. If you have a *collection of elements*, you can organize them in many different ways. They can be arrays, linked lists, queues, hash tables, sets, and so on. Each of these collections will have its own unique set of operations, but there's usually one operation that you might want to perform on all of them – *traverse the entire collection from beginning to end, one element at a time*. Oh, and you want to traverse the elements in such a way that *you don't need to know the internal structure of the collection*. And you may want to be able to traverse the collection backwards, and you may want to have several traversals going on at the same time.

That's what the Iterator pattern is for.[9] The Iterator pattern creates an object that allows you to traverse a collection, one element at a time.

Because of the requirement that you don't need to know about the internal structure of the collection, an Iterator object doesn't care about sorting order; it just returns each object as it's stored in the collection, one at a time from first to last. The simplest iterator needs just two methods

- *hasNext()*: Which returns a true if there is an element to be retrieved, i.e. we've not reached the end of the collection yet; and false if there's no elements left.

- *getNextElement()*: Which returns the next element in the collection.

---

[9]Gamma et. al, 1995.

In the Iterator Pattern, we have an Iterator interface that is implemented to make a concrete Iterator object that is used by a concrete Collections object. Both of these are used by a client that creates the Collection and gets the iterator from there. Figure 11-4 is the UML version of this from Gamma et. al.

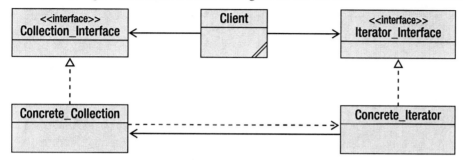

Figure 11-4. An example of using the Iterator Pattern

You can see that the client class uses the Collection and the Iterator interfaces, and the `Concrete_Iterator` is part of and uses the `Concrete_Collection`. Note that the `Collection_Interface` will contain an abstract method to create an iterator for the Collection. This method is implemented in the `Concrete_Collection` class and when the client calls the method, a `Concrete_Iterator` is created and passed to the client to use.

Starting in version 1.2, Java contained the **Java Collections Framework** (JCF) that included a number of new classes and interfaces to allow you to create collections of objects, including an ***Iterator*** interface. All of these new types contained iterators. Java even included (just for collections of type List) an expanded Iterator called a ***ListIterator***. With the ListIterator you can go backwards through the list.

Typical Iterator code in Java using both the *Iterator* and the *ListIterator* implementations:

```
/**
 * Iterate through elements Java ArrayList using an Iterator
 * We then use ListIterator to go backwards through the same
 * ArrayList
 */

import java.util.ArrayList;
import java.util.Iterator;
import java.util.ListIterator;

public class ArrayListIterator {
    public static void main(String[] args) {
        //create an ArrayList object
        ArrayList<Integer> arrayList = new ArrayList<Integer>();
        //Add elements to Arraylist
        arrayList.add(1);
        arrayList.add(3);
        arrayList.add(5);
        arrayList.add(7);
        arrayList.add(11);
        arrayList.add(13);
        arrayList.add(17);
```

```
    //get an Iterator object for ArrayList

    Iterator iter = arrayList.iterator();

    System.out.println("Iterating through ArrayList elements");
    while(iter.hasNext()) {
        System.out.println(iter.next());
    }

    ListIterator list_iter = arrayList.listIterator(arrayList.size());

    System.out.println("Iterating through ArrayList backwards");
    while(list_iter.hasPrevious()) {
        System.out.println(list_iter.previous());
    }
  }
}
```

Note that when we create the *ListIterator* object, we pass it the number of elements in the *ArrayList*. This is to set the cursor that the *ListIterator* object uses to point to just past the last element in the *ArrayList* so it can then look backwards using the *hasPrevious()* method. In both the *Iterator* and *ListIterator* implementations in Java, the *cursor* always points between two elements so that the *hasNext()* and *hasPrevious()* method calls make sense; for example, when you say *iter.hasNext()*, you're asking the iterator if there is a next element in the collection. Figure 11-5 is the abstraction of what the cursors look like.

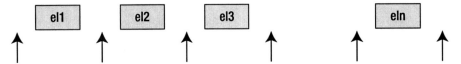

Figure 11-5. Cursors in the Iterator Abstraction

Finally, some iterators will allow you to insert and delete elements in the collection while the iterator is running. These are called *robust iterators*. The Java *ListIterator* interface (not the *Iterator*) allows both insertion (via the *add()* method) and deletion (via the *remove()* method) in an iterator with restrictions. The *add()* method only adds to the position immediately before the one that would be the next element retrieved by a *next()* or immediately after the next element that would be returned by a *previous()* method call. The *remove()* method can only be called between successive *next()* or *previous()* method calls, it can't be called twice in a row, and never immediately after an *add()* method call.

The Observer Pattern

I love NPR's *Talk of the Nation: Science Friday* radio show (http://sciencefriday.com). But I hardly get to listen to it when it is broadcast because it's on from 2:00–4:00 PM EST on Fridays and, because I work for a living (snicker), I can't listen to it then. But I subscribe to the podcast and so every Saturday morning I get a new podcast of *SciFri* so I can listen to it on my iPod while I mow the lawn. If I ever get tired of *SciFri*, I can just unsubscribe and I won't get any new podcasts. That, ladies and gentlemen, is the *Observer Pattern*.

According to the Gang of Four, the Observer Pattern "...defines a one-to-many dependency between objects so that when one object changes state, all of its dependents are notified and updated automatically."[10] So in my SciFri example, NPR is the "publisher" of the SciFri podcast, and all of us who "subscribe" (or register) to the podcast are the observers. We wait for the *SciFri* state to change (a new podcast gets created) and then we get updated automatically by the publisher. How the updates happen differentiates between two different types of Observer – push and pull. In a *push Observer*, the Publisher (also known as the Subject in object-oriented speak) changes state and then *pushes* the new state out to all the Observers. In a *pull Observer*, the Subject changes state, but doesn't provide a full update until the Observers ask for it – they *pull* the update from the Subject. In a variation of the *pull* model, the Subject may provide a minimal update to all the Observers notifying them that the state has changed, but the Observers still need to ask for the details of the new state.

So with the Observer pattern, we need a Subject interface so that the Subject and the Observer and the Client all can tell what the state interface they're using is. We also need an Observer interface that just tells us how to update an Observer. Our publisher will then implement the Subject interface and the different "listeners" will implement the Observer interface. Figure 11-6 is a UML diagram of this.

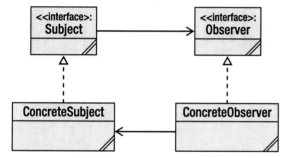

Figure 11-6. The canonical Observer Pattern

The client class is missing, but it will use both the ConcreteSubject and ConcreteObserver classes. Here's a simple implementation of a *push model* version of all of these. Remember, it's *push model* because the *ConcreteSubject* object is notifying all the *Observers* whether they request it or not.

First, the Subject interface that tells us how to register, remove, and notify the Observers.

```
public interface Subject
{
    public void addObserver(Observer obs);
    public void removeObserver(Observer obs);
    public void notifyAllObservers();
}
```

Next, the implementation of the Subject interface. This class is the real publisher, so it also needs the attributes that form the state of the Subject. In this simple version we use an *ArrayList* to hold all the Observers.

```
import java.util.ArrayList;
```

---

[10]Gamma et. al, 1995.

```java
public class ConcreteSubject implements Subject
{
    private ArrayList<Observer> observerList;
        // these two variables are our state
    private int foo;
    private String bar;

    public ConcreteSubject() {
        observerList = new ArrayList<Observer>();
        this.foo = 0;
        this.bar = "Hello";
    }

    public void addObserver(Observer obs) {
        observerList.add(obs);
    }

    public void removeObserver(Observer obs) {
        observerList.remove(obs);
    }

    public void notifyAllObservers() {
        for (Observer obs: observerList) {
            obs.update(this.foo, this.bar);
            }
    }

    public void setState(int foo, String bar) {
        this.foo = foo;
        this.bar = bar;
        notifyAllObservers();
    }
}
```

Next, the Observer interface that tells us how to update our Observers.

```java
public interface Observer
{
    public void update(int foo, String bar);
}
```

And then the implementation of the Observer interface.

```java
public class ConcreteObserver implements Observer
{
    private int foo;
    private String bar;
    Subject subj;

    /**
     * Constructor for objects of class ConcreteObserver
     */
    public ConcreteObserver(Subject subj) {
```

```
            this.subj = subj;
            subj.addObserver(this);
    }

    public void update(int foo, String bar)
    {
            this.foo = foo;
            this.bar = bar;
            show();
    }

    private void show() {
            System.out.printf("Foo = %s Bar = %s\n", this.foo, this.bar);
    }
}
```

And finally, the driver program that creates the publisher and each of the observers and puts them all together.

```
public class ObserverDriver
{
    public static void main(String [] args) {
        ConcreteSubject subj = new ConcreteSubject();

        ConcreteObserver obj = new ConcreteObserver(subj);

        subj.setState(12, "Monday");
        subj.setState(17, "Tuesday");
    }
}
```

And the output of executing the driver (which all comes from the show() method in the ConcreteObserver object will look like:

```
Foo = 12 Bar = Monday

Foo = 17 Bar = Tuesday
```

In many ways, the Observer design pattern works like the Java events interface. In Java you create a class that registers as a "listener" (our Observer) for a particular event type. You also create a method that is the actual observer and which will respond when the event occurs. When an event of that type occurs, the Java events object (our Subject) notifies your observer by making a call to the method you wrote, passing the data from the event to the observer method – Java events use the *push model* of the Observer pattern.

For example, if you create a *Button* object in a Java program, you use the *addActionListener()* method of the *Button* object to register to observe *ActionEvent*s. When an *ActionEvent* occurs all the *ActionListener*s are notified by having a method named *actionPerformed()* called. This means that your *Button* object must implement the *actionPerformed()* method to handle the event.

The Strategy Pattern

Sometimes you have an application where you have several ways of doing a single operation or you have several different behaviors, each with a different interface. One of the ways to implement something like this is using a `switch` statement like so:

```
switch (selectBehavior) {
        case Behavior1:
                Algorithm1.act(foo);
                break;
        case Behavior2:
                Algorithm2.act(foo, bar);
                break;
        case Behavior3:
                Algorithm3.act(1, 2, 3);
                break;
}
```

The problem with this type of construct it that if you add another behavior, you need to change this code and potentially all the other code that has to select different behaviors. Not good.

The Strategy design pattern gets you around this. It says that if you have several behaviors (algorithms) you need to select from dynamically, you should make sure that they all adhere to the same interface – a `Strategy` interface – and then that they are selected dynamically via a driver, called the `Context`, that is told which to call by the client software. The Strategy pattern embodies two of our fundamental object-oriented design principles—*encapsulate the idea that varies* and *code to an interface, not an implementation.* Figure 11-7 is what a Strategy setup will look like.

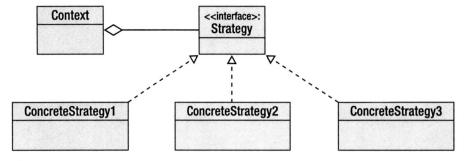

Figure 11-7. A typical Strategy Pattern layout

Some examples of when you might use the Strategy pattern are

- Capture video using different compression algorithms

- Compute taxes for different types of entities (people, corporations, non-profits)

- Plot data in different formats (line graphs, pie charts, bar graphs)

- Compress audio files using different formats

In each of these examples you can think of having the application program telling a driver – the `Context` – which of the strategies to use and then asking the Context to perform the operation.

As an example, let's say you are a newly minted CPA and you're trying to write your own software to compute your customers tax bills. (Why a CPA would write her own tax program, I have no idea; work with me on this.) Initially, you've divided your customers into individuals who only file personal income taxes, corporations who file corporate income taxes, and not-for-profit organizations who file hardly any taxes at all. Now, all of these groups have to compute taxes so the behavior of a class to compute taxes should be the same for all; but they'll compute taxes in different ways. So what we need is a Strategy setup that will use the same interface – to encapsulate what varies in our application, and to code the concrete classes to an interface – and allow our client class to select which type of tax customer to use. Figure 11-8 is a diagram of what our program will look like.

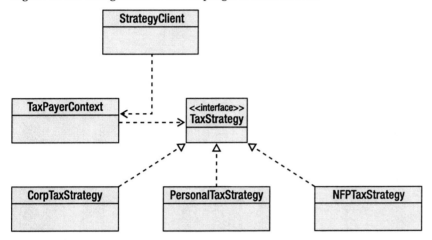

Figure 11-8. Using the Strategy pattern to select a Tax behavior

We create a TaxStrategy interface that all the concrete TaxStrategy classes will implement.

```
public interface TaxStrategy {
  public double computeTax(double income);
}
```

Since the only thing that varies here is how the tax is computed, our TaxStrategy interface just includes the *computeTax()* method.

Then we create each of the concrete TaxStrategy classes, each of which implement the tax computation for that particular type of customer

```
public class PersonalTaxStrategy implements TaxStrategy {
    private final double RATE = 0.25;

    public double computeTax(double income) {
        if (income <= 25000.0) {
            return income * (0.75 * RATE);
        } else {
            return income * RATE;
        }
    }
}
```

```
public class CorpTaxStrategy implements TaxStrategy {

    private final double RATE = 0.45;

    public double computeTax(double income) {
        return income * RATE ;
    }
}

public class NFPTaxStrategy implements TaxStrategy {
    private final double RATE = 0.0;

    public double computeTax(double income) {
        return income * RATE;
    }
}
```

Next, we create the Context class that does the heavy lifting of creating strategy objects requested by the client program and executing the correct ones.

```
public class TaxPayerContext {
    private TaxStrategy strategy;
    private double income;
    /** constructor for Context */
    public TaxPayerContext(TaxStrategy strategy, double income) {
        this.strategy = strategy;
        this.income = income;
    }
    public double getIncome() {
        return income;
    }
    public void setIncome(double income) {
        this.income = income;
    }
    public TaxStrategy getStrategy() {
        return strategy;
    }
    public void setStrategy(TaxStrategy strategy) {
        this.strategy = strategy;
    }
    public double computeTax() {
        return strategy.computeTax(income);
    }
}
```

Note that here we write a separate version of the *computeTax()* method (we're not overriding the method because we're not extending any of the concrete classes – the Strategy pattern uses composition, not inheritance). This version calls the *computeTax()* method of the strategy that the client has selected.

Finally, we implement the client that controls who gets instantiated and when.

```
public class StrategyClient {
        public static void main(String [] args) {
                double income;
```

```
        TaxPayerContext tp;

        income = 35000.00;
        tp = new TaxPayerContext(new PersonalTaxStrategy(),
                                                          income);

        System.out.println("Tax is " + tp.computeTax());

        tp.setStrategy(new CorpTaxStrategy());
        System.out.println("Tax is " + tp.computeTax());
    }
}
```

The client class selects which algorithm to use and then gets the context object to execute it. This way we've encapsulated the tax computation in separate classes. We can easily add new customer types just by adding new concrete TaxStrategy classes and making the change in the client to use that new concrete type. Piece of cake!

Conclusion

Design Patterns are a reusable, commonly occurring core solution to a design problem. They are not a finished design. Rather a design pattern is a template you can use to solve similar problems in many different domains. Design patterns offer you proven strategies for solving common proglems and so they can help speed up your design process. And because these patterns describe *proven solutions* they can help reduce defects in your design as well.

Be careful, though. Like all design techniques, design patterns are heuristics and so there will be cases where they just don't fit. Trying to squeeze a pattern into a problem where it just doesn't belong is adking for trouble.

The goal of design patterns is to define a common vocabulary for design. They may not get us all the way there but design patterns, plus the design principles described in Chapter 10, get us a long way down that road.

References

Alexander, C., S. Ishikawa, et al. *A Pattern Language: Towns, Buildings, Construction.* (Oxford, UK: Oxford University Press, 1977.)

Freeman, E. and E. Freeman *Head First Design Patterns.* (Sebastopol, CA: O'Reilly Media, Inc., 2004.)

Gamma, E., Helm, R., Johnson, R., Vlissides. *Design Patterns: Elements of Reusable Object-Oriented Software.* (Boston, MA: Addison-Wesley, 1995.)

Krasner, G. E. and S. T. Pope. "A cookbook for using the Model-View-Controller user interface paradigm in Smalltalk-80." *Journal of Object-Oriented Programming* 1(3): 26-49. 1988.

Lieberherr, K., I. Holland, et al. *Object-Oriented Programming: An Objective Sense of Style.* OOPSLA '88, Association for Computing Machinery, 1988.

Martin, R. C. *Agile Software Development: Principles, Patterns, and Practices.* (Upper Saddle River, NJ: Prentice Hall, 2003.)

Code Construction

Mostly, when you see programmers, they aren't doing anything. One of the attractive things about programmers is that you cannot tell whether or not they are working simply by looking at them. Very often they're sitting there seemingly drinking coffee and gossiping, or just staring into space. What the programmer is trying to do is get a handle on all the individual and unrelated ideas that are scampering around in his head.

—Charles M. Strauss

Great software, likewise, requires a fanatical devotion to beauty. If you look inside good software, you find that parts no one is ever supposed to see are beautiful too. I'm not claiming I write great software, but I know that when it comes to code I behave in a way that would make me eligible for prescription drugs if I approached everyday life the same way. It drives me crazy to see code that's badly indented, or that uses ugly variable names.

—Paul Graham, "Hackers and Painters," 2003

Well, finally we're getting to the real heart of software development – writing the code. The assumption here is that you already *do* know how to write code in at least one programming language; this chapter presents examples in a few languages, each chosen for the appropriate point being made. The purpose of this chapter is to provide some tips for writing *better* code. Because we can all write better code.

For plan-driven process folks (see Chapter 2), coding is the tail that wags the development-process dog. Once you finish detailed requirements, architecture, and detailed design, the code should just flow out of the final design, right? Not. In 20 years of industry software development experience, I never saw this happen. Coding is hard; translating even a good, detailed design into code takes a lot of thought, experience, and knowledge, even for small programs. Depending on the programming language you are using and the target system, programming can be a very time-consuming and difficult task. On the other hand, for very large projects that employ dozens or even hundreds of developers, having a very detailed design is critical to success, so don't write off the plan-driven process just yet.

For the agile development process folks, coding is it. The agile manifesto (`http://agilemanifesto.org`) says it at the very beginning, "Working software over comprehensive documentation." Agile developers favor creating code early and often; they believe in delivering software to their customers frequently, and using feedback from the customers to make the code better. They welcome changes in requirements and see them as an opportunity to refactor the code and make the product more usable for their customer. This doesn't mean that coding gets any easier when using an agile process; it means that your focus is different. Rather than focus on requirements and design and getting them nailed down as early as possible, in agile processes you focus on delivering working code to your customer as quickly and as often as possible. You change the code often, and the entire team owns all the code and so has permission to change anything if it's appropriate.

Your code has two audiences:

- The machine that's the target of the compiled version of the code, what will actually get executed.

- The people, including yourself, who will *read* it in order to understand it and modify it.

To those ends, your code needs to fulfill the requirements, implement the design, and also be readable and easy to understand. We'll be focusing on the readability and understandability parts of these ends first, and then look at some issues related to performance and process. This chapter will not give you all the hints, tips, and techniques for writing great code; there are entire books for that, some of which are in the references at the end of this chapter. Good luck!

Before we continue, I'd be remiss if I didn't suggest the two best books on coding around. The first is Steve McConnell's *Code Complete 2: A Practical Handbook of Software Construction*, a massive, 960-page, tome that takes you through what makes good code.[1] McConnell discusses everything from variable names, to function organization, to code layout, to defensive programming, to controlling loops. It is in McConnell's book where the "software construction" metaphor comes from. The metaphor suggests that building a software application is similar to constructing a building. Small buildings (Fido's dog house, for example) are easier to build, require less planning, and are easier to change (refactor) if something goes wrong. Larger buildings (your house) require more detail, more planning, and more coordination largely because it's more than a one-person job. Really big buildings (skyscrapers) require many detailed levels of both design and planning, close coordination, and many processes to handle change and errors. Although the building construction model isn't perfect – it doesn't handle incremental development well and McConnell also talks about an accretion model where one layer of software is added to an existing layer much like a pearl is created in an oyster – the metaphor gives you a clear view of the idea that software gets much more complicated and difficult to build, the larger it gets.

The second classic book is Hunt and Thomas', *The Pragmatic Programmer*.[2] The book is organized as 46 short sections containing 70 tips that provide a clear vision of how you should act as a programmer. It provides practical advice on a range of topics from source code control, to testing, to assertions, to the DRY principle, some of which we'll cover later in this chapter. Hunt and Thomas themselves do the best job of describing what the book and what pragmatic programming is all about,

Programming is a craft. At its simplest, it comes down to getting a computer to do what you want it to do (or what your user wants it to do). As a programmer, you are

---

[1] McConnell, S. *Code Complete 2: A Practical Handbook of Software Construction*. Redmond, WA, Microsoft Press, 2004).

[2] Hunt, A. and D. Thomas. *The Pragmatic Programmer: From Journeyman to Master*. (Boston, MA: Addison-Wesley, 2000).

part listener, part advisor, part interpreter, and part dictator. You try to capture elusive requirements and find a way of expressing them so that a mere machine can do them justice. You try to document your work so that others can understand it, and you try to engineer your work so that others can build on it. What's more, you try to do all this against the relentless ticking of the project clock. You work small miracles every day. It's a difficult job.[3]

A coding example

In *Code Complete,* Steve McConnell gives an example of bad code that is worth examining so we can begin to see what the issues of readability, usability, and understandability are about. I've converted it from C++ to Java, but the example is basically McConnell's.[4] Here's the code; we'll look for what's wrong with it.

```
void HandleStuff(CORP_DATA inputRec, int crntQtr, EMP_DATA empRec, Double estimRevenue,
    double ytdRevenue, int screenx, int screeny, Color newColor, Color prevColor, StatusType
    status, int expenseType) {
int i;
for ( i = 0; i < 100; i++ )
        {
        inputRec.revenue[i] = 0;
        inputRec.expense[i] = corpExpense[crntQtr][i];
        }
UpdateCorpDatabase( empRec );
estimRevenue = ytdRevenue * 4.0 / (double) crntQtr;
newColor = prevColor;
status = SUCCESS;
if ( expenseType == 1 ) {
        for ( i = 0; i < 12; i++ )
                profit[i] = revenue[i] - expense.type1[i];
        }
else if ( expenseType == 2 ) {
                profit[i] = revenue[i] - expense.type2[i];
        }
else if ( expenseType == 3 )
                profit[i] = revenue[i] - expense.type3[i];
                }
```

So what's wrong with this code? Well, what isn't? Let's make a list

- Because this is Java, it should have a *visibility modifier.* No, it's not required, but you should always put one in. You are not writing for the compiler here, you are writing for the human. Visibility modifiers make things explicit for the human reader.

---

[3] Hunt, 2000.
[4] McConnell, 2004, p. 162.

- The method name is terrible. HandleStuff doesn't tell you anything about what the method does.

- Oh, and the method does too many things. It seems to compute something called profit based on an expenseType. But it also seems to change a color and indicate a success. Methods should be small. They should do just one thing.

- Where are the comments? There is no indication of what the parameters are or what the method is supposed to do. All methods should tell you at least that.

- The layout is just awful. And it's not consistent. The indentation is wrong. Sometimes the curly braces are part of the statement, and sometimes they're separators. And are you sure that that last right curly brace really ends the method?

- The method doesn't protect itself from bad data. If the crntQtr variable is zero, then the division in line 8 will return a divide-by-zero exception.

- The method uses magic numbers including 100, 4.0, 12, 2, and 3. Where do they come from? What do they mean? Magic numbers are bad.

- The method has way too many input parameters. If we knew what the method was supposed to do maybe we could change this.

- There are also at least two input parameters – screenx and screeny – that aren't used at all. This is an indication of poor design; this method's interface may be used for more than one purpose and so it is "fat," meaning it has to accommodate all the possible uses.

- The variables corpExpense and profit are not declared inside the method, so they are either instance variables or class variables. This can be dangerous. Because instance and class variables are visible inside every method in the class, we can also change their values inside any method, generating a side effect. Side effects are bad.

- Finally, the method doesn't consistently adhere to the Java naming conventions. Tsk, tsk.

So this example is terrible code for a bunch of different reasons. In the rest of the chapter we'll take a look at the general coding rules that are violated here and give suggestions for how to make your code correct, readable, and maintainable.

Functions and Methods and Size, Oh My!

First things first. Your classes, functions, and methods should all *do just one thing*. This is the fundamental idea behind encapsulation. Having your methods do just one thing isolates errors and makes them easier to find. It encourages re-use because small, single feature methods are easier to use in different classes. Single feature (and single layer of abstraction) classes are also easier to re-use.

Single feature implies small. Your methods/functions should be small. And I mean small – 20 lines of executable code is a good upper bound for a function. Under no circumstances should you write 300 line functions. I know, I've done it. It's not pretty. Back in Chapter 7 we talked about *stepwise refinement* and *modular decomposition*. Taking an initial function definition and re-factoring it so that it does just a single small thing will decompose your function into two or more smaller, easier to understand and easier to maintain functions. Oh, and as we'll see in Chapter 14, smaller functions are easier to test because they require fewer unit tests (they have fewer ways to get through the code). As the book said, *Small is Beautiful.*

Formatting, Layout, and Style

Formatting, layout, and style are all related to how your code looks on the page. It turns out that, as we saw above, that how your code looks on the page is also related to its correctness. McConnell's *Fundamental Theorem of Formatting* says "good visual layout shows the logical structure of a program."[5] Good visual layout not only makes the program more readable, it helps reduce the number of errors because it shows how the program is structured. The converse is also true; a good logical structure is easier to read. So the objectives of good layout and formatting should be

- to accurately represent the logical structure of your program;

- to be consistent so there are few exceptions to whatever style of layout you've chosen;

- to improve readability for humans; and

- to be open to modifications. (You do know you're code is going to be modified, right?)

General Layout Issues and Techniques

Most layout issues have to do with laying out blocks of code; there are different types of block layout, some of which are built into languages, some you get to choose on your own. The three most prevalent kinds of block layouts are built-in block boundaries, begin-end block boundaries, and emulating built-in blocks.

Some languages have built-in block boundaries for every control structure in the language. In this case you have no choice; because the block boundary element is a language feature you must use it. Languages that have built-in block boundaries include Ada, PL/1, Lisp and Scheme, and Visual Basic. As an example, an if-then statement in Visual Basic looks like

```
if income > 25000 then
        statement1
        statement2
else
        statement3
        ...
end if
```

You can't write a control structure in Visual Basic without using the ending block element, so blocks are easier to find and distinguish.

But, most languages don't have built-in block boundary lexical elements. Most languages use a begin-end block boundary requirement. With this requirement, a block is a sequence of zero or more statements (where a statement has a particular definition) that is delimited by *begin* and *end* lexical

---

[5] McConnell, 2004.

elements. The most typical begin and end elements are the keywords **begin** and **end**, or left and right curly braces **{** and **}**. So, for example

Pascal:

```
if income > 25000 then
        begin
                statement1;
                statement2
        end
else
        statement3;
```

C/C++/Java:

```
if (income > 25000)
{
        statement1;
        statement2;
} else
        statement3;
```

Note in both examples that a single statement is considered a block and does not require the block delimiter elements. Note also in Pascal the semi-colon is the statement *separator* symbol, so is required between statements, but because **else** and **end** are not the end of a statement, you don't use a semi-colon right before **else** or **end** (confused? most people are); in C, C++, and Java, the semi-colon is the statement *terminator* symbol, and must be at the end of every statement. This is easier to remember and write; you just pretty much put a semi-colon everywhere except after curly braces. Simplicity is good.

Finally, when we format a block we can try to emulate the built-in block boundary in languages that don't have it by requiring that every block use the block delimiter lexical elements.

C/C++/Java:

```
if (income > 25000) {
        statement1;
        statement2;
} else {
        statement3;
}
```

In this example, we want to pretend that the left and right curly braces are part of the control structure syntax, and so we use them to delimit the block, no matter how large it is. To emphasize that the block delimiter is part of the control structure, we put it on the same line as the beginning of the control statement. We can then line up the closing block boundary element with the beginning of the control structure. This isn't a perfect emulation of the built-in block element language feature, but it comes pretty close and has the advantage that you're less likely to run into problems with erroneous indentation like the following:

C/C++/Java:

```
if (income > 25000)
```

```
        statement1;
        statement2;
        statement3;
```

In this example, the erroneous indentation for statement2 and statement3 can lead the reader to believe that they are part of the if statement. The compiler is under no such illusions.

Overall, using an emulating block-boundaries style works very well, is readable, and clearly illustrates the logical structure of your program. It's also a great idea to put block boundaries around every block, including just single statement blocks. That lets you eliminate the possibility of the erroneous indentation error above. So if you say

```
if (income > 25000) {
        statement1;
}
```

it's then clear that in

```
if (income > 25000) {
        statement1;
}
        statement2;
        statement3;
```

that statement2 and statement3 are not part of the block, regardless of their indentation. It also means that you can now safely add extra statements to the block without worrying about whether they are in the block or not

```
if (income > 25000) {
        statement1;
        statement2;
        statement3;
        statement4;
        statement5;
}
```

White Space

White space is your friend. You wouldn't write a book with no spaces between words, or line breaks between paragraphs, or no chapter divisions, would you? Then why would you write code with no white space? White space allows you to logically separate parts of the program and to line up block separators and other lexical elements. It also lets your eyes rest between parts of the program. Resting your eyes is a good thing. The following are some suggestions on the use of white space:

- Use blank lines to separate groups (just like paragraphs).

- Within a block align all the statements to the same tab stop (the default tab width is normally four spaces).

- Use indentation to show the logical structure of each control structure and block.

- Use spaces around operators.

- In fact, use spaces around array references and function/method arguments as well.

- Do not use double indentation with begin-end block boundaries.

Block and Statement Style Guidelines

As mentioned previously, the "emulating block boundaries" style works well for most block-structured languages.

- Use more parentheses than you think you'll need. I especially use parentheses around all my arithmetic expressions – mostly just to make sure I haven't screwed up the precedence rules.

```
fx = ((a + b) * (c + d)) / e;
```

- Format single statement blocks consistently. Using the emulating block-boundaries technique:

```
if (average > MIN_AVG) {
    avg = MIN_AVG;
}
```

- For complicated conditional expressions, put separate conditions on separate lines.

```
if (('0' <= inChar && inChar <= '9') ||
    ('a' <= inChar && inChar <= 'z') ||
    ('A' <= inChar && inChar <= 'Z')) {
        mytext.addString(inChar);
        mytext.length++;
}
```

- Wrap individual statements at column 70 or so. This is a holdover from the days of 80-column punch cards, but it's also a great way to make your code more readable. Having very long lines of code forces your readers to scroll horizontally, or it makes them forget what the heck was at the beginning of the line!

- Don't use goto, no matter what Don Knuth says.[6] Some languages, like Java, don't even have goto statements. Most don't need them (assembly languages excepted). Take the spirit of Knuth's paper and only use gotos where they make real sense and make your program more readable and understandable.

- Use only one statement per line. (Do not write code as if you were entering the annual International Obfuscated C Code Contest! www.ioccc.org.) This

```
g.setColor(Color.blue); g.fillOval(100, 100, 200, 200);
mytext.addString(inChar);mytext.length++;System.out.println();
```

- is legal, but just doesn't look good, and it's easy to just slide right over that statement in the middle. This

---

[6] Knuth, D. "Structured Programming with goto Statements." *ACM Computing Surveys* 6(4): 261-301. 1974.

```
g.setColor(Color.blue);
g.fillOval(100, 100, 200, 200);

mytext.addString(inChar);
mytext.length++;
System.out.println();
```

- looks much, much better.

Declaration Style Guidelines

Just like in writing executable code, your variable declarations need to be neat and readable.

- Use only one declaration per line. Well, I go both ways on this one. While I think that

```
int max,min,top,left,right,average,bottom,mode;
```

- is a bit crowded; I'd rewrite this as

```
int max, min;
int top, bottom;
int left, right;
int average, mode;
```

- Not one per line, but the variables that are related are grouped together. That makes more sense to me.

- Declare variables close to where they are used. Most procedural and object-oriented programming languages have a *declaration before use* rule, requiring that you declare a variable before you can use it in any expression. In the olden days, say in Pascal, you had to declare variables at the top of your program (or subprogram) and you couldn't declare variables inside blocks. This had the disadvantage that you might declare a variable pages and pages before you'd actually use it. (But see the section later in this chapter where I talk about how long your functions should be.)

    - These days you can normally declare variables in any block in your program. The scope of that variable is the block in which it is declared and all the blocks inside that block.

    - This tip says that it's a good idea to declare those variables in the closest block in which they are used. That way you can see the declaration and the use the variables *right there*.

- Order declarations sensibly

    - Group by types and usage (see the previous example).

    - Use white space to separate your declarations. Once again, white space is your friend. The key idea in these last couple of tips is to make your declarations visible and to keep them near the code where they will be used.

- Don't nest header files – ever! (This is for you C and C++ programmers.) Header files are designed so that you only need to define constants, declare global variables, and declare function prototypes once, and you can then re-use the header file in some (possibly large) number of source code files. Nesting header files hides some of those declarations inside the nested headers. This is bad – because visibility is good. It allows you to erroneously include a header file more than once, which leads to redefinitions of variables and macros and errors.

  The only header files you might nest in your own header files are system headers like stdio.h or stdlib.h and I'm not even sure I like that.

- Don't put source code in your header files – ever! (Again, this is for you C and C++ programmers.) Headers are for declarations, not for source code. Libraries are for source code. Putting a function in a header file means that the function will be re-defined every place you include the header. This can easily lead to multiple definitions – which the compiler may not catch until the link phase. The only source that should be in your headers are macro definitions in #define pre-processor statements and even those should be used carefully.

Commenting Style Guidelines

Just like white space, comments are your friend. Every programming book in existence tells you to put comments in your code – and none of them (including this one) tell you just where to put comments, and what a good comment should look like. That's because how to write good, informative comments falls in the "it depends" category of advice. A good, informative comment depends on the *context* in which you are writing it, so general advice is pretty useless. The only good advice about writing comments is – just do it. Oh, and since you'll change your code – do it again. That's the second hardest thing about comments – keeping them up to date. So here's my piece of advice, write comments when you first write your program. This gives you an idea of *where* they should be. Then, when you finish your unit testing of a particular function, write a final set of comments for that function by updating the ones that are already there. That way, you'll come pretty close to having an up-to-date set of comments in the released code.

- Indent a comment with its corresponding statement. This is important for readability because then the comment and the code line up.

```
/* make sure we have the right number of arguments */
if (argc < 2) {
    fprintf(stderr, "Usage: %s <filename>\n", argv[0]);
    exit(1);
}
```

- Set off block comments with blank lines. Well, I go both ways on this one. If you line up the start and end of the block comments on lines by themselves, then you don't need the blank lines. If, on the other hand, you stick the end of comment marker at the end of a line, you should use a blank line to set it apart from the source code. So if you do this

```
/*
 * make sure we have the right number of arguments
 * from the command line
 */
```

```c
if (argc < 2) {
    fprintf(stderr, "Usage: %s <filename>\n", argv[0]);
    exit(1);
}
```

- you don't need the blank line; but if you do

```c
/* make sure we have the right number of arguments
   from the command line */

if (argc < 2) {
    fprintf(stderr, "Usage: %s <filename>\n", argv[0]);
    exit(1);
}
```

- then you do (but I wouldn't recommend this style in the first place).

- Don't let comments wrap – use block comments instead. This usually occurs if you tack a comment onto the end of a line of source code

```c
if (argc < 2) { // make sure we have the right number of arguments from the
command line
```

- Don't do this. Make this a block comment above the if statement instead (see the bullet point above). It's just way easier to read.

- All functions/methods should have a header block comment. The purpose of this bit of advice is so that your reader knows what the method is supposed to do. The necessity of this is mitigated if you use good identifier names for the method name and the input parameters. Still, you should tell the user what the method is going to do and what the return values, if any are. See the tip below for the version of this advice for Java programmers. In C++ we can say:

```cpp
#include <string>
/*
 * getSubString() - get a substring from the input string.
 *  The substring starts at index start
 *  and goes up to but doesn't include index stop.
 *  returns the resulting substring.
 */
string getSubString(string str, int start, int stop) { }
```

- In Java use JavaDoc comments for all your methods. JavaDoc is built into the Java environment and all Java SDKs come with the program to generate JavaDoc web pages, so why not use it? JavaDoc can provide a nice overview of what your class is up to at very little cost. Just make sure and keep those comments up to date!

```java
/**
 * getSubString() - get a substring from the input string.
 *      The substring starts at index start
 *      and goes up to but doesn't include index stop.
 * @param str the input string
 * @param start the integer starting index
 * @param stop the integer stopping index
 * @return the resulting substring.
```

```
 */
String getSubString(String str, int start, int stop) { }
```

- Use fewer, but better comments. This is one of those useless motherhood and apple pie pieces of advice that everyone feels obliged to put in any discussion of comments. OK, so you don't need to comment ever line of code. Everyone knows that

```
index = index + 1;      // add one to index
```

  - is pretty stupid. So don't do it. Enough said.

- "Self-documenting code" is an ideal. Self documenting code is the Holy Grail of lazy programmers who don't want to take the time to explain their code to readers. Get over it. Self documenting code is the Platonic ideal of coding that assumes that everyone who reads your code can also read your mind. If you have an algorithm that's at all complicated, or input that is at all obscure, you need to explain it. Don't depend on the reader to grok every subtlety of your code. Explain it. Just do it.

Identifier Naming Conventions

As Rob Pike puts it so well in his terrific white paper on programming style, "Length is not a virtue in a name; clarity of expression *is*."[7] As Goldilocks would put it, you need identifier names that are not too long, not too short, but just right. Just like comments, this means different things to different people. Common sense and readability should rule.

- All identifiers should be descriptive.
  Remember, someday you may be back to look at your code again. Or, if you're working for a living, somebody else will be looking at your code. Descriptive identifiers make it much, much easier to read your code and figure out what you were trying to do at 3:00 AM. A variable called `interestRate` is much easier to understand than `ir`. Sure, `ir` is shorter and faster to type, but believe me, you'll forget what it stood for about 10 minutes after you ship that program. Reasonably descriptive identifiers can save you a lot of time and effort.

- `OverlyLongVariableNamesAreHardToRead` (and type)
  On the other hand, don't make your identifiers too long. For one thing they are hard to read, for another they don't really add anything to the context of your program, they use up too much space on the page, and finally, they're just plain ugly.

- `Andtheyareevenharderwhenyoudontincludeworddivisions`

---

[7] Pike, Rob, *Notes on Programming in C*, retrieved from
`http://www.literateprogramming.com/pikestyle.pdf` on 29 September 2010. 1999.

Despite what Rob Pike says [Pike80, p. 2], using camel case (those embedded capital letters that begin new words in your identifiers) can make your code easier to read. Especially if the identifier isn't overly long. At least to me, `maxPhysAddr` is easier to read than `maxphysaddr`.

- And single-letter variable names are cryptic, but useful.

Using single letter variable names for things like mortgage payments, window names, or graphics objects is not a good example of readability. M, w, and g don't mean anything even in the context of your code. `mortpmnt`, `gfxWindow`, `gfxObj` have more meaning. The big exception here is variables intended as index values – loop control variables and array index variables. Here, `i`, `j`, `k`, `l`, `m`, etc. are easily understandable, although I wouldn't argue about using `index`, or `indx` instead.

```
for (int i = 0; i < myArray.length; i++) {
    myArray[i] = 0;
}
```

- looks much better and is just as understandable as

```
for (int arrayIndex = 0; arrayIndex < myArray.length; arrayIndex++) {
    myArray[arrayIndex] = 0;
}
```

- Adhere to the programming language naming conventions when they exist.

  - Somewhere, sometime, you'll run into a document called Style Guide or something like that. Nearly every software development organization of any size has one. Sometimes you're allowed to violate the guidelines, and sometimes during a code review you'll get dinged for not following the guidelines and have to change your code.

  - If you work in a group with more than one developer, style guidelines are a good idea. They give all your code a common look and feel and they make it easier for one developer to make changes to code written by somebody else.

  - A common set of guidelines in a Style Guide is about naming conventions. Naming conventions tell you what your identifier names should look like for each of the different kind of identifiers. Java has a common set of naming conventions:

    - For classes and interfaces: The identifier names should be nouns, using both upper and lowercase alphanumerics and with the first character of the name capitalized.

```
public class Automobile {}
public interface Shape {}
```

    - For methods: The identifier names should be verbs, using both upper and lowercase alphanumerics and with the first character of the name in lower case.

```
private double computeAverage(int [] list)
```

    - For variables: The identifier names should use both upper and lowercase alphanumerics, with the first character of the name in lower case. Variable names should not start with $ or _ (underscore).

```
    double average;
    String firstSentence;
```

- For all identifiers (except constants), camel case should be used, so that internal words are capitalized.

```
long myLongArray;
```

- For constants: All letters should be uppercase and words should be separated by underscores.

```
static final int MAX_WIDTH = 80;
```

Defensive Programming

By defensive programming we mean that your code should protect itself from bad data. The bad data can come from user input via the command line, a graphical text box or form, or a file. Bad data can also come from other routines in your program via input parameters like in the first example above.

How do you protect your program from bad data? Validate! As tedious as it sounds, you should always check the validity of data that you receive from outside your routine. This means you should check the following

- Check the number and type of command line arguments.

- Check file operations.

    - Did the file open?

    - Did the read operation return anything?

    - Did the write operation write anything?

    - Did we reach EOF yet?

- Check all values in function/method parameter lists.

    - Are they all the correct type and size?

- You should always initialize variables and not depend on the system to do the initialization for you.

What else should you check for? Well, here's a short list:

- Null pointers (references in Java)

- Zeros in denominators

- Wrong type

- Out of range values

As an example, here's a C program that takes in a list of house prices from a file and computes the average house price from the list. The file is provided to the program from the command line.

```
/*
 * program to compute the average selling price of a set of homes.
 * Input comes from a file that is passed via the command line.
```

```
 * Output is the Total and Average sale prices for
 * all the homes and the number of prices in the file.
 *
 * jfdooley
 */
#include <stdlib.h>
#include <stdio.h>

int main(int argc, char **argv)
{
        FILE *fp;
        double totalPrice, avgPrice;
        double price;
        int numPrices;

        /* check that the user entered the correct number of args */
        if (argc < 2) {
                fprintf(stderr,"Usage: %s <filename>\n", argv[0]);
                exit(1);
        }

        /* try to open the input file */
        fp = fopen(argv[1], "r");
        if (fp == NULL) {
                fprintf(stderr, "File Not Found: %s\n", argv[1]);
                exit(1);
        }
        totalPrice = 0.0;
        numPrices = 0;

        while (!feof(fp)) {
                fscanf(fp, "%10lf\n", &price);
                totalPrice += price;
                numPrices++;
        }

        avgPrice = totalPrice / numPrices;
        printf("Number of houses is %d\n", numPrices);
        printf("Total Price of all houses is $%10.2f\n", totalPrice);
        printf("Average Price per house is $%10.2f\n", avgPrice);

        return 0;
}
```

Assertions Can Be Your Friend

Defensive programming means that using assertions is a great idea if your language supports them. Java, C99, and C++ all support assertions. Assertions will test an expression that you give them and if the expression is false, it will throw an error and normally abort the program. You should use error handling code for errors you think might happen – erroneous user input, for example – and use assertions for errors that should *never* happen – off by one errors in loops, for example. Assertions are great for testing your program, but because you should remove them before giving programs to customers (you don't want the program to abort on the user, right?) they aren't good to use to validate input data.

Exceptions and Error Handling

We've talked about using assertions to handle truly bad errors, ones that should never occur in production. But what about handling "normal" errors? Part of defensive programming is to handle errors in such a way that no damage is done to any data in the program or the files it uses, and so that the program stays running for as long as possible (making your program robust).

Let's look at exceptions first. You should take advantage of built-in exception handling in whatever programming language you're using. The exception handling mechanism will give you information about what bad thing has just happened. It's then up to you to decide what to do. Normally in an exception handling mechanism you have two choices, handle the exception yourself, or pass it along to whoever called you and let them handle it. What you do and how you do it depends on the language you're using and the capabilities it gives you. We'll talk about exception handling in Java later.

Error Handling

Just like with validation, you're most likely to encounter errors in input data, whether it's command line input, file handling, or input from a graphical user interface form. Here we're talking about errors that occur at run time. Compile time and testing errors are covered in the next chapter on debugging and testing. Other types of errors can be data that your program computes incorrectly, errors in other programs that interact with your program, the operating system for instance, race conditions, and interaction errors where your program is communicating with another and your program is at fault.

The main purpose of error handling is to have your program survive and run correctly for as long as possible. When it gets to a point where your program cannot continue, it needs to report what is wrong as best as it can and then exit gracefully. Exiting is the last resort for error handling. So what should you do? Well, once again we come to the "it depends" answer. What you should do depends on what your program's context is when the error occurs and what its purpose is. You won't handle an error in a video game the same way you handle one in a cardiac pacemaker. In every case, your first goal should be – try to recover.

Trying to recover from an error will have different meanings in different programs. Recovery means that your program needs to try to either ignore the bad data, fix it, or substitute something else that is valid for the bad data. See McConnell[8] for a further discussion of error handling. Here are a few examples of how to recover from errors,

- You might just *ignore the bad data and keep going,* using the next valid piece of data. Say your program is a piece of embedded software in a digital pressure gauge. You sample the sensor that returns the pressure 60 times a second. If the sensor fails to deliver a pressure reading once, should you shut down the gauge? Probably not; a reasonable thing to do is just skip that reading and set up to read the next piece of data when it arrives. Now if the pressure sensor skips several readings in a row, then something might be wrong with the sensor and you should do something different (like yell for help).

---

[8] McConnell, 2004.

- You might *substitute the last valid piece of data* for a missing or wrong piece. Taking the digital pressure gauge again, if the sensor misses a reading, since each time interval is only a sixtieth of a second, it's likely that the missing reading is very close to the previous reading. In that case you can substitute the last valid piece of data for the missing value.

- There may be instances where you don't have any previously recorded valid data. Your application uses an asynchronous event handler, so you don't have any history of data, but your program knows that the data should be in a particular range. Say you've prompted the user for a salary amount and the value that you get back is a negative number. Clearly no one gets paid a salary of negative dollars, so the value is wrong. One way (probably not the best) to handle this error is to *substitute the closest valid value in the range*, in this case a zero. Although not ideal, at least your program can continue running with a valid data value in that field.

- In C programs, nearly all system calls and most of the standard library functions return a value. You should test these values! Most functions will return values that indicate success (a non-negative integer) or failure (a negative integer, usually -1). Some functions return a value that indicates how successful they were. For example, the printf() family of functions returns the number of characters printed, and the scanf() family returns the number of input elements read. Most C functions also set a global variable named errno that contains an integer value that is the number of the error that occurred. The list of error numbers is in a header file called errno.h. A zero on the errno variable indicates success. Any other positive integer value is the number of the error that occurred. Because the system tells you two things, (1) an error occurred, and (2) what it thinks is the cause of the error, you can do lots of different things to handle it, including just *reporting the error* and bailing out. For example, if we try to open a file that doesn't exist, the program

```
#include <stdio.h>
#include <stdlib.h>
#include <errno.h>

int main(int argc, char **argv)
{
    FILE *fd;
    char *fname = "NotAFile.txt";

    if ((fd = fopen(fname, "r")) == NULL) {
        perror("File not opened");
        exit(1);
    }
    printf("File exists\n");
    return 0;
}
```

- will return the error message

```
File not opened: No such file or directory
```

- if the file really doesn't exist. The function perror() reads the errno variable and using the string provided plus a standard string corresponding to the error number, writes an error message to the console's standard error output. This program could also prompt the user for a different file name or it could substitute a default file name. Either of these would allow the program to continue rather than exiting on the error.

- There are other techniques to use in error handling and recovery. These examples should give you a flavor of what you can do within your program. The important idea to remember here is to attempt recovery if possible, but most of all, *don't fail silently!*

Exceptions in Java

Some programming languages have built-in error reporting systems that will tell you when an error occurs, and leave it up to you to handle it one way or another. These errors that would normally cause your program to die a horrible death are called *exceptions*. Exceptions get *thrown* by the code that encounters the error. Once something is thrown, it's usually a good idea if someone *catches* it. This is the same with exceptions. So there are two sides to exceptions that you need to be aware of when you're writing code:

- When you have a piece of code that can encounter an error you *throw* an exception. Systems like Java will throw some exceptions for you. These exceptions are listed in the Exception class in the Java API documentation (see http://download.oracle.com/javase/6/docs/api). You can also write your own code to throw exceptions. We'll have an example later in the chapter.

- Once an exception is thrown, somebody has to *catch* it. If you don't do anything in your program, this *uncaught exception* will percolate through to the Java Virtual Machine (the JVM) and be caught there. The JVM will kill your program and provide you with a stack backtrace that should lead you back to the place that originally threw the exception and show you how you got there. On the other hand, you can also write code to encapsulate the calls that might generate exceptions and catch them yourself using Java's S **try...catch** mechanism. Java requires that some exceptions must be caught. We'll see an example later.

Java has three different types of exceptions – checked exceptions, errors, and unchecked exceptions. *Checked exceptions* are those that you should catch and handle yourself using an exception handler; they are exceptions that you should anticipate and handle as you design and write your code. For example, if your code asks a user for a file name, you should anticipate that they will type it wrong and be prepared to catch the resulting **FileNotFoundException**. Checked exceptions must be caught.

Errors on the other hand are exceptions that usually are related to things happening outside your program and are things you can't do anything about except fail gracefully. You might try to catch the error exception and provide some output for the user, but you will still usually have to exit.

The third type of exception is the *runtime exception*. Runtime exceptions all result from problems within your program that occur as it runs and almost always indicate errors in your code. For example, a **NullPointerException** nearly always indicates a bug in your code and shows up as a runtime exception. Errors and runtime exceptions are collectively called *unchecked exceptions* (that would be because you usually don't try to catch them, so they're unchecked). In the program below we deliberately cause a runtime exception:

CHAPTER 12 ⬚ CODE CONSTRUCTION

```
public class TestNull {
  public static void main(String[] args) {
      String str = null;
      int len = str.length();
  }
}
```

This program will compile just fine, but when you run it you'll get this as output:

```
Exception in thread "main" java.lang.NullPointerException

        at TestNull.main(TestNull.java:4)
```

This is a classic runtime exception. There's no need to catch this exception because the only thing we can do is exit. If we do catch it, the program might look like:

```
public class TestNullCatch {
        public static void main(String[] args) {
                String str = null;

                try {
                        int len = str.length();
                } catch (NullPointerException e) {
                        System.out.println("Oops: " + e.getMessage());
                        System.exit(1);
                }
        }
}
```

which gives us the output

```
Oops: null
```

Note that the **getMessage()** method will return a String containing whatever error message Java deems appropriate – if there is one. Otherwise it returns a null. This is somewhat less helpful than the default stack trace above.

Let's rewrite the short C program above in Java and illustrate how to catch a *checked exception.*

```
import java.io.*;
import java.util.*;

public class FileTest
{
        public static void main(String [] args)
        {
                File fd = new File("NotAFile.txt");
                System.out.println("File exists " + fd.exists());
```

```
        try {
                FileReader fr = new FileReader(fd);
        } catch (FileNotFoundException e) {
                System.out.println(e.getMessage());
        }
    }
}
```

and the output we get when we execute `FileTest` is

```
File exists false

NotAFile.txt (No such file or directory)
```

By the way, if we don't use the **try-catch** block in the above program, then it won't compile. We get the compiler error message

---

```
FileTestWrong.java:11: unreported exception java.io.FileNotFoundException; must be caught or
declared to be thrown

            FileReader fr = new FileReader(fd);
```

```
                             ^
```

```
1 error
```

Remember, checked exceptions **must** be caught. This type of error doesn't show up for unchecked exceptions. This is far from everything you should know about exceptions and exception handling in Java; start digging through the Java tutorials and the Java API!

The Last Word on Coding

Coding is the heart of software development. Code is what you produce. But coding is hard; translating even a good, detailed design into code takes a lot of thought, experience, and knowledge, even for small programs. Depending on the programming language you are using and the target system, programming can be a very time-consuming and difficult task. That's why taking the time to make your code readable and have the code layout match the logical structure of your design is essential to writing code that is understandable by humans and that works. Adhering to coding standards and conventions, keeping to a consistent style, and including good, accurate comments will help you immensely during debugging and testing. And it will help you six months from now when you come back and try to figure out what the heck you were thinking here.

And finally,

I am rarely happier than when spending an entire day programming my computer to perform automatically a task that it would otherwise take me a good ten seconds to do by hand.

—Douglas Adams, "Last Chance to See"

References

Hunt, A. and D. Thomas. *The Pragmatic Programmer: From Journeyman to Master*. (Boston, MA: Addison-Wesley, 2000).

Knuth, D. "Structured Programming with goto Statements." *ACM Computing Surveys* 6(4): 261-301. 1974.

Krasner, G. E. and S. T. Pope. "A cookbook for using the Model-View-Controller user interface paradigm in Smalltalk-80." *Journal of Object-Oriented Programming* 1(3): 26-49. 1988.

Lieberherr, K., I. Holland, et al. *Object-Oriented Programming: An Objective Sense of Style*. OOPSLA '88, Association for Computing Machinery, 1988.

Martin, R. C. *Agile Software Development: Principles, Patterns, and Practices*. (Upper Saddle River, NJ: Prentice Hall, 2003).

McConnell, S. *Code Complete 2: A Practical Handbook of Software Construction*. Redmond, WA, Microsoft Press, 2004).

Pike, Rob, *Notes on Programming in C*, retrieved from `http://www.literateprogramming.com/pikestyle.pdf` on 29 September 2010. 1999.

CHAPTER 13

Debugging

As soon as we started programming, we found to our surprise that it wasn't as easy to get programs right as we had thought. Debugging had to be discovered. I can remember the exact instant when I realized that a large part of my life from then on was going to be spent in finding mistakes in my own programs.

—Maurice Wilkes, 1949

It is a painful thing to look at your own trouble and know that you yourself and no one else has made it.

—Sophocles

Congratulations! You've finished writing your code so now it's time to get it working. I know. You're thinking, "I can write perfect code; I'm careful. I won't have any errors in my program." Get over it. Every programmer thinks this at one point or another. There's just no such thing as a perfect program. Humans are imperfect (thankfully). So we all make mistakes when we write code. After writing code for over 40 years I've gotten to the point where most of the time my programs that are less than about 20 lines long don't have any *obvious* errors in them and lots of times they even compile the first time. I think that's a pretty good result. You should shoot for that.

Getting your program to work is a process with three parts, the order of which is the subject of some debate. The three parts are

- Debugging

- Reviewing/inspecting

- Testing

Debugging is the process of finding the *root cause* of an error and fixing it. This doesn't mean treating the symptoms of an error by coding around it to make it go away; it means to find the real reason for the error and fixing that piece of code so the error is removed. Debugging is normally done once you finish writing the code and before you do a code review or unit testing (but see test-driven development later in this chapter).

Reviewing (or inspecting) is the process of reading the code as it sits on the page and *looking for errors.* The errors can include errors in how you've implemented the design, other kinds of logic errors, wrong comments, etc. Reviewing code is an inherently **static** process because the program isn't running on a computer – you're reading it off a screen or a piece of paper. So although reviewing is very good for finding static errors, it can't find dynamic or interaction errors in your code. That's what testing is for. We'll talk more about reviews and inspections in the next chapter.

Testing, of course is the process of **finding errors** in the code, as opposed to fixing them, which is what debugging is all about. Testing occurs, at minimum, at the following three different levels:

- *Unit testing*: Where you test small pieces of your code, notably at the function or method level.

- *Integration testing*: Where you put together several modules or classes that relate to each other and test them together.

- *System testing*: Where you test the entire program from the user's perspective; this is also called *black-box testing*, because the tester doesn't know how the code was implemented, all they know is what the requirements are and so they're testing to see if the code as written implements all the requirements correctly.

We'll focus on debugging in this chapter.

What's an Error, Anyway?

We define three types of errors in code

- Syntactic errors

- Semantic errors

- Logic errors

Syntactic errors are errors you make with respect to the syntax of the programming language you're using. Spelling a keyword wrong, failing to declare a variable before you use it, forgetting to put that closing curly brace in a block, forgetting the return type of a function, and forgetting that semi-colon at the end of a statement are all typical examples of syntactic errors. Syntactic errors are by far the easiest to find, because the compiler finds nearly all of them for you. Compilers are very rigid taskmasters when it comes to enforcing lexical and grammar rules of a language so if you get through the compilation process with no errors **and no warnings**, then it's very likely your program has no syntax errors left. Notice the "and no warnings" in the previous sentence. You should *always* compile your code with the strictest syntax checking turned on, and you should *always* eliminate all errors and warnings before you move on to reviews or testing. If you are sure you've not done anything wrong syntactically, then that's just one less thing to worry about while you're finding all the other errors! And the good news is that modern integrated development environments (IDEs) do this for you automatically once you've set up the compiler options. So once you set the warning and syntax checking levels, every time you make a change, the IDE will automatically re-compile your file and let you know about any syntactic errors!

Semantic errors, on the other hand, occur when you fail to create a proper sentence in the programming language. You do this because you have some basic misunderstanding about the grammar rules of the language. Not putting curly braces around a block, accidentally putting a semi-colon after the condition in an `if` or `while` statement in C/C++ or Java, forgetting to use a `break;` statement at the end of a `case` statement inside a `switch`, are all classic examples of semantic errors. Semantic errors are harder to find because they are normally syntactically correct pieces of code so the compiler passes your program and it compiles correctly into an object file. It's only when you try to execute your program that semantic errors surface. The good news is that they're usually so egregious that they show up pretty much immediately. The bad news is they can be very subtle. For example, in this code segment

```
while (j < MAX_LEN);
{
        // do stuff here
        j++;
}
```

the semi-colon at the end of the `while` statement's conditional expression is usually very hard to see, your eyes will just slide right over it; but its effect is to either put the program into an infinite loop, because the loop control variable `j` is never being incremented, or to never execute the loop, but then erroneously execute the block because it is no longer semantically connected to the `while` statement.

The third type of error, *logic errors*, are by far the most difficult to find and eradicate. A logic error is one that occurs because you've made a mistake in translating the design into code. These errors include things like computing a result incorrectly, off-by-one errors in loops (which can also be a semantic error if your off-by-one error is because you didn't understand array indexing, for example), misunderstanding a network protocol, returning a value of the wrong type from a method, and so on. With a logic error, either your program seems to execute normally, but you get the wrong answers, or it dies a sudden and horrible death because you've walked off the end of an array, tried to dereference a null pointer, or tried to go off and execute code in the middle of a data area. It's not pretty.

Unit testing involves finding the errors in your program, and debugging involves finding the root cause and fixing those errors. Debugging is about finding out why an error occurs in your program. You can look at errors as opportunities to learn more about the program, and about how you work and approach problem solving. Because after all, debugging is a problem solving activity, just as developing a program is problem solving. Look at debugging as an opportunity to learn about yourself and improve your skill set.

What Not To Do

Just like in any endeavor, particularly problem solving endeavors, there's a wrong way and a right way to approach the task. Here are a few things you shouldn't do as you approach a debugging problem.[1]

First of all, *don't guess about where the error might be.* This implies that (1) you don't know anything about the program you're trying to debug, and (2) you're not going about the job of finding the root cause of the error systematically. Stop, take a deep breath, and start again.

Don't fix the symptom, fix the problem. Lots of times you can "fix" a problem by forcing the error to go away by adding code. This is particularly true if the error involves an outlier in a range of values. The temptation here is to special case the outlier by adding code to handle just that case. Don't do it! You haven't fixed the underlying problem here; you've just painted over it. Trust me, there's some other special case out there waiting to break free and squash your program. Study the program, figure out what it's doing at that spot, and fix the problem. You'll thank me later.

Avoid denial. It's always tempting to say "the compiler must be wrong" or "the system must be broken" or "Ralph's module is obviously sending me bad data" or "that's impossible" or some such excuse. Buck up here, developer. If you just "changed one thing" and the program breaks, then guess who probably just injected an error into the program? Or at the very least uncovered one? Review the quote from Sophocles at the beginning of this chapter, "... *you yourself and no one else has made it.*" You will make mistakes. We all do. The best attitude to display is, "by golly, this program can't beat me, I'm going to fix this thing!" One of the best discussions of careful coding and how hard it is to write correct

---

[1] McConnell, S. *Code Complete 2: A Practical Handbook of Software Construction.* (Redmond, WA: Microsoft Press, 2004).

programs is the discussion of how to write binary search in Column 5 of Jon Bentley's *Programming Pearls.*[2] You should read it.

An Approach to Debugging

Here's an approach to debugging that will get the job done. Remember, you're solving a problem here and the best way to do that is to have a systematic way of sneaking up on the problem and whacking it on the head. The other thing to remember about debugging is that, like a murder mystery, you're working backwards from the conclusion.[3] The bad thing has already happened – your program failed. Now you need to examine the evidence and work backwards to a solution.

1. Reproduce the problem reliably.

2. Find the source of the error.

3. Fix the error (just that one).

4. Test the fix (now you've got a regression test for later).

5. Optionally look for other errors in the vicinity of the one you just fixed.

Reproduce the Problem Reliably

This is the key first step. If your error only shows up periodically it will be much, much harder to find. The classic example of how hard this can be is the "but it works fine on my computer" problem. This is the one sentence you never want to hear. This is why people in tech support retire early. Reproducing the problem – in different ways if possible – will allow you to see what's happening and will give you a clear indication of where the problem is occurring. Luckily for you, most errors are easy to find. Either you get the wrong answer and you can look for where the print statement is located and work backwards from there, or your program dies a horrible death and the system generates a stack trace for you. The Java Virtual Machine does this automatically for you. With other languages, you may need to use a debugger to get the stack trace.

Remember, errors are not random events. If you think the problem is random, then it's usually one of the following:

- *An initialization problem:* This can be that you're depending on a side effect of the variable definition to initialize the variable and it's not acting as you expect.

- *A timing error:* Something is happening sooner or later than you expect.

- *A dangling pointer problem:* You returned a pointer from a local variable and the memory in which that local variable was stored has been given back to the system.

- *A buffer overflow or walking off the end of an array:* You have a loop that iterates through a collection and you're walking off the end and stomping on either a piece of code, or another variable or the system stack.

---

[2] Bentley, J. *Programming Pearls, 2nd Edition.* (Reading, MA, Addison-Wesley: 2000).

[3] Kernighan, B. W. and R. Pike. *The Practice of Programming.* (Boston, MA, Addison-Wesley, 1999).

- *A concurrency issue (a race condition)*: In a multi-threaded application or in an application that uses shared memory you've not synchronized your code and a variable you need to use is getting overwritten by someone else before you can get to it.

Reproducing the problem is not enough, however. You should reproduce it using the simplest test case that will cause the error to occur. It's a matter of eliminating all the other possibilities so you can focus on the single one (well, maybe one or two) that probably causes the error. One way to do this is to try to reproduce the problem using half the data you had the first time. Pick one half or the other. If the error still occurs, try it again. If the error doesn't happen, try the other half of the data. If there's still no error, then try with three-quarters of the data. You get the idea. You'll know when you've found the simplest case because with anything smaller the behavior of the program will change; either the error will disappear, or you'll get a slightly different error.

Find the Source of the Error

Once you can reproduce the problem from the outside, you can now find where the error is occurring. Once again, we need to do this systematically. For most errors this is easy. There are a number of techniques you can use.

- *Gather data*: Since you've now got a test case that will reproduce the error, gather data from running the test case. The data can include what kinds of input data cause the error, what do you have to do to get it to appear – the exact steps you need to execute, how long it takes to appear, and what exactly happens. Once you have this data you can form an hypothesis on where the error is in the code. For most types of errors, you'll have some output that is correct and then either the program crashes or you get bad output. That will help isolate the error.

- *Read the code*: What a concept! The first thing you should do once you've run your test case is examine the output, make a guess where the error might be (look at the last thing that got printed and find that print statement in the program), and then sit back, grab a cup of coffee, and just read the code. Understanding what the code is trying to do in the area where the error occurs is key to figuring out what the fix should be. It's also key to finding the source of the error in the first place. Nine times out of ten, if you just sit back and read the code for five minutes or so you'll find just where the error is. Don't just grab the keyboard and start hacking away. Read the code.

- *Insert print statements*: The simplest thing to do once you figure out what output is incorrect is to start putting print statements at that point and at other interesting points in the code. Interesting points can be the entrance and exit to functions, "Entering sort routine", "Exiting partition routine", and so on. When using an integrated development environment (IDE) there are built-in debugging features, including setting breakpoints, watchpoints, the ability to step through code, etc. that make inserting print statements less useful. I'll come back to some of these below.

- You can also put print statements at the top and bottom of loops, at the beginning of the then and else blocks of if-statements, in the default case of a switch statement, etc. Unless something very spooky is going on you should be able to isolate where the error is occurring pretty quickly using this method. Once again, work your way backwards from the point where you think the error makes itself known. Remember that many times where an error *exhibits* its behavior may be many lines of code after where the error actually *occurs*.

- In some languages you can encase your print statements inside debugging blocks that you can turn on and off on the command line when you compile. In C/C++ you can insert

```
#ifdef DEBUG
                    printf("Debug statement in sort routine\n");
#endif
```

- blocks in various places and then when you compile the program you can either put a #define DEBUG in a header file or you can compile using gcc -DDEBUG foo.c and the printf function call will be included in your program. Leaving out the #define or the -DDEBUG will remove the printf function call from the executable program (but not your source). Beware though that this technique makes your program harder to read because of all the DEBUG blocks scattered around the code. You should remove DEBUG blocks before your program releases. Unfortunately, Java doesn't have this facility because it doesn't have a pre-processor. However all is not lost. You can get the same effect as the #ifdef DEBUG by using a named boolean constant. Here's an example of code:

```
public class IfDef {
        final static boolean DEBUG = true;

        public static void main(String [] args) {
                System.out.printf("Hello, World \n");

                if (DEBUG) {
                    System.out.printf("max(5, 8) is %d\n", Math.max(5, 8));
                        System.out.printf("If this prints, the code was
    included\n");
                }
        }
}
```

- In this example we set the boolean constant DEBUG to true when we want to turn the DEBUG blocks on, and we'll then turn it to false when we want to turn them off. This isn't perfect because you have to re-compile every time you want to turn debugging on and off, but you have to do that with the C/C++ example above as well.

- *Look for patterns*: The next thing to try is to see if there's a pattern to the code or the error that you've seen before. As you gain more programming experience and get a better understanding of how you program and what kind of mistakes you make, this will be easier.

- The extra semi-colon at the end of the while loop above is one example of a mistake that can be a pattern. Another is

```
for (int j = 0; j <= myArray.length; j++) {
    // some code here
}
```

- where you will step off the end of the array because you're testing for <= rather than <. This is the classic off-by-one error.

- A classic in C/C++ is using one = where you meant to use two == in a conditional expression. Say you're checking an array of characters for a particular character in a C/C++ program

```
for (int j = 0; j < length; j++) {
            if (c = myArray[j]) {
                    pos = j;
                    break;
            }
}
```

- the single equals sign will cause the if statement to stop early every time; pos will always be zero. By the way, Java doesn't let you get away with this. It gives you an error that says the type of the assignment expression is not a boolean.

```
TstEql.java:10: incompatible types
found   : char
required: boolean
                if (c = myArray[j]) {
                      ^
1 error
```

- This is because in Java, just like in C and C++ an assignment operator returns a result and every result has a type. In this case, the result type is char but the if-statement is expecting a boolean expression there. The Java compiler checks for this because it's more strongly typed than C and C++; their compilers don't do the check.

- Forgetting a break statement in a switch is another.

```
switch(selectOne) {
            case 'p':      operation = "print";
                                break;
            case 'd':      operation = "display";
            default:       operation = "blank";
                                break;
}
```

- will reset *operation* to *blank* because there is no break statement after the second case.

- *Explain the code to someone.* How many times have you started explaining a problem to one of your peers and two minutes later, all of a sudden, you solve it. When you start explaining the problem to someone else, you're really explaining it to yourself as well. That's when the inspiration can hit. Give it a try.

- *Other problems.* I've only scratched the surface of the possible errors you can make and find in your code. Because there are nearly an infinite number of programs you can write in any given programming language, there are nearly an infinite number of ways to insert errors into them. Memory leaks, typing mistakes, side effects from global variables, failure to close files, not putting a default case in a switch statement, accidentally overriding a method definition, bad return types, hiding a global or instance variable with a local variable, there are thousands of them.

Don't be discouraged, though. Most errors you'll make really are simple. Most of them you'll catch during code reviews and unit tests. The ones that escape into system test or (heaven forbid) released code are the really interesting ones. Debugging is a great problem solving exercise. Revel in it.

Debugging Tools

So far the only debugging tools we've talked about using are compilers to remove syntax errors and warnings, print statements you can insert in your code to give you data on what is happening where, and inline debugging statements that you can compile in or out. There are other tools you can use that will help you find the source of an error. The first among these are debuggers.

Debuggers are special programs that execute instrumented code and allow you to peek inside the code as it's running to see what's going on. Debuggers allow you to stop your running code (breakpoints), examine variable values as the code executes (watchpoints), step into and out of functions, and even make changes to the code and the data while the program is running. Debuggers are the easiest way to get a stack trace for C and C++ programs. For C and C++ developers, the gdb debugger that comes with nearly all Unix and Linux systems (and the development tool packages for Mac OS X and Windows) is usually the debugger of choice. For Java, Gdb is also integrated in some interactive development environments like Eclipse (`www.eclipse.org/`), and also comes with a graphical user interface in the DDD debugger (`www.gnu.org/software/ddd/`). The NetBeans IDE (www.netbeans.org) comes with its own graphical debugger. The Java debuggers in Eclipse and NetBeans allow you to set breakpoints at individual lines of code, they let you watch variables values change via watchpoints, and they allow you to step through the code one line or one method at a time. Gdb does all the things mentioned above and more, but you should use it, and any other debugger cautiously. Debuggers, by their nature, have tunnel vision when it comes to looking at code. They are great at showing you all the code for the current function, but they don't give you a feel for the organization of the program as a whole. They also don't give you a feel for complicated data structures and it's hard to debug multi-threaded and multi-process programs using a debugger. Multi-threaded programs are particularly hard for a number of reasons, one of which is that while executing timing is crucial for the different threads, and running a multi-threaded program in a debugger changes the timing.

Fix the Error (Just That One)!

Once you've found where the error is, you need to come up with a fix for it. Most of the time the fix is obvious and simple because the error is simple. That's the good news. But sometimes while you can find the error, the fix isn't obvious, or the fix will entail rewriting a large section of code. In cases like this be careful! Take the time necessary to understand the code, and then rewrite the code and fix the error correctly. The biggest problem in debugging is haste.

When you are fixing errors remember two things:

- Fix the actual error; don't fix the symptom.

- Only fix one error at a time.

This second item is particularly important. We've all been in situations where you're fixing an error and you find another one in the same piece of code. The temptation is to fix them both right then and there. Resist! Fix the error you came to fix. Test it and make sure the fix is correct. Integrate the new code back into the source code base. Then you can go back to step 1 and fix the second error. You might ask, "Why do all this extra work when I can just make the fix right now?"

Well, here's the situation. By the time you get to this step in the debugging process you already have a test for the first error, you've educated yourself about the code where the error occurs, you're ready to make that one fix. Why should you confuse the issue by fixing two things now? Besides, you don't have a test for the second error. So how do you test that fix? Trust me, it's a little more work, but doing the fixes one at a time will save you lots of headaches down the road.

Test the Fix

Well, this sounds obvious, doesn't it? But you'd be surprised how many fixes don't get tested. Or if they're tested, it's a simple test with generic sample data and no attempt to see if your fix broke anything else.

First of all, re-run the original test that uncovered the error. Not just the minimal test that you came up with in step 1, but the first test that caused the error to appear. If that test now fails (in the sense that the error does not occur any more), then that's a good sign you've at least fixed the proximate cause of the error. Then run every other test in your regression suite (see the next chapter for more discussion on regression tests) so you can make sure you've not re-broken something that was already fixed. Finally, integrate your code into the source code base, check out the new version and test the entire thing. If all that still works, then you're in good shape. Go have a beer.

Look for More Errors

Well, if there was one error in a particular function or method, then there might be another, right? So while you're here, you might as well take a look at the code in the general vicinity of the error you just fixed and see if anything like it happens again. This is another example of looking for patterns. Patterns are there because developers make the same mistakes over and over again (we're human, after all). Grab another cup of coffee and a doughnut and read some more code. It won't hurt to take a look at the whole module or class and see if there are other errors or opportunities for change. In the agile world, this is called *refactoring*. This means rewriting the code to make it simpler. Making your code simpler will make it clearer, easier to read, and it will make finding that next error easier. So have some coffee and read some code.

Source Code Control

In some of the paragraphs above we've made mention of a source code base and integrating changes into that base. That is a sneaky way of starting a brief discussion of *source code control*, also known as *software version control*.

Whenever you work on a project, whether you are the only developer or you are part of a team, you should keep backups of the work you're doing. That's what a version control system (VCS) does for you, but with a twist. A VCS will not only keep a backup of all the files you create during a project, but it will keep track of all the changes you've made to them, so that in addition to saying, "Give me the latest version of PhoneContact.java," you can say, "I want the version of PhoneContact.java from last Thursday."

A VCS keeps a *repository* of all the files you've created and added to it for your project. The repository can be a flat file or a more sophisticated database. A client program allows you access the repository and retrieve different versions of one or more of the files stored there. Normally, if you just ask the VCS for a particular file or files, you get the latest version. Whatever version of the file you extract from the repository, it's called the *working copy* in VCS-speak. Extracting the file is called a *check out.*

If you are working on a project all alone, then the working copy you check out from the VCS repository is the only one out there and any changes that you make will be reflected in the repository when you check the file back in. The cool part of this is that if you make a change and it's wrong, you can just check out a previous version that doesn't have the change in it. The other interesting part of a VCS is when there is more than one developer working on a project. When you're working on a development team, it's quite likely that somebody else on the team may check out the same file that you did. This brings up the problem of file sharing. The problem here is if both of you make changes to the file and then both want to check the file back into the repository who gets to go first and whose changes end up in the repository? Ideally, both, right?

Well, maybe not. Say Alice and Bob both check out PhoneContact.java from the repository and each of them makes changes to it. Bob checks his version of PhoneContact.java back into the repository and goes to lunch. A few minutes later Alice checks in her version of PhoneContact.java. Two problems occur. (1) if Alice hasn't made any changes in the same lines of code that Bob did, her version is still newer than Bob's and it hides Bob's version in the repository. Bob's changes are still there, but they are now in an older version than Alice's. (2) Worse, if Alice did make changes to some of the same code that Bob did, then her changes actually overwrite Bob's and main.c is a very different file. Bummer. So we don't want either of these situations to occur. How do we avoid this problem?

Version control systems use the following two different strategies to avoid this collision problem.:

- lock-modify-unlock
- copy-modify-merge

Using Lock-Modify-Unlock

The first strategy is *lock-modify-unlock*. In this strategy, Bob checks out PhoneContact.java and locks it for edit. This means that Bob now has the only working copy of PhoneContact.java that can be changed. If Alice tries to check out PhoneContact.java she gets a message that she can only check out a read-only version and so can't check it back in until Bob gives up his lock. Bob makes his changes, checks PhoneContact.java back in, and then releases the lock. Alice can now check out and lock an editable version of PhoneContact.java (which now includes Bob's changes) and make her own changes and check the file back in, giving up her lock. The lock-modify-unlock strategy has the effect of serializing changes in the repository.

This *serialization of changes* is the biggest problem with lock-modify-unlock. While Bob has the file checked out for editing, Alice can't make her changes. She just sits around twiddling her thumbs until Bob is done. Alice's boss doesn't like this thumb twiddling stuff. However, there is an alternative.

Using Copy-Modify-Merge

The second strategy is *copy-modify-merge*. In this strategy, Alice and Bob are both free to check out editable copies of PhoneContact.java. Let's say that Alice makes her changes first and checks her new version of the file back into the repository and goes out for cocktails. When Bob is finished making his changes he tries to check his new version of PhoneContact.java into the repository only to have the VCS tell him his version of the file is "out of date;" Bob can't check in. What happened here? Well, the VCS stamps each file that's checked out with a timestamp and a version number. It also keeps track of what is checked out and who checked it out and when. It checks those values when you try to check in.

When Bob tried to check in, his VCS realized that the version of the code he was trying to check in was older than the current version (the new one that Alice had checked in earlier), so it let him know that. So what is Bob to do? That's where the third part of copy-modify-merge comes in. Bob needs to tell the VCS to merge his changes with the current version of PhoneContact.java and then check in the updated version. This all works just fine if Alice and Bob have changed different parts of the file. If their changes do not conflict, then the VCS can just do the merge automatically and check in the new file. A problem occurs if Alice and Bob have made changes to the same lines of code in the file. In that case, Bob must do a manual merge of the two files. Bob has to do this because the VCS isn't smart enough to choose between the conflicting changes. Usually, a VCS will provide some help in doing the merge, but ultimately the merge decision must be Bob's.

copy-modify-merge is the strategy used by most version control systems these days, including the popular open-source version control system, subversion (`http://subversion.apache.org`).[4] There is one problem (well, okay, more than one, but we'll just talk about this one) with copy-modify-merge. If your repository allows you to store binary files, you can't merge them. Say you have two versions of the same jpg file. How do you decide which of the bits is correct? So in this case the VCS (subversion included) will require you to use lock-modify-unlock.

Git (http://git.scm.com), the other candidate for most popular open-source version control system, uses a model that has each developer have a local repository of the entire development history. When a developer makes a change to a file, the changes are copied to the other local repositories. Git uses a model called an incomplete merge along with a number of plug-in merge tools to coordinate merges across repositories. Git's main virtue is speed. It may be the fastest distributed VCS around.

One Last Thought on Coding and Debugging – Pair Programming

Pair programming is a technique to improve software quality and programmer performance. It's been around for many years, but only recently been formalized [Williams00]. In pair programming two people share one computer and one keyboard. One person "drives," controlling the keyboard and writing the code, and the other "navigates," watching for errors in the code, suggesting changes and test cases. Periodically the driver and the navigator switch places. Pairs can work together for long periods of time on a project, or pairs can change with each programming task. Pair programming is particularly popular in agile development environments; in the *Extreme Programming* process, all developers are required to pair program and no code that has not been written by two people is allowed to be integrated into the project [Beck00]. There have been several studies[5] that show that pair programming decreases the number of errors in code and improves the productivity of programmers. So this is our final debugging technique – pair program!

Conclusion

Just like writing good, efficient code, debugging is a skill that all programmers need to acquire. Being a careful coder will mean you have less debugging to do, but there will always be debugging. Programmers

---

[4] Collins-Sussman, B., Fitzpatrick, B. W., and Pilato, C. M. *Version Control with Subversion.* (Sebastapol, CA: O'Reilly Press, 2010). Retrieved from `http://svnbook.red-bean.com/` on 15 October 2010.

[5] Cockburn, A. and L. Williams. The Costs and Benefits of Pair Programming. *Extreme Programming Examined.* (Boston, MA: Addison-Wesley Longman, 2001). Page 592.

are all human and we'll always make mistakes. Having a basket of debugging skills will help you find the root causes of errors in your code faster and it will help you from injecting more errors. The combination of reviews (Chapter 15), debugging and unit testing – as we'll see in the next chapter – is the knock-out punch that a developer uses to release defect-free code.

References

Bentley, J. *Programming Pearls, 2nd Edition.* (Reading, MA, Addison-Wesley: 2000).

Chelf, B. "Avoiding the most common software development goofs." Retrieved from `www.embedded.com/show/Article.jhtml?articleID=192800005` on October 2, 2006.

Cockburn, A. and L. Williams. The Costs and Benefits of Pair Programming. *Extreme Programming Examined.* (Boston, MA: Addison-Wesley Longman, 2001). Page 592.

Collins-Sussman, B., Fitzpatrick, B. W., and Pilato, C. M. *Version Control with Subversion.* (Sebastapol, CA: O'Reilly Press, 2010). Retrieved from `http://svnbook.red-bean.com/` on 15 October 2010.

Kernighan, B. W. and R. Pike. *The Practice of Programming.* (Boston, MA, Addison-Wesley, 1999).

McConnell, S. *Code Complete 2: A Practical Handbook of Software Construction.* (Redmond, WA: Microsoft Press, 2004).

CHAPTER 14

Unit Testing

More than the act of testing, the act of designing tests is one of the best bug preventers known. The thinking that must be done to create a useful test can discover and eliminate bugs before they are coded — indeed, test-design thinking can discover and eliminate bugs at every stage in the creation of software, from conception to specification, to design, coding and the rest.

—Boris Beizer

You can see a lot by just looking.

—Yogi Berra

As was emphasized in the last chapter, nobody's perfect, including software developers. In Chapter 13 we talked about different things to look for when you *know* there are errors in your code. Now we're going to talk about how to *find* those errors. Of the three types of errors in your code, the compiler will find the syntax errors and the occasional semantic error. In some language environments, the run-time system will find others (to your users chagrin). The rest of the errors are found in two different ways – testing, and code reviews and inspections. In this chapter, we'll discuss testing, when to do it, what it is, how to do it, what your tests should cover, and the limitations of testing. In the next chapter we'll talk about code reviews and inspections.

There are three levels of testing in a typical software development project: unit testing, integration testing, and system testing. *Unit testing* is typically done by you, the developer. With unit testing, you're testing individual methods and classes, but you're generally not testing larger configurations of the program. You're also not usually testing interfaces or library interactions – except those that your method might actually be using. Because you are doing unit testing, you know how all the methods are written, what the data is supposed to look like, what the method signatures are, and what the return values and types should be. This is known as *white-box testing*. It should really be called *transparent-box testing*, because the assumption is you can see all the details of the code being tested.

Integration testing is normally done by a separate testing organization. This is the testing of a collection of classes or modules that interact with each other; its purpose is to test interfaces between modules or classes and the interactions between the modules. Testers write their tests with knowledge of the interfaces but not with information about *how* each module has been implemented. From that perspective the testers are users of the interfaces. Because of this, integration testing is sometimes called *gray-box testing*. Integration testing is done after unit tested code is integrated into the source code base.

A partial or complete version of the product is built and tested, to find any errors in how the new module interacts with the existing code. This type of testing is also done when errors in a module are fixed and the module is re-integrated into the code base.

System testing is normally done by a separate testing organization. This is the testing of the entire program (the system). System testing is done on both internal baselines of the software product and on the final baseline that is proposed for release to customers. The separate testing organization uses the requirements and writes their own tests without knowing anything about how the program is designed or written. This is known as *black-box testing* because the program is opaque to the tester except for the inputs it takes and the outputs it produces. The job of the testers at this level is to make sure that the program implements all the requirements. Black box testing can also include stress testing, usability testing, and acceptance testing. End users may be involved in this type of testing.

The Problem with Testing

So, if we can use testing to find errors in our programs, why don't we find all of them? After all, we wrote the program, or at least the fix or new feature we just added, so we must understand what we just wrote. We also wrote the tests. So why do so many errors escape into the next phase of testing or even into users hands?

Well, there are two reasons we don't find all the errors in our code. First, we're not perfect. This seems to be a theme here. But we're not. If we made mistakes when we wrote the code, why should we assume we won't make some mistakes when we read it or try to test and fix it? This happens for even small programs, but it's particularly true for larger programs. If you have a 50,000 line program, that's a lot to read and understand and you're bound to miss something. Also, static reading of programs won't help you find those dynamic interactions between modules and interfaces. So we need to test more intelligently and combine both static (code reading) and dynamic (testing) techniques to find and fix errors in programs.

The second reason that errors escape from one testing phase to another and ultimately to the user is that software, more than any other product that humans manufacture, is very complex. Even small programs have many pathways through the code and many different types of data errors that can occur. This large number of pathways through a program is called a *combinatorial explosion*. Every time you add an **if** statement to your program, you double the number of possible paths through the program. Think about it; you have one path through the code if the conditional expression in the **if** statement is true, and a different path if the conditional expression is false. Every time you add a new input value you increase complexity and increase the number of possible errors. This means that, for large programs, you can't possibly test every possible path through the program with every possible input value. There are an exponential number of code path/data value combinations to test every one.

So what to do? Well, if brute force won't work, then you need a better plan. That plan is to identify those use cases that are the most probable and test those. You need to identify the likely input data values and the boundary conditions for data, and figure out what the likely code paths will be and test those. That, it turns out, will get you most of the errors. Steve McConnell says in *Code Complete* that a combination of good testing and code reviews can uncover more than 95% of errors in a good-sized program.[1] That's what we need to shoot for.

---

[1] McConnell, S. *Code Complete 2: A Practical Handbook of Software Construction*. (Redmond, WA: Microsoft Press, 2004.)

That Testing Mindset

There's actually another problem with testing – you. Well, actually, you, the developer. You see, developers and testers have two different, one might say adversarial, roles to play in code construction. Developers are there to take a set of requirements and produce a design that reflects the requirements and write the code that implements the design. Your job as a developer is to *get code to work*.

A tester's job, on the other hand, is to take those same requirements and your code and *get the code to break*. Testers are supposed to do unspeakable, horrible, wrenching things to your code in an effort to get the errors in it to expose themselves to the light of day. Their job is to break stuff. You the developer then get to fix it. This is why being a tester can be a very cool job.

You can see where this might be an adversarial relationship. You can also see where developers might make pretty bad testers. If your job is to make the code work, you're not focused on breaking it. So your test cases may not be the nasty, mean test cases that someone whose job it is to break your code may come up with. In short, because they're trying to build something beautiful, *developers make lousy testers*. Developers tend to write tests using typical, clean data. They tend to have an overly optimistic view of how much of their code that a test will exercise. They tend to write tests assuming that the code will work; after all it's their code, right?

This is why most software development organizations have a *separate testing team*, particularly for integration and system testing. The testers write their own test code, create their own frameworks, do the testing of all new baselines and the final release code, and report all the errors back to the developers who then must fix them. The one thing testers normally *do not* do is unit testing. Unit testing is the developer's responsibility, so you're not off the hook here. You do need to think about testing, learn how to write tests, how to run them, and how to analyze the results. You need to learn to be mean to your code. And you still need to fix the errors.

When to Test?

Before I get around to discussing just how to do unit testing and what things to test, let's talk about *when* to test. Current thinking falls into two areas: the more traditional approach is to write your code, get it to compile, so you've eliminated the syntax errors, and then write your tests and do your unit testing *after* you feel the code for a function or a module is finished. This has the advantage that you've understood the requirements and written the code and while you were writing the code you had the opportunity to think about test cases. Then you can write clear test cases. In this strategy testing and debugging go hand in hand and occur pretty much simultaneously. It allows you to find an error, fix it, and then re-run the failed test right away.

A newer approach that flows out of the agile methodologies, especially out of Extreme Programming, is called *test-driven development* (TDD). With TDD, you write your unit tests *before* you write any code. Clearly if you write your unit tests first, they will all fail – at most you'll have the stub of a method to call in your test. But that's a good thing because in TDD your goal when you write code is to *get all the tests to pass*. So if you've written a bunch of tests, you then write just enough code to make all the tests pass and then you know you're done! This has the advantage of helping you keep your code lean, which implies simpler and easier to debug. You can write some new code, test it; if it fails write some more code, if it passes, stop. It also gives you, right up front, a set of tests you can run whenever you make a change to your code. If the tests all still pass, then you haven't broken anything by making the changes. It also allows you to find an error, fix it, and then re-run the failed test right away.

So which way is better? Well, the answer is another of those "it depends" things. Generally, writing your tests first gets you in the testing mind-set earlier and gives you definite goals for implementing the code. On the other hand, until you do it a lot and it becomes second nature, writing tests first can be hard because you have to visualize what you're testing. It forces you to come to terms with the requirements and the module or class design early as well. That means that design/coding/testing all pretty much happen at once. This can make the whole code construction process more difficult. TDD works well for small to medium sized projects (as do agile techniques in general), but it may be more difficult for very large programs. TDD also works quite well when you are pair programming. In pair programming, the driver is writing the code while the navigator is watching for errors and thinking about testing. With TDD, the driver is writing a *test* while the navigator is thinking of more tests to write and thinking ahead to the code. This process tends to make writing the tests easier and then flows naturally into writing the code.

Give testing a shot both before and after and then you can decide which is best.

What to Test?

Now that we've talked about different phases of testing and when you should do your unit testing, it's time to discuss just *what* to test. What you're testing falls into two general categories: *code coverage* and *data coverage*.

- *Code coverage* has the goal of executing every line of code in your program at least once with representative data so you can be sure that all the code functions correctly. Sounds easy? Well, remember that combinatorial explosion problem for that 50,000 line program.

- *Data coverage* has the goal of testing representative samples of good and bad data, both input data and data generated by your program, with the objective of making sure the program handles data and particularly data errors correctly.

Of course there is overlap between code coverage and data coverage; sometimes in order to get a particular part of your program to execute you have to feed it bad data, for example. We'll separate these as best we can and come together when we talk about writing actual tests.

Code Coverage: Test Every Statement

Your objective in code coverage is to test every statement in your program. In order to do that, you need to keep several things in mind about your code. Your program is made up of a number of different types of code, each of which you need to test.

First, there's *straight line code*. Straight line code illuminates a single path through your function or method. Normally this will require one test – per different data type (see below for data coverage).

Next there is *branch coverage*. With branch coverage you want to test everywhere your program can change directions. That means you need to look at control structures here. Take a look at every *if* and *switch* statement, and every complex conditional expression – those that contain AND and OR operators in them. For every *if* statement you'll need two tests – one for when the conditional expression is **true** and one for when it's **false**. For every *switch* statement in your method you'll need a separate test for each *case* clause in the switch, including the *default* clause (all your **switch** statements have a **default** clause, right?). The logical and (**&&**) and or (**||**) operators add complexity to your conditional expressions, so you'll need extra test cases for those.

Ideally, you'll need four test cases for each (F-F, F-T, T-F, T-T), but if the language you are using uses short-cut evaluation for logical operators, as do C/C++ and Java, then you can reduce the number of test cases. For the or operator you'll still need two cases if the first sub-expression is **false**, but you can just use a single test case if the first sub-expression evaluates to **true** (the entire expression will always be true). For the and operator, you'll only need a single test if the first sub-expression evaluates to **false** (the result will always be false) but you need both tests if the first sub-expression evaluates to **true**.

Then there is *loop coverage*. This is similar to branch coverage above. The difference here is that in *for*, *while*, or *do-while* loops you have the best likelihood of introducing an *off-by-one error* and you need to test for that explicitly. You'll also need a test for a "normal" run through the loop, but you'll need to test for a couple of other things too. First will be the possibility for the pre-test loops that you never enter the loop body – the loop conditional expression fails the very first time. Then you'll need to test for an infinite loop – the conditional expression never becomes false. This is most likely because you don't change the loop control variable in the loop body, or you do change it, but the conditional expression is wrong from the get-go. For loops that read files, you normally need to test for the *end-of-file* marker (EOF). This is another place where errors could occur either because of a premature end-of-file or because (in the case of using standard input) end-of-file is never indicated.

Finally, there are *return values*. In many languages, standard library functions and operating system calls all return values. For example, in C, the **fprintf** and **fscanf** functions return the number of characters printed to an output stream and the number of input elements assigned from an input stream, respectively. But hardly anyone ever checks these return values.[2] You should!

Note that Java is a bit different than C or C++. In Java many of the similarly offending routines will have return values declared **void** rather than **int** as in C or C++. So the above problem occurs much less frequently in Java than in other languages. It's not completely gone however. While the **System.out.print()** and **System.out.println()** methods in Java are both declared to return **void**, the **System.out.printf()** method returns a **PrintStream** object that is almost universally ignored. In addition, it's perfectly legal in Java to call a **Scanner**'s **next()** or **nextInt()** methods or any of the methods that read data and not save the return value in a variable. Be careful out there.

Data Coverage: Bad Data Is Your Friend?

Remember in the chapter on Code Construction we talked about *defensive programming*, and that the key to defending your program was watching out for bad data, detecting and handling it so that your program can recover from bad data or at least fail gracefully. Well, this is where we see if your defenses are worthy. Data coverage should examine two types of data, good data and bad data. Good data is the typical data your method is supposed to handle. These tests will test data that is the correct type and within the correct ranges. They are just to see if your program is working normally. This doesn't mean you're completely off the hook here. There are still a few cases to test. Here's the short list:

- **Test boundary conditions.** This means to test data near the edges of the range of your valid data. For example, if your program is computing average grades for a course, then the range of values is between 0 and 100 inclusive. So you should test grades at, for example, 0, 1, 99, and 100. Those are all valid grades. But you should also test at -1, and 101. Both of these are invalid values, but are close to the range. In addition, if you are assigning letter grades, you need to check at the upper and lower boundaries of each letter grade value. So if an F is any grade below a 60, you need to check 59, 60, and 61. If you're going to have an off-by-one error, that's where to check.

- **Test typical data values.** These are valid data fields that you might normally expect to get. For the grading example above, you might check 35, 50, 67, 75, 88, 93, and so on. If these don't work you've got other problems.

---

[2] Kernighan, B. W. and R. Pike. *The Practice of Programming.* (Boston, MA: Addison-Wesley, 1999.)

- **Test pre- and post-conditions**. Whenever you enter a control structure – a loop or a selection statement, or make a function call, you're making certain assumptions about data values and the state of your computations. These are pre-conditions. And when you exit that control structure, you're making assumptions about what those values are now. These are post-conditions. You should write tests that make sure that your assumptions are correct by testing the pre- and post-conditions. In languages that have assertions (including C, C++, and Java), this is a great place to use them.

Testing valid data and boundary conditions is one thing, but you also need to test bad data.

- **Illegal data values**. You should test data that is blatantly illegal to make sure that your data validation code is working. We already mentioned testing illegal data near the boundaries of your data ranges. You should also test some that are blatantly out of the range.

- **No data**. Yup, test the case where you are expecting data and you get nothing. This is the case where you've prompted a user for input and instead of typing a value and hitting the return key, they just hit return. Or the file you've just opened is empty. Or you're expecting three files on the command line and you get none. You've got to test all of these cases.

- **Too little or too much data**. You have to test the cases where you ask for three pieces of data and only get two. Also the cases where you ask for three and you get ten pieces of data.

- **Uninitialized variables**. Most language systems these days will provide default initialization values for any variable that you declare. But you should still test to make sure that these variables are initialized correctly. (Really, you should not depend on the system to initialize your data anyway; you should always initialize it yourself.)

Characteristics of Tests

Robert Martin, in his book *Clean Code* describes a set of characteristics that all unit tests should have using the acronym F.I.R.S.T.:[3]

Fast. Tests should be fast. If your tests take a long time to run, you're liable to run them less frequently. So make your tests small, simple, and fast.

Independent. Tests should not depend on each other. In particular, one test shouldn't set up data or create objects that another test depends on For example, the JUnit testing framework for Java has separate set-up and tear-down methods that make the tests independent. We'll examine JUnit in more detail later on.

---

[3] Martin, R. C. *Clean Code: A Handbook of Agile Software Craftsmanship*. (Upper Saddle River, NJ: Prentice-Hall, 2009.)

Repeatable. You should be able to run your tests any time you want, in any order you want, including after you've added more code to the module.

Self-Validating. The tests should either just pass or fail; in other words, their output should just be boolean. You shouldn't have to read pages and pages of a log file to see if the test passed or not.

Timely. This means you should write the tests when you need them, so that they're available when you want to run them. For agile methodologies that use TDD, this means write the unit tests first, just before you write the code that they will test.

Finally, its important that just like your functions, your tests should only test one thing; there should be a single concept for each test. This is very important for your debugging work because if each test only tests a single concept in your code, a test failure will point you like a laser at the place in your code where your error is likely to be.

How to Write a Test

Before we go any further, let's look a bit deeper into how to write a unit test. We will do this by hand now to get the feel for writing tests and we'll examine how a testing framework helps us when we talk about JUnit in the next section. We'll imagine that we are writing a part of an application and go from there. We'll do this in the form of a user story, as it might be done in an Extreme Programming (XP) environment.[4]

In XP the developers and the customer get together to talk about what the customer wants. This is called *exploration*. During exploration the customer writes a series of *stories* that describe features that they want in the program. These stories are taken by the developers and broken up into *implementation tasks* and estimated. Pairs of programmers take individual tasks and implement them using TDD. We'll present a story, break it up into a few tasks, and implement some tests for the tasks just to give you and idea of the unit testing process.

The Story

We want to take as input a flat file of phone contacts and we want to sort the file alphabetically and produce an output table that can be printed.

Really, that's all. Stories in XP projects are typically very short – the suggestion is that they be written on 3 × 5 index cards.

So we can break this story up into a set of tasks. By the way, this will look suspiciously like a design exercise; it is.

The Tasks

We need a class that represents a phone contact.

We need to create a phone contact.

---

[4] Newkirk, J. and R. C. Martin. *Extreme Programming in Practice.* (Boston, MA, Addison-Wesley, 2001.)

> We need to read a data file and create a list of phone contacts. (This may look like two things, but it's really just one thing – converting a file in to a list of phone contacts.)
>
> We need to sort the phone contacts alphabetically by last name.
>
> We need to print the sorted list.

The Tests

First of all, we'll collapse the first two tasks above into a single test. It makes sense once we've created a phone contact class to make sure we can correctly instantiate an object; in effect we're testing the class' constructors. So let's create a test.

In our first test we'll create an instance of our phone contact object and print out the instance variables to prove it was created correctly. We have to do a little design work first. We have to figure out what the phone contact class will be called and what instance variables it will have.

A reasonable name for the class is **PhoneContact**, and as long as it's alright with our customer, the instance variables will be **firstName**, **lastName**, **phoneNumber**, and **emailAddr**. Oh, and they can all be String variables. It's a simple contact list. For this class we can have two constructors. A default constructor that just initializes the contacts to null and a constructor that takes all four values as input arguments and assigns them. That's probably all we need at the moment. Here's what the test may look like:

```
public class TestPhoneContact
{
    /**
     * Default constructor for test class TestPhoneContact
     */
    public TestPhoneContact() {
    }

    public void testPhoneContactCreation() {
        String fname = "Fred";
        String lname = "Flintstone";
        String phone = "800-555-1212";
        String email = "fred@knox.edu";

        PhoneContact t1 = new PhoneContact();
        System.out.printf("Phone Contact reference is %H\n", t1);

        PhoneContact t2 = new PhoneContact(fname, lname, phone, email);
        System.out.printf("Phone Contact:\n Name = %s\n Phone = %s\n Email = %s\n",
                        t2.getName(), t2.getPhoneNum(),
                        t2.getEmailAddr());
    }
}
```

Now this test will fail to begin with because we've not created the **PhoneContact** class yet. That's okay. So let's do that now. The **PhoneContact** class will be simple, just the instance variables, the two constructors, and getter and setter methods for the variables. A few minutes later we have:

```
public class PhoneContact {
    /**
     * instance variables
```

```
    */
    private String lastName;
    private String firstName;
    private String phoneNumber;
    private String emailAddr;

    /**
     * Constructors for objects of class PhoneContact
     */
    public PhoneContact() {
        lastName = "";
        firstName = "";
        phoneNumber = "";
        emailAddr = "";
    }

    public PhoneContact(String firstName, String lastName,
                        String phoneNumber, String emailAddr) {
        this.lastName = lastName;
        this.firstName = firstName;
        this.phoneNumber = phoneNumber;
        this.emailAddr = emailAddr;
    }

    /**
     * Getter and Setter methods for each of the instance variables
     */
    public String getName() {
        return this.lastName + ", " + this.firstName;
    }

    public String getLastName() {
        return this.lastName;
    }

    public String getFirstName() {
        return this.firstName;
    }

    public String getPhoneNum() {
        return this.phoneNumber;
    }

    public String getEmailAddr() {
        return this.emailAddr;
    }

    public void setLastName(String lastName) {
        this.lastName = lastName;
    }

    public void setFirstName(String firstName) {
```

```
            this.firstName = firstName;
        }

        public void setPhoneNum(String phoneNumber) {
            this.phoneNumber = phoneNumber;
        }

        public void setEmailAddr(String emailAddr) {
            this.emailAddr = emailAddr;
        }
}
```

The last thing we need is a driver for the test we've just created. This will complete the *scaffolding* for this test environment.

```
public class TestDriver
{
    public static void main(String [] args)
    {
        TestPhoneContact t1 = new TestPhoneContact();

        t1.testPhoneContactCreation();
    }
}
```

Now, when we compile and execute the **TestDriver** we'll get displayed on the output console something like this:

Phone Contact reference is 3D7DC1CB

Phone Contact:

 Name = Flintstone, Fred

 Phone = 800-555-1212

 Email = fred@knox.edu

The next task is to read a data file and create a phone contact list. Here, before we figure out the test or the code we need to decide on some data structures.

Since the story says "flat file of phone contacts" we can just assume we're dealing with a text file where each line contains phone contact information. Say the format mirrors the **PhoneContact** class and is "first_name last_name phone_number email_addr" one entry per line.

Next we need a list of phone contacts that we can sort later and print out. Because we want to keep the list alphabetically by last name, we can use a **TreeMap** Java Collections type to store all the phone contacts. Then we don't even need to sort the list because the **TreeMap** class keeps the list sorted for us. It also looks like we'll need another class to bring the **PhoneContact** objects and the list operations together. So what's the test look like?

Well, in the interest of keeping our tests small and to adhere to the "a test does just one thing" maxim, it seems like we could use two tests after all, one to confirm that the file is there and can be opened, and one to confirm that we can create the **PhoneContact** list data structure. For the file opening test, it looks like we'll need a new class that represents the phone contact list. We can just stub that class out for now, creating a simple constructor and a stub of the one method that we'll need to test. That way we can write the test (which will fail because we don't have a real method yet). The file opening test looks like

```java
public void testFileOpen() {
    String fileName = "phoneList.txt";

    PhoneContactList pc = new PhoneContactList();
    boolean fileOK = pc.fileOpen(fileName);

    if (fileOK == false) {
        System.out.println("Open Failed");
        System.exit(1);
    }
}
```

which we add to the testing class we created before. In the **TestDriver** class above we just add the line

t1.testFileOpen();

to the **main()** method. Once this test fails, you can then implement the new class, and fill in the stubs that we created above. The new **PhoneContactList** class then looks like

```java
import java.util.*;
import java.io.*;

public class PhoneContactList
{
    private TreeMap<String, PhoneContact> phoneList;
    private Scanner phoneFile;

    /**
     * Constructors for objects of class PhoneContactList
     */
    public PhoneContactList() {
    }

    public PhoneContactList(PhoneContact pc)
    {
        phoneList = new TreeMap<String, PhoneContact>();
        phoneList.put(pc.getLastName(), pc);
    }

    public boolean fileOpen(String name)
    {
        try {
            phoneFile = new Scanner(new File(name));
            return true;
        } catch (FileNotFoundException e) {
            System.out.println(e.getMessage());
            return false;
        }
```

```
        }
}
```
So this is how your test-design-develop process will work. Try creating the rest of the tests we listed above and finish implementing the **PhoneContactList** class code. Good luck.

JUnit: A Testing Framework

In the previous section, we created our own test scaffolding, and hooked our tests into it. Many development environments have the facilities to do this for you. One of the most popular for Java is the JUnit testing framework that was created by Eric Gamma and Kent Beck (see **www.junit.org**).

JUnit is a framework for developing unit tests for Java classes. It provides a base class called TestCase that you extend to create a series of tests for the class you are creating. JUnit contains a number of other classes, including an assertion library used for evaluating the results of individual tests, and several applications that run the tests you create. A very good FAQ for JUnit is at **http://junit.sourceforge.net/doc/faq/faq.htm#overview_1**.

To write a test in JUnit, you must import the framework classes and then extend the **TestCase** base class. A very simple test would look like this:

```
import junit.framework.TestCase;

public class SimpleTest extends TestCase {

        public SimpleTest(String name) {
                super(name);
        }

        public void testSimpleTest() {
                LifeUniverse lu = new LifeUniverse();
                int answer = lu.ultimateQuestion();
                assertEquals(42, answer);
        }
}
```

Note that the single-argument constructor is required. The **assertEquals()** method is one of the assertion library (**junit.framework.Assert**) methods which, of course, tests to see if the expected answer (the first parameter) is equal to the actual answer (the second parameter). There are many other **assert*()** methods. The complete list is at **http://junit.sourceforge.net/javadoc/**.

Because JUnit is packaged in a Java jar file, you either need to add the location of the jar file to your Java CLASSPATH environment variable, or add it to the line when you compile the test case from the command line. For example, to compile our simple test case we would use this:

```
% javac -classpath $JUNIT_HOME/junit.jar SimpleTest.java
```

where **$JUNIT_HOME** is the directory where you installed the **junit.jar** file.

Executing a test from the command line is just as easy as compiling. There are two ways to do it. The first is to use one of the JUnit pre-packaged runner classes, which takes as its argument the name of the test class

```
java -cp .:./junit.jar junit.textui.TestRunner SimpleTest
```

which results in

```
.
Time: 0.001
```

```
OK (1 test)
```

where there is a dot for every test that is run, the time the entire test suite required, and the results of the tests.

You can also execute the **JUnitCore** class directly, also passing the name of the test class as an argument to the class

```
java -cp .:./junit.jar org.junit.runner.JUnitCore SimpleTest
```

which results in

```
JUnit version 4.8.2
.
Time: 0.004
```

```
OK (1 test)
```

JUnit is included in many standard integrated development environments (IDEs). BlueJ, NetBeans, and Eclipse all have JUnit plug-ins, making the creation and running of unit test cases nearly effortless.

For example, with our example above and using BlueJ, we can create a new Unit Test class and use it to test our *PhoneContact* and *PhoneContactList* classes. See Figure 14-1.

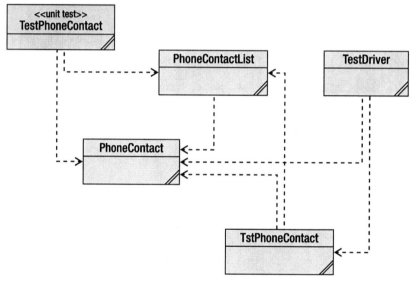

Figure 14-1.The PhoneContact Test UML diagrams

Our test class, **TestPhoneContact** now looks like:

```
public class TestPhoneContact extends junit.framework.TestCase
{
    /**
     * Default constructor for test class TestPhoneContact
     */
    public TestPhoneContact(String name)
```

```java
{
    super(name);
}

/**
 * Sets up the test fixture.
 * Called before every test case method.
 */
protected void setUp()
{
}

/**
 * Tears down the test fixture.
 * Called after every test case method.
 */
protected void tearDown()
{
}

public void testPhoneContactCreation() {
    String fname = "Fred";
    String lname = "Flintstone";
    String phone = "800-555-1212";
    String email = "fred@knox.edu";

    PhoneContact pc = new PhoneContact(fname, lname, phone, email);
    assertEquals(lname, pc.getLastName());
    assertEquals(fname, pc.getFirstName());
    assertEquals(phone, pc.getPhoneNum());
    assertEquals(email, pc.getEmailAddr());
}

public void testFileOpen() {
    String fileName = "phoneList.txt";

    PhoneContactList pc = new PhoneContactList();
    boolean fileOK = pc.fileOpen(fileName);
    assertTrue(fileOK);

    if (fileOK == false) {
        System.out.println("Open Failed, File Not Found");
        System.exit(1);
    }
}
}
```

To run this set of tests in BlueJ, we select Test All from the drop-down menu shown in Figure 14-2.

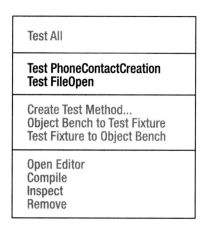

Figure 14-2. The JUnit Menu - Select Test All to run the tests

Because we don't have a **phoneList.txt** file created yet, we get the output shown in Figure 14-3.

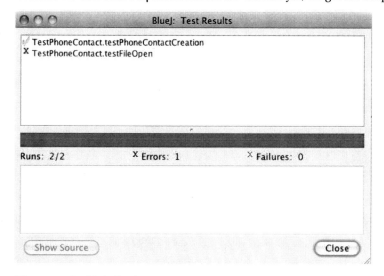

Figure 14-3. JUnit Testing output

Here, we note that the **testFileOpen()** test has failed.

   Every time we make any changes to our program we can add another test to the **TestPhoneContact** class and re-run all the tests with a single menu selection. The testing framework makes is much easier to create individual tests and whole suites of tests that can be run every time you make a change to the program. This lets us know every time we make a change if we've broken something or not. Very cool.

Testing Is Good

At the end of the day, unit testing is a critical part of your development process. Done carefully and correctly, it can help you remove the vast majority of your errors even before you integrate your code into the larger program. TDD, where you write tests first and then write the code that makes the tests succeed, is an effective way to catch errors in both low-level design and coding and allows you to easily and quickly create a regression test suite that you can use for every integration and every baseline of your program.

Conclusion

From your point of view as the developer, unit testing is the most important class of testing your program will undergo. It's the most fundamental type of testing, making sure your code meets the requirements of the design at the lowest level. Despite the fact that developers are more concerned with making sure their program works than with breaking it, developing a good unit testing mindset is critical to your development as a mature, effective programmer. Testing frameworks make this job much easier than in the past and so learning how your local testing framework operates and learning to write good tests is a skill you should work hard at. Better that you should find your own bugs than the customer.

References

Kernighan, B. W. and R. Pike. *The Practice of Programming.* (Boston, MA: Addison-Wesley, 1999.)

Martin, R. C. *Clean Code: A Handbook of Agile Software Craftsmanship.* (Upper Saddle River, NJ: Prentice-Hall, 2009.)

McConnell, S. *Code Complete 2: A Practical Handbook of Software Construction.* (Redmond, WA: Microsoft Press, 2004.)

Newkirk, J. and R. C. Martin. *Extreme Programming in Practice.* (Boston, MA, Addison-Wesley, 2001.)

CHAPTER 15

Walkthroughs, Code Reviews, and Inspections

Our objective with Inspections is to reduce the Cost of Quality by finding and removing defects earlier and at a lower cost. While some testing will always be necessary, we can reduce the costs of test by reducing the volume of defects propagated to test.

—Ron Radice (2002)

When you catch bugs early, you also get fewer compound bugs. Compound bugs are two separate bugs that interact: you trip going downstairs, and when you reach for the handrail it comes off in your hand.

—Paul Graham (2001)

Here's a shocker: your main quality objective in software development is to get a working program to your user that meets all their requirements and has no defects. That's right: your code should be perfect. It meets all the user's requirements and it has no errors in it when you deliver it. Impossible, you cry? Can't be done? Well, *software quality assurance* is all about trying to get as close to perfection as you can – albeit within time and budget. (You knew there was a catch, didn't you?)

Software quality is usually discussed from two different perspectives, the user's and the developer's. From the user's perspective, quality has a number of characteristics – things that your program must do in order to be accepted by the user – among which are:[1]

- *Correctness*: The software has to work, period.

- *Usability*: It has to be easy to learn and easy to use.

---

[1] McConnell, S. *Code Complete 2: A Practical Handbook of Software Construction.* (Redmond, WA: Microsoft Press, 2004.)

- *Reliability.* It has to stay up and be available when you need it.

- *Security.* The software has to prevent unauthorized access and it has to protect your data.

- *Adaptability.* It should be easy to add new features.

From the developer's perspective, things are a bit different. The developer wants to see the following:

- *Maintainability.* It has to be easy to make changes to the software.

- *Portability.* It has to be easy to move the software to a different platform.

- *Readability.* Many developers won't admit this, but you do need to be able to read the code.

- *Understandability.* The code needs to be designed in such a way that a new developer can understand how it all hangs together.

- *Testability.* Well, at least the testers think that your code should be easy to test. Code that is created in a modular fashion, with short functions that do only one thing, is much easier to understand and test than code that is all just one big main() function.

Software Quality Assurance (SQA) has three legs to it:

- *Testing.* Finding the errors that surface while your program is executing, also known as *dynamic analysis.*

- *Debugging.* Getting all the obvious errors out of your code, the ones that are found by testing it.

- *Reviews.* Finding the errors that are inherently in your code as it sits there, also known as *static analysis.*

Many developers – and managers – think that you can test your way to quality. You can't. As we saw in the last chapter, tests are limited. You often can't explore every code path, you can't test every possible data combination, and often your tests themselves are flawed. Tests can only get you so far. As Edsger Dijkstra famously said, "...program testing can be a very effective way to show the presence of bugs, but it is hopelessly inadequate for showing their absence."[2]

Reviewing your code – reading it and looking for errors on the page – provides another mechanism for making sure that you've implemented the user's requirements and the resulting design correctly. In fact, most development organizations that use a plan-driven methodology will not only review code, they'll also review the requirements document, the architecture, the design specification, the test plan, the tests themselves, and the user documentation. In short, all the *work products* produced by the software development organization. Organizations that use an agile development methodology don't necessarily have all the documents mentioned above, but they do have requirements, user stories, user documentation, and especially code to review. In this chapter we'll focus on reviewing your code.

---

[2] Dijkstra, E. "The Humble Programmer." *CACM* **15**(10): 859-866. 1972.

Walkthroughs, Reviews, and Inspections – Oh My!

Testing alone is not a particularly effective way of finding errors in your code. In many cases, the combination of unit testing, integration testing, and system testing will only find about 50% or so of the errors in your program.[3] But, if you add some type of code review (reading the code to find errors) to your testing regimen you can bring that percentage up to between 93% and 99% of all the errors in your code. Now that's an objective to shoot for.

There are three types of reviews that are typically done, and they work their way up from very informal techniques, to very formal methodologies. These reviews are typically done either right after you've got a clean compile of your code and before you unit test, or right after you finish your unit testing. It's better to do the reviews right after unit testing. Then you've got your changes made, you've got a clean compile, and you've done the first round of testing. That's a great time to have someone else take a look at your code.

Walkthroughs

Walkthroughs, also known as *desk checks* or *code reads*, are the least formal type of a review. Walkthroughs are normally used to confirm small changes to code, say a line or two, that you have just made to fix an error. If you've just added a new method to a class, or you've changed more than about 10 lines of code, under no circumstances should you do a walkthrough. Do a code review instead.

Walkthroughs involve two or at most three people: the author of the code and the reviewer. The author's job in a walkthrough is to explain to the reviewer what the change is supposed to do and to point out where the change was made. The reviewer's job is to understand the change and then read the code. Once the reviewer reads the code she makes one of two judgments; either she agrees that the change is correct, or she does not. If not, the author has to go back, fix the code again, and then do another walkthrough. If the reviewer thinks the change is correct, then the author can integrate the changed code back into the code base for integration testing.

If you're using an agile methodology and you're pair programming, a code walkthrough will happen naturally as you are implementing a task. The driver is writing the code and the navigator is looking over her shoulder, checking for errors and thinking ahead. In this case it's acceptable to use a walkthrough for a larger piece of code, but for a complete task, or better yet, for each user story that is implemented, you should do a code review or an inspection.

Code Reviews

Code reviews, on the other hand, are somewhat more formal than a walkthrough. Code reviews are what most software developers do. You should always do a code review if you've changed a substantial amount of code, or if you've added new code to an existing program. As mentioned, agile programmers should do code reviews when they finish a user story. Code reviews are real meetings.

There are usually between three and five attendees at a code review. The people who attend a code review should each bring a different perspective to the meeting.

---

[3] McConnell, 2004.

- The moderator of the code review is usually the author. It's the moderator's job to call the meeting, send out the work to be reviewed well before the meeting time, and to run the code review meeting. The moderator may also take notes at the meeting.

- There should be one or more developers at the meeting; someone who is working on the same project as the author. This person will bring detailed knowledge of the project to the meeting and assume that perspective.

- There should be a tester at the code review. This person brings the testing perspective and not only reads the code being reviewed, but thinks about ways the code should be tested.

- Finally, there should be an experienced developer present who is not on the same project as the author. This person is the "disinterested third-party" who represents the quality perspective. Their job at the code review is to understand the code and get the author to explain the changes clearly. This person provides a more strategic vision about the code and how it fits into the project.

Oh, and no managers are allowed at code reviews. The presence of a manager changes the dynamics of the meeting and makes the code review less effective. People who might be willing to honestly critique a piece of code among peers will clam up in the presence of a manager; this doesn't help find errors. No managers, please.

The objective of a code review is to find errors in the code. It is not to fix them. Code reviews are informal enough that some discussion of fixes may occur, but that should be kept to a minimum. Before the code review meeting, all the participants should go over the materials sent out by the moderator and prepare a list of errors they find. This step is critical to making the review meeting efficient and successful. Do your homework!

This list should be given to the moderator at the beginning of the meeting. The author (who may also be the moderator) goes through the code changes, explaining them and how they either fix the error they were intended to fix, or add the new feature that was required. If an error or a discussion leads the review meeting off into code that was not in the scope of the original review – Stop! Be very careful about moving off into territory that hasn't been pre-read. You should treat any code not in the scope of the review as a black box. Schedule another meeting instead. Remember, the focus of the code review is on a single piece of code and finding errors in that piece of code. Don't be distracted.

A computer and projector are essential at the code review so that everyone can see what's going on all the time. A second computer should be used so that someone (usually the author) can take notes about errors found in the code. A code review should not last more than about two hours or review more than about 200–500 lines of code because everyone's productivity will begin to suffer after about that amount of time or reading.

After the code review, the notes are distributed to all the participants and the author is charged with fixing all the errors that were found during the review. If you run out of time, then another review is scheduled. While metrics aren't required for code reviews, the moderator should at least keep track of how many errors were found, how many lines of code were reviewed, and if appropriate, the severity of each of the errors. These metrics are very useful to gauge productivity and should be used in planning the next project.

Code Inspections

Code inspections are the most formal type of review meeting. The sole purpose of an inspection is to find defects in a document. Inspections can be used to review planning documents, requirements, designs, or code, in short, any work product that a development team produces. Code inspections have specific rules regarding how many lines of code to review at once, how long the review meeting must be, and how much preparation each member of the review team should do, among other things. Inspections are typically used by larger organizations because they take more time and effort than walkthroughs or code reviews. They are also used for mission and safety-critical software where defects can cause harm to users. The most widely known inspection methodology was invented by Michael Fagan in 1976. Fagan's process was the first formal software inspection process proposed and as such, has been very influential. Most organizations that use inspections use a variation of the original Fagan software code inspection process.[4] Code inspections have several very important criteria, including:

- Inspections use checklists of common error types to focus the inspectors.

- The focus of the inspection meeting is solely on finding errors; no solutions are permitted.

- Reviewers are required to prepare beforehand; the inspection meeting will be canceled if everyone isn't ready.

- Each participant in the inspection has a distinct role.

- All participants have had inspection training.

- The moderator is not the author and has had special training in addition to the regular inspection training.

- The author is always required to follow up on errors reported in the meeting with the moderator.

- Metrics data is always collected at an inspection meeting.

Inspection Roles

The following are the roles used in code inspections:

- *Moderator.* The moderator gets all the materials from the author, decides who the other participants in the inspection should be, and is responsible for sending out all the inspection materials and scheduling and coordinating the meeting. Moderators must be technically competent; they need to understand the inspection materials and keep the meeting on track. The moderator schedules the inspection meeting and sends out the checklist of common errors for the reviewers to peruse. They also follow-up with the author on any errors found in the inspection, so they must understand the errors and the corrections. Moderators attend an additional inspection-training course to help them prepare for their role.

---

[4] Fagan, M. "Design and Code Inspections to Reduce Errors in Program Development." *IBM Systems Journal* 15(3): 182-211. 1976.

- *Author:* The author distributes the inspection materials to the moderator. If an Overview meeting is required, the author chairs it and explains the overall design to the reviewers. Overview meetings are discouraged in code inspections, because they can "taint the evidence" by injecting the author's opinions about the code and the design before the inspection meeting. Sometimes, however, if many of the reviewers are not familiar with the project an Overview meeting is necessary. The author is also responsible for all rework that is created as a result of the inspection meeting. During the inspection the author answers questions about the code from the reviewers, but does nothing else.

- *Reader:* The reader's role is to read the code. Actually, the reader is supposed to paraphrase the code, not read it. This implies that the reader has a good understanding of the project, its design and the code in question. The reader does not explain the code; he just paraphrases it. The author should answer any questions about the code. That said, if the author has to explain too much of the code that is usually considered a defect to be fixed; the code should be refactored to make it simpler.

- *Reviewers:* The reviewers do the heavy lifting in the inspection. A reviewer can be anyone with an interest in the code who is not the author. Normally reviewers are other developers from the same project. As in code reviews it's usually a good idea to have a senior person who is not on the project also be a reviewer. There are usually between two and four reviewers in an inspection meeting. Reviewers must do their pre-reading of the inspection materials and are expected to come to the meeting with a list of errors that they have found. This list is given to the Recorder.

- *Recorder:* Every inspection meeting has a recorder. The recorder is one of the reviewers and is the person who takes notes at the inspection meeting. The recorder merges the defect lists of the reviewers and classifies and records errors found during the meeting. The recorder prepares the inspection report and distributes it to the meeting participants. If the project is using a defect management system, then it is up to the Recorder to enter defect reports for all major defects from the meeting into the system.

- *Managers:* As with code reviews, managers are not invited to code inspections.

Inspection Phases and Procedures

Fagan inspections have seven phases that must be followed for each inspection:[5]

1. Planning

2. The Overview meeting

3. Preparation

---

[5] Fagan, M. "Advances in Software Inspections." *IEEE Trans on Software Engineering* 12(7): 744-751. 1986.

4. The Inspection meeting

5. The Inspection report

6. Rework

7. Follow up

Planning

In the Planning phase, the moderator organizes and schedules the meeting and picks the participants. The moderator and the author get together to discuss the scope of the inspection materials – for code inspections typically between 200 and 500 uncommented lines of code will be reviewed. The author then distributes the code to be inspected to the participants.

The Overview Meeting

An Overview meeting is necessary if several of the participants are unfamiliar with the project or its design and they need to come up to speed before they can effectively read the code. If an Overview meeting is necessary, the author will call it and run the meeting. The meeting itself is mostly a presentation by the author of the project architecture and design. As mentioned, Overview meetings are discouraged, because they have a tendency to taint the evidence. Like the Inspection meeting itself, Overview meetings should last no longer than two hours.

Preparation

In the Preparation phase, each reviewer reads the work to be inspected. Preparation should take no more than 2–3 hours. The amount of work to be inspected should be between 200 and 500 uncommented lines of code or between 30 and 80 pages of text. A number of studies have shown that reviewers can typically review about 125–200 lines of code per hour. In Fagan inspections, the preparation phase is required. The inspection meeting can be canceled if the reviewers have not done their preparation. The amount of time each reviewer spent in preparation is one of the metrics that is gathered at the inspection meeting.

The Inspection Meeting

The moderator is in charge of the Inspection meeting. Her job during the meeting is to keep the meeting on track and focused. The Inspection meeting should last no more than two hours. If there is any material that has not been inspected at the end of that time, a new meeting is scheduled. At the beginning of the meeting, the reviewers turn in their list of previously discovered errors to the recorder.

During the meeting the reader paraphrases the code and the reviewers follow along. The author is there to clarify any details and answer any questions about the code and otherwise does nothing. The recorder writes down all the defects reported, their severity and their classification. Solutions to problems are strongly discouraged. Participants are encouraged to have a different meeting to discuss solutions.

We should look for a minute at defect types and severity as reported in a Fagan inspection. Fagan specifies only two types of defects: *minor* and *major*. Minor defects are typically typographic errors, errors in documentation, small user interface errors, and other miscellany that don't cause the software to fail. All other errors are major defects. This is a bit extreme. Two levels are usually not sufficient for most development organizations. Most organizations will have at least a five level defect structure:

1. **Fatal:** Yes, your program dies; can you say core dump?

2. **Severe:** A major piece of functionality fails and there is no workaround for the user. Say that in a first-person shooter game, the software doesn't allow you to re-load your main weapon and doesn't let you switch weapons in the middle of a fight. That's bad.

3. **Serious:** The error is severe, but with a workaround for the user. The software doesn't let you re-load your main weapon, but if you switch weapons and then switch back you can re-load.

4. **Trivial:** A small error, either wrong documentation or something like a minor user interface problem. For example, a text box is 10 pixels too far from its prompt in a form.

5. **Feature request:** A brand new feature for the program is desired. This isn't an error; it's a request from the user (or marketing) for new functionality in the software. In a game this could be new weapons, new character types, new maps or surroundings, and so on. This is version 2.

In most organizations, software is not allowed to ship to a user with known severity 1 and 2 errors still in it. But severity 3 errors really make users unhappy, so realistically, no known severity 1 through 3 errors are allowed to ship. Ideally, of course, no errors ship, right?

In a Fagan inspection meeting it is usually up to the recorder to correctly classify the severity of the major defects found in the code. This classification can be changed later. In the Fagan inspection process all severity 1 through 3 defects are required to be fixed.

Inspection Report

Within a day of the meeting, the recorder distributes the Inspection report to all participants. The central part of the report is the defects that were found in the code at the meeting.

The report also includes metrics data, including

- The number of defects found

- The number of each type of defect by severity and type

- The time spent in preparation; total time in person-hours and time per participant

- The time spent in the meeting; clock time and total person-hours

- The number of uncommented lines of code or pages reviewed

Rework and Follow Up

The author fixes all the severity 1 through 3 defects found during the meeting. If enough defects were found, or if enough refactoring or code changes had to occur, then another inspection is scheduled. How much is enough? Amounts vary. McConnell says 5% of the code,[6] but this author has typically used 10% of the code inspected. So if you inspected 200 lines of code and you had to change 20 or more of them in the rework, then you should have another inspection meeting. If it's less than 10%, the author and the moderator can do a walkthrough. Regardless of how much code is changed, the moderator must check all the changes as part of the follow up. As part of the rework another metric should be reported – the amount of time required by the author to fix each of the defects reported. This metric, plus the number of defects found during the project are critical to doing accurate planning and scheduling for the *next* project. This metric is easier to keep track of if developers use a defect tracking system.

Summary of Review Methodologies

Table 15-1 summarizes the characteristics of the three review methodologies we've examined. Each has its place and you should know how each of them works. The important thing to remember is that reviews and testing go hand in hand and both should be used to get your high-quality code out the door.

Table 15-1. Comparison of Review Methodologies

Properties	Walkthrough	Code Review	Code Inspection
Formal moderator training	No	No	Yes
Distinct participant roles	No	Yes	Yes
Who drives the meeting	Author	Author/moderator	Moderator
Common error checklists	No	Maybe	Yes
Focused review effort	No	Yes	Yes
Formal follow up	No	Maybe	Yes
Detailed defect feedback	Incidental	Yes	Yes
Metric data collected and used	No	Maybe	Yes
Process improvements	No	No	Yes

---

[6] McConnell, 2004.

Defect Tracking Systems

Most software development organizations and many open source development projects will use an automated defect tracking system to keep track of defects found in their software and to record requests for new features in the program. One of the most popular open source defect tracking systems is Bugzilla (**www.bugzilla.org**).

Defect tracking systems keep track of a large amount of information about each defect found and entered. A typical defect tracking system will keep track of at least the following:

- The number of the defect (assigned by the tracking system itself)

- The current state of the defect in the system (Open, Assigned, Resolved, Integrated, Closed)

- The fix that was made to correct the error

- The files that were changed to make the fix

- What baseline the fix was integrated into

- What tests were written and where they are stored (ideally, the tests are stored along with the fix)

- The result of the code review or inspection

Defect tracking systems assume that at any given time a defect report is in some state that reflects where it is in the process of being fixed. A typical defect tracking system can have upwards of ten (10) states for each defect report.

Figure 16-1 shows the states of a typical defect tracking system and the flow of a defect report through the system. In brief, all defects start out as New. They are then assigned to a developer for Analysis. The developer decides whether the reported defect is:

- A duplicate of one already in the system

- Not a defect and so should be rejected

- A real defect that should be worked on by someone

- A real defect whose resolution can be postponed to a later date

Defects that are worked on are eventually fixed and move to the Resolved state. The fix must then be subjected to a code review. If the code review is successful, the defect fix is then Approved. From Approved, the fix is scheduled for integration into the next baseline of the product, and if the integration tests of that baseline are successful, the defect is Closed. Whew!

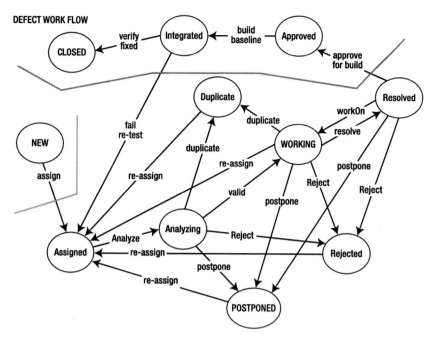

DEFECT WORK FLOW

Figure 15-1. Defect tracking system workflow

Conclusion

A second set of eyes on your code is always a good thing. Code that is reviewed by others is improved and brings you closer to the Platonic ideal of defect-free software. Walkthroughs, code reviews, and formal code inspections each have their place in the array of tools used to improve code quality. The more of these tools you have in your toolbox, the better programmer you are. The combination of reviews, debugging and unit testing will find the vast majority of defects in your code[7] and is the best thing that a developer can do to help release great code.

References

Ackerman, A., et al. (1989). "Software Inspections: An Effective Verification Process." *IEEE Software* **6**(3): 31-36. 1989.

Dijkstra, E. "The Humble Programmer." *CACM* **15**(10): 859-866. 1972.

Doolan, P. "Experience with Fagan's Inspection Method." *Software - Practice & experience* **22**(2): 173-182. 1992.

---

[7] McConnell, 2004.

Dunsmore, A., M. Roper, et al. "Practical Code Inspection Techniques for Object-Oriented Systems: An Experimental Comparison." *IEEE Software* **20**(4): 21-29. 2003.

Fagan, M. "Design and Code Inspections to Reduce Errors in Program Development." *IBM Systems Journal* 15(3): 182-211. 1976.

Fagan, M. "Advances in Software Inspections." *IEEE Trans on Software Engineering* 12(7): 744-751. 1986.

Martin, R. C. *Agile Software Development: Principles, Patterns, and Practices.* (Upper Saddle River, NJ: Prentice Hall, 2003.)

McConnell, S. *Code Complete 2: A Practical Handbook of Software Construction.* (Redmond, WA: Microsoft Press, 2004.)

CHAPTER 16

Wrapping It all Up

All programmers are optimists. Perhaps this modern sorcery especially attracts those who believe in happy endings and fairy godmothers. Perhaps the hundreds of nitty frustrations drive away all but those who habitually focus on the end goal. Perhaps it is merely that computers are young, programmers are younger, and the young are always optimists.

—Frederick Brooks, Jr.[1]

It's the only job I can think of where I get to be both an engineer and an artist. There's an incredible, rigorous, technical element to it, which I like because you have to do very precise thinking. On the other hand, it has a wildly creative side where the boundaries of imagination are the only real limitation.

—Andy Hertzfeld

Reading Alex E. Bell's[2] and Mark Guzdial's[3] "Viewpoint" columns in the August 2008 issue of *Communications of the ACM*, I was struck by the synergy of the two articles. One is a cautionary tale about the tools to use in professional software development, and the other is, at least in part, a cautionary tale about language and syntax use in teaching programming. This got me to thinking about all the silver bullets we've tried in both development and education, and why most of them don't matter to real software development. This seems like an appropriate way to wrap up this discussion on software development.

---

[1] Brooks, F. P. *The Mythical Man-Month : Essays on Software Engineering, Silver Anniversary Edition.* (Boston, MA: Addison-Wesley, 1995.)

[2] Bell, A. E. "Software Development Amidst the Whiz of Silver Bullets," *Communications of the ACM*, 51, 8 (August 2008), 22-24.

[3] Guzdial, M. "Paving the Way for Computational Thinking," *Communications of the ACM*, 51, 8 (August 2008), 25-27.

What Have You Learned?

As I've said more than once in this book, software development is hard. I don't think that everyone can do it, and of those that can, I think few do it extremely well all the time. That, of course, is the attraction. Nobody really wants to work on easy problems. The challenge is to work on something you've never done before, something you might not even know if you can solve. That's what has you coming back to creating software again and again.

Software development is one of the most creative things a human can do. Out of nothing, one takes a problem, wrestles with it, explores it, pokes at it, rips it apart and puts it back in a different form, comes up with that bit of inspiration that leads to a solution, and then converts it into an artifact that others can use effortlessly. Having others use your program to solve their problems is just the coolest thing.

Writing software is a humbling experience. It is so hard to get software right and so easy to get wrong. In writing software, I've learned to embrace failure. Failure is an exciting and frustrating part of the process. From failure, you learn about yourself: you learn how you approach problems, you learn the types of mistakes you're prone to make, and you learn how to work around them. Failure teaches you perseverance because you just have to keep working until the program does.

Small teams build most software, and they build the best software. Small, highly motivated and empowered teams are the most productive. Small teams also tend to use a slimmed down development process. Unless you work for a large company that's desperate to be at SEI Capability Maturity Model Level 5,[4] your processes can be very sparse. Detailed problem descriptions, brainstorming design sessions, simple configuration management, code reviews, and a separate testing team take care of everything necessary to create almost defect-free code. Process flexibility, communication, and ownership are the keys to project success.

A lot of really good software gets written, tested, and shipped every year; much more than the alleged "failure" numbers would have one believe.[5] The key issue that divides plan-driven development and agile development is the recognition of the constant changes in requirements. The best thing about agile development is that it recognizes this fact and builds refactoring into its process.

Simple tools are the most effective. Simple tools allow you to cut to the heart of a problem and examine it closely with nothing in your way. They allow you to take it out, hold it in your hands, turn it over, and poke at it quickly and easily. Simple tools also allow you to join them together to do more complicated things. I'll just point you to Stephen Jenkins' article on "Old School" programming.[6] He's said it much better than I could.

Coding, debugging, and unit testing are at least as important as design. Experience gives a good programmer a deep sense of design and a wealth of patterns to draw on; experience gives a great programmer a deep, intimate knowledge of the programming language that is their tool. It's this deep, intimate knowledge that produces beautiful code.

The process of debugging a long, complex program is an immensely rewarding endeavor. Isolating a problem, uncovering your mistakes, building debugging scaffolding, hypothesizing a solution,

---

[4] Paulk, M. C. *The Capability Maturity Model: Guidelines for Improving the Software Process.* (Reading, MA: Addison-Wesley, 1995.)

[5] Glass, R. "The Standish Report: Does It Really Describe a Software Crisis?," *Communications of the ACM*, 49, 8 (August 2006), 15-16.

[6] Jenkins, S. B. "Musings of an 'Old-School' Programmer," *Communications of the ACM*, 49, 5 (May 2006), 124-126.

reworking a design, finally identifying the error, and then creating a correct fix gives one such a rush of elation and satisfaction that it's at times nearly overwhelming.

What to Do Next?

So now that you've read all about software development and maybe tried some of the examples, what do you do next? How do you become a better software developer? Well, here are some suggestions.

Write code, write lots of code: Experience helps a lot. Programming is a craft that requires practice and constant reinforcement. It's very likely that you'll need to learn a whole new set of tools and programming languages every ten years or so. So having written lots of code will make that task easier.

Learn simple tools: Simple tools give you flexibility. They also help you learn the fundamental skills that you can then take to more complicated IDEs. And when those IDEs get replaced – as they will – you can fall back on the simple tools till you learn the new IDE.

Read about problem solving and design: People have been solving problems for several thousand years now and people have been designing things for nearly that long. Writings in other areas can communicate common problem solving strategies that also work for software development. Don't ignore Polya's *How to Solve It* book. It was written to solve math problems, but it translates very, very well to software.[7] Also don't ignore the classics in the computer science literature, like Dijkstra's *Structured Programming* book,[8] Brooks classic *The Mythical Man-Month*,[9] Bentley's *Programming Pearls*,[10] McConnell's *Rapid Development*,[11] and Beck's *Extreme Programming Explained*.[12]

Read about programming and read about programmers: There is a plethora of literature on programming. A number of books have been mentioned in the previous chapters. Two that bear repeating are Hunt and Thomas' *The Pragmatic Programmer*[13] and McConnell's *Code Complete 2*.[14] It's also a great idea to see how other programmers work. There is a developing literature in computing on how great programmers think, work and generally write great code. Two notable books are Lammer's *Programmers At Work*[15] and Oram and Wilson's *Beautiful Code*.[16]

---

[7] Polya, G. *How To Solve It: A New Aspect of Mathematical Method, 2nd Edition*. (Princeton, NJ: Princeton University Press, 1957.)

[8] Dahl, O. J., E. Dijkstra, et al. *Structured Programming*. (London, UK: Academic Press, 1972.)

[9] Brooks, 1995.

[10] Bentley, J. *Programming Pearls, 2nd Edition*. (Reading, MA: Addison-Wesley, 2000.)

[11] McConnell, S. *Rapid Development: Taming Wild Software Schedules*. (Redmond, WA: Microsoft Press, 1996.)

[12] Beck, K. *Extreme Programming Explained: Embrace Change*. (Boston, MA: Addison-Wesley, 2006.)

[13] Hunt, A. and D. Thomas. *The Pragmatic Programmer: From Journeyman to Master*. (Boston, MA: Addison-Wesley, 2000.)

[14] McConnell, S. *Code Complete 2*. (Redmond, WA: Microsoft Press, 2004.)

[15] Lammers, S. *Programmers At Work*. (Redmond, WA: Microsoft Press, 1986.)

Talk to other programmers: Books are an okay way to gather information, but talking to your peers can't be beat. A side effect of pair programming is that you get to see how someone else works, how they approach problems, how they code, debug, and write tests. Code review meetings are a great way to learn how others work. Code reviews also reinforce Gerald Weinberg's idea of *egoless programming*.[17] Once you get over the idea that you "own" the code in a software product (your employer owns it; read some of those documents you had to sign on the first day of work), you gain the ability to look at your code and the code of your co-workers objectively and you can learn from it.

Join the ACM and the IEEE-CS: The Association for Computing Machinery (ACM) `www.acm.org` and the IEEE Computer Society (IEEE-CS) `www.computer.org` are the two main professional organizations for computer scientists. Their journals contain a wealth of information about all things related to computers and computing, their conferences are worth attending, and online they have free books and courses for members. You will not regret joining one or both of them.

Be humble: The following quote from Dijkstra says it all. Software development is hard. Programs are very complex, and programs of any size are extremely hard to understand completely. Besides being one of the most creative things that humans have ever done, computer software is one of the most complex. Be humble. Work hard. Have fun!

> *The competent programmer is fully aware of the strictly limited size of his own skull; therefore he approaches the programming task in full humility...*

> —Edsger Dijkstra[18]

And lastly, I couldn't resist a quote that had both the words *magic* and *computer* in it...

> *The magic of myth and legend has come true in our time. One types the correct incantation on a keyboard, and a display screen comes to life, showing things that never were nor could be.... The computer resembles the magic of legend in this respect, too. If one character, one pause, of the incantation is not strictly in proper form, the magic doesn't work. Human beings are not accustomed to being perfect, and few areas of human activity demand it. Adjusting to the requirement for perfection is, I think, the most difficult part of learning to program.*

> —Frederick Brooks

---

[16] Oram, A. and G. Wilson, Eds. *Beautiful Code: Leading Programmers Explain How They Think.* (Sebastopol, CA: O'Reilly Media, Inc, 2007.)

[17] Weinberg, G. M. *The Psychology of Computer Programming, Silver Anniversary Edition.* (New York, NY: Dorset House, 1988.)

[18] Dijkstra, E. "The Humble Programmer," *CACM* **15**(10): 859-866. 1972.

CHAPTER 16 ■ WRAPPING IT ALL UP

References

Beck, K. *Extreme Programming Explained: Embrace Change.* (Boston, MA: Addison-Wesley, 2006.)

Bell, A. E. "Software Development Amidst the Whiz of Silver Bullets," *Communications of the ACM*, 51, 8 (August 2008), 22-24.

Bentley, J. *Programming Pearls, 2nd Edition.* (Reading, MA: Addison-Wesley, 2000.)

Brooks, F. P. *The Mythical Man-Month : Essays on Software Engineering, Silver Anniversary Edition.* (Boston, MA: Addison-Wesley, 1995.)

Dahl, O. J., E. Dijkstra, et al. *Structured Programming.* (London, UK: Academic Press, 1972.)

Dijkstra, E. "The Humble Programmer," *CACM* 15(10): 859-866. 1972.

Glass, R. "The Standish Report: Does It Really Describe a Software Crisis?," *Communications of the ACM*, 49, 8 (August 2006), 15-16.

Guzdial, M. "Paving the Way for Computational Thinking," *Communications of the ACM*, 51, 8 (August 2008), 25-27.

Hunt, A. and D. Thomas. *The Pragmatic Programmer: From Journeyman to Master.* (Boston, MA: Addison-Wesley, 2000.)

Jenkins, S. B. "Musings of an 'Old-School' Programmer," *Communications of the ACM*, 49, 5 (May 2006), 124-126.

Lammers, S. *Programmers At Work.* (Redmond, WA: Microsoft Press, 1986.)

McConnell, S. *Rapid Development: Taming Wild Software Schedules.* (Redmond, WA: Microsoft Press, 1996.)

McConnell, S. *Code Complete 2.* (Redmond, WA: Microsoft Press, 2004.)

Oram, A. and G. Wilson, Eds. *Beautiful Code: Leading Programmers Explain How They Think.* (Sebastopol, CA: O'Reilly Media, Inc, 2007.)

Paulk, M. C. *The Capability Maturity Model: Guidelines for Improving the Software Process.* (Reading, MA: Addison-Wesley, 1995.)

Polya, G. *How To Solve It: A New Aspect of Mathematical Method, 2nd Edition.* (Princeton, NJ: Princeton University Press, 1957.)

Weinberg, G. M. *The Psychology of Computer Programming, Silver Anniversary Edition.* (New York, NY: Dorset House, 1988.)

225

Index

F

■ X, Y, Z

CPSIA information can be obtained at www.ICGtesting.com
Printed in the USA
237358LV00011B/4/P